A Pocketful of Hope

A Book of Devotions for the Family

By Mary C. Crowley

Think Mink!
Women Who Win
You Can Too
A Pocketful of Hope

A Pocketful of Hope

A Book of Devotions for the Family

Mary C. Crowley

Fleming H. Revell Company
Old Tappan, New Jersey

Unless otherwise identified, all Scripture quotations are from the King James Version of the Bible.

Scripture quotations identified TLB are taken from the Living Bible, copyright 1971 by Tyndale House Publishers, Wheaton, IL. Used by permission.

Scripture quotations identified RSV are from the Revised Standard Version of the Bible, copyrighted 1946, 1952, © 1971 and 1973.

Library of Congress Cataloging in Publication Data
Crowley, Mary C.
   A pocketful of hope.

   1. Women—Prayer-books and devotions. 2. Devotional calendars.
I. Title.
BV4844.C75   242'.2   81-11955
ISBN 0-8007-1272-2   AACR2

ACKNOWLEDGMENTS

The poem "The Challenge" Copyright © 1972 by W. Heartsill Wilson is used by permission of the author.

Excerpts from *Be Somebody* by Mary C. Crowley, Copyright © 1974 by Crescendo Publications, Inc., used by permission of Crescendo Publications, Inc., P. O. Box 28218, Dallas, Texas 75228.

"Some Men Die In Shrapnel" by Robert D. Abrahams, from "The Night They Burned Shanghai" in the *Saturday Evening Post*. Used by permission of the author.

Excerpt from "Make Someone Happy," Copyright © 1960 by Betty Comden, Adolph Green & Jule Styne. Stratford Music Corp., owner, & Chappell & Co., Inc., Administrator of publication and allied rights for the Western Hemisphere. International Copyright Secured. ALL RIGHTS RESERVED. Used by permission.

"Tribute" by Roy Croft, from *Leaves of Gold* edited by Clyde Lytle, Copyright © 1978, Coslett Publishing Company.

Excerpt from "Stopping by Woods on a Snowy Evening" from THE POETRY OF ROBERT FROST edited by Edward Connery Lathem. Copyright 1923, © 1969 by Holt, Rinehart and Winston. Copyright 1951 by Robert Frost. Reprinted by permission of Holt, Rinehart and Winston, Publishers.

Excerpt from *Tyranny of the Urgent* by Charles E. Hummel. © 1967 by Inter-Varsity Christian Fellowship of the USA and used by permission of InterVarsity Press.

Excerpt from "Renascence" by Edna St. Vincent Millay from COLLECTED POEMS, Harper & Row. Copyright 1917, 1945 by Edna St. Vincent Millay.

Excerpt from "Living for Jesus" Copyright 1917 Heidelberg

FOREWORD

It was very early, but Mary had already had her private time sharing the day's beginning at breakfast which she had cooked for her husband. She could have been any loving wife paying full attention to her husband's needs as he started the day with food and communication before hurrying off to work. Now we were sitting cozily together at her big, round breakfast table, chatting over a cup of tea, the telephone at her elbow. "You won't mind if I make this hospital call?" she asked, and then dialed. Her voice was soon warm and sympathetic, asking whether the night had been a painful one and assuring a woman who had had an operation the day before that improvement would begin to be noticed soon and that she would pray for her. After inquiring about each of the woman's children by name and promising she would call again, Mary turned to me as she hung up. "That is one of my dear managers [her business employs 30,000 people, with over 700 managers] who is having a hard time." Before we finished our time together a few other calls had been "sandwiched" or "slipped" in—but it seemed more as if we were being joined at the table by people walking in the door, than the usual feeling of a "telephone interruption." Mary talked to her daughter in another state, to a grandchild, to her son, and to another employee. We had prayer for many people, including those she wanted to pray for, those in my family, and those at L'Abri. We blended deep discussion about practical matters in our lives with seeking the Lord's help for each other and for those for whom we had personal responsibility.

This is a tiny "snapshot" of Mary Crowley, a person who lives what she talks about, who is very honest and real in her attempt to live on the basis of the Bible—not just attempting to "hear" the Word, but to DO it. Mary is an incredibly rare person in this twentieth century—an extremely successful business woman who has integrity, who treats human beings as human, who keeps her promises made so clearly to the Lord and to others (as much as it is possible to keep them in the midst of a fallen world where finiteness and limitedness and unexpected illness and accidents hinder at times), and whose giving consists of a tremendous diversity of "costs." The cost of giving includes so much more than a sharing of material things if it is to be in accordance with thoughtful love and true concern for others. It includes a giving of self ... which has no set of "how to" rules, but is to be original, creative, and diverse from day to day.

"Reality" is a word that covers a lot. A "skin-deep" imitation of having the Lord as Lord of one's life, cannot substitute for reality. Mary is *real*. As you listen to her talk, as you hear her favorite portions of scripture, you get a glimpse of her own day-by-day manner of walking in a growing reality of communication with the Lord. Her giving is a giving of time, talents, energy, thought, prayer, emotion, love, communication—not only in groups but also with compassion on a person-to-person basis—all sorts of original kinds of comfort and help to people. For a Christian, giving includes taking prayer seriously in interceding faithfully for people we love and care about—this is a natural part of Mary's daily life, it is not "put on." Her devotions in her own life are not tacked on bits of "epilogue" nor are they religious bits of habit in the formality of a proper opening, but an essential part of her life, as natural to her as breathing.

One of the most important things about Mary is her courage to speak and act on the basis of what she believes to be right and to fit in with truth. It is not simply bringing about a spiritual feeling or a comfortable feeling from day to day that counts, but growing in relationship with the God who exists, who is the Creator, and whose Word is truth. Truth, and the actions based on truth, are important. Living life in watertight compartments so that religion has nothing to do with business, or social actions, or law and government, is to forget that people act on what they really believe to be true—and that there must be a consistency in action as well as in belief. It is consistency in the totality of life that we all need to strive for, blending what we *say* with what we *do* in the whole of life, so that the Lord is recognized as Lord of every part of our lives. In this respect it is a joy to relate the fact that Mary has used her opportunities to speak out against abortion and infanticide, and euthanasia, courageously standing on the absolutes of the Bible, as well as compassionately attempting to care for the needs of people who need her personal help in these as well as other areas. Perfect? No, no one can do everything perfectly, but an attempt to live and work in some measure of balance in the totality of life seems to be very present.

Come again to a hot Dallas afternoon where in a store selling Texas boots and cowboy hats and bluejeans, Mary is giving a group of children the excitement of choosing boots and hats. Look at her, tired and perspiring, sitting right down on the floor with a glass of orange juice, smiling at each child, giving bits of advice, looking delightedly at a breathless little four-year-old boy as he holds perfectly still while a hat is being tried on and feathers chosen. Her joy in giving joy is so personal that it involves her in the details of a child's dream, as well as in dreaming up new ways of cheering up adults with surprises! Who else would have thought of taking 750 people to a supermarket and giving them each a cart full of things they could otherwise not afford to buy? No one was hired to stand there while this went on, ready to pay the total. Mary herself nodded and smiled with pleasure as she wrote the check to cover the 750 grocery carts full of special food for Christmas.

When the Lord instructed the Israelites not to gather all the crops during the harvest time, but to leave something in their fields to be gathered by people who had less, He unfolded a pattern of involvement in the needs of others by sharing a personal territory. Mary opens the way for so many to "glean" in her "fields" at different periods of harvest. The beautiful reality of truth is that Jesus has said, ". . . Inasmuch as ye have done it unto one of the least of these my brethren, ye have done it unto me" (Matthew 25:40). Whether flowers by a sick-bed, a scholarship for a young person, a little boy's dreamed-of cowboy hat, food for a group of missionaries, a party for discouraged workers, a phone call to a frightened or depressed friend, help in an urgent drive to make truth known, seemingly earthshaking projects or trivial treats, Mary has taken literally God's admonition to give compassionately to others with a wholehearted generosity and involvement which is sheer hard work. "When I was sick you visited me . . . when I was hungry you fed me . . ." (*see* Matthew 25:35, 36). How else can we be involved in doing things directly for the Lord? Mary has written a book of daily devotions, but the "book" that can be read so vividly by all who know her is the day-by-day life which spills over with true devotion to the Lord and her "doing" things for Him in what she is doing for others—the least of His children.

A Pocketful of Hope

A Book of Devotions for the Family

JANUARY 1

Therefore if any man be in Christ, he is a new creature: old things are passed away; behold, all things are become new.
2 CORINTHIANS 5:17

Another year is dawning
Dear Father, let it be
In working or in waiting,
Another year with Thee.

Another year of leaning
Upon Thy loving breast,
Another year of trust
Of quiet, happy rest.

Another year of mercies,
Of faithfulness and grace,
Another year of gladness
And the showing of Thy Face.

Another year of progress,
Another year of praise,
Another year of proving,
Thy presence all the days.

Another year of service,
Of witness for Thy love,
Another year of training
For holier work above.

> Another year is dawning,
> Dear Father, let it be,
> On earth, or else in heaven,
> Another year for Thee.
> FRANCES R. HAVERGAL

Dear God, help us to fill the pages of this new book with love, truth, and honor in Thy name and for Thy sake.

JANUARY 2

Come unto me all ye that labour and are heavy laden, and I will give you rest.

MATTHEW 11:28

Great peace have they which love thy law: and nothing shall offend them.

PSALMS 119:165

The upright shall have good things in possession.

PROVERBS 28:10

These are the promises to claim this year.

What have we now? The love of God set upon us beyond all change, power with God through prayer in time of need, the providence of God to watch over us, the angels of God to minister to us, and the Spirit of God to do His will within us.

It has been the practice of our family when we come together at Christmastime or New Year's, to claim a promise of God for the coming year. Will you join with us this year and claim one, or all, of these for your very own?

Dear Lord, today we claim promises from Your vast store that will mean a great deal to each of us. Help them to be a source of Your strength for us through the coming days of this New Year.

JANUARY 3

And I will make my covenant between me and thee, and will multiply thee exceedingly.

GENESIS 17:2

This is a new year, a time for making resolutions. Nowhere do we read about the resolutions of the apostles, but in many places we read about their actions. Perhaps that should tell us that God is much more interested in our acts than in our resolutions. We can still make resolutions, and it is a good thing to do, but we must be forever at it if we are to accomplish them.

In his dream, a man came to the end of the year and came to God's storehouse of blessings. He went to the angel in charge and said, "We have had enough of war, conflict, and killings. We need some goodwill, peace, and love." The angel said, "You misunderstand. We don't store fruits here, only seeds." We all have the seeds of goodwill, peace, harmony, love, but it is up to us to plant them, cultivate them, tend them, and—through the grace of God—help them grow to maturity.

Father, may our New Year's resolutions be pleasing to Thee, rooting out things that are bad, sowing things that are good, and with Your love and encouragement, coming to a bountiful harvest.

JANUARY 4

Every day will I bless thee; and I will praise thy name for ever and ever.

PSALMS 145:2

"Good morning, Lord, it's Mary again."
You might call this a morning prayer of gratitude and praise after a day of extensive oral surgery. Jesus answered my prayer of the day before and helped me get through with serenity and pleasantness.

I always believe in thanking Him for answered prayer. This morning when I woke up, I was so grateful to feel clearheaded.

The song that came to my mind immediately was "To God Be the Glory, Great Things He Hath Done." I love that song. It has always meant a great deal to me, and it means even more to me since I learned the story about it from the Billy Graham Crusades. Cliff Barrows reminded us of the background of this hymn. It was written by a precious blind lady, Fanny Crosby, sometime before 1875. It was not immediately used or applauded in its native land. Apparently the song was taken to England by Ira D. Sankey, the wonderful song leader of that period, who went to England with the evangelist, D. L. Moody. It was published first in England in 1874 and is still used there today. It was there in 1954 that Cliff Barrows, with the Billy Graham team, found the hymn.

The words so beautifully express the praise and wonder of God's great works and our potential in Him that Cliff brought it back, and it has been sung since that time in all the crusades and has been put in the crusade songbooks:

To God be the glory, great things He hath done!
  So loved He the world that He gave us His son,
Who yielded His life an atonement for sin
  And opened the Lifegate that all may go in.

Praise the Lord, praise the Lord, let the earth hear His voice!
  Praise the Lord, praise the Lord, let the people rejoice!
Oh come to the Father through Jesus, the Son
  And give Him the glory, Great things He hath done!

Dear Lord, You do such great and glorious things in our lives and in our world. Help us to see them as from Your hand and always to give the glory unto Thee.

JANUARY 5

But they that wait upon the Lord shall renew their strength; they shall mount up with wings as eagles; they shall run, and not be weary; and they shall walk, and not faint.

                                                        Isaiah 40:31

Through the years, many have asked, "Who motivates you; what sustains you?" Simply and succinctly, my sustenance, my motivation, is compressed into a few sentences from the Thirty-seventh Psalm:

Fret not thyself . . . Trust in the Lord, and do good; so shalt thou dwell in the land, and verily thou shall be fed. Delight thyself also in the Lord; and he shall give thee the desires of thine heart. Commit thy way unto the Lord; trust also in him; and he shall bring it to pass. . . . Rest in the Lord, and wait patiently for him: fret not thyself because of him who prospereth in his way, . . . Cease from anger, and forsake wrath: . . . The steps of a good man are ordered by the Lord: and he delighteth in his way, Though he fall, he shall not be utterly cast down: for the Lord upholdeth him with his hand.

I am not good, but I work everlastingly trying to become better. (None can be called good, but God.) What JOY and EN-COURAGEMENT to know that though I slip, He does not fall. The Lord upholdeth with HIS HAND.

Then my added strength comes from the promise in James (1:5-8, 22) which I claim daily:

If any of you lack wisdom, let him ask of God, that giveth to all men liberally, and upbraideth not; and it shall be given him. But let him ask in faith, nothing wavering. For he that wavereth is like a wave of the sea driven with the wind and tossed. For let not that man think that he shall receive any thing of the Lord. A double minded man is unstable in all his ways. . . . But be ye doers of the word, and not hearers only.

Dear Father, thank You for always holding my hand—to keep me from falling and to lead me to that higher, nobler, better thing You have for me.

JANUARY 6

Delight thyself also in the Lord; and he shall give thee the desires of thine heart.

PSALMS 37:4

Keep a song in your heart!

The way to be happy is to make others happy. Helping others is the secret of all success. If you set out in the pursuit of happiness for yourself, you will find that happiness will elude you. But if you set out with a real urgency to bring springtime into the wintry monotony of the lives with which you come in contact . . . if *that* becomes your primary goal, you will find that happiness will fall upon you as a by-product of what you have done for others.

Keep your eyes off yourself and on the greater purpose; let that purpose permeate your thinking and your speaking, and you will accomplish your objectives.

You see, when we do our absolute *best,* the Lord will fill in the gaps and make everything come out sure and right and glorious—but He will not fill in the gaps until *we* do our BEST!

The good Lord takes care of His own, and if we do our very best and truly believe, **He will see us through.**

Father,
Thank You for loving me.
Thank You for being my Father—my mother—my friend.
Thank You for the time You've picked me up when I've fallen.
Thank You for loving me when I've hurt Your loving heart.
Thank You for health and strength and ability to do my work.
Thank You for my work and the dear people with whom I work;
Make me pleasant to them and helpful, because Jesus loves me.

JANUARY 7

Jesus answered and said unto them, Verily, I say unto you, If ye have faith, and doubt not, ye shall not only do this which is done to the fig tree, but also if ye shall say unto this mountain, Be thou removed, and be thou cast into the sea; it shall be done.

MATTHEW 21:21

The Bible promises that whatever we ask in the name of Jesus and according to His will we shall have, or it shall come to pass. Now I want you to realize just what this means. In the first place, it means that we are to enter into this promise by laying claim to it. God has made a promise and we must claim it. Second, we must recognize the Person to whom we pray. We are addressing the Creator of the universe who loves and cares for our needs. Third, we must come to realize the power of prayer. If we depend upon work, we get only what man can accomplish, but when we depend upon prayer, we get what God can do. It takes both for us to realize God's promise.

O Lord, we want Your power in our lives, and we claim the promises You have made to accomplish in us great and mighty things.

JANUARY 8

If we confess our sins, he is faithful and just to forgive us our sins, and to cleanse us from all unrighteousness.

1 JOHN 1:9

A new heart also will I give you, and a new spirit will I put within you . . .

EZEKIEL 36:26

When we consider the power of prayer in our lives, we should realize that it has a threefold function. In the first place, it has the power to cleanse us. This *cleansing* power brings with it a new sense of courage which springs from a pure, clean heart.

In addition to cleansing, prayer has a *conforming* power in our lives. As we pray, we are brought into the presence and will of God. The only way we can become more like God is through the study of His Word and through communication with Him in prayer.

Finally, prayer has a *changing* power. It transforms our lives, because prayer moves God and He moves people. As we pray, we can sense how God changes attitudes. As attitudes change, people also change, and then *things* begin to change. Prayer is the greatest instrument ever placed at man's disposal, for through it we have access to the power of God.

O God, why do we go on powerless and ineffective when through prayer we can gain access to everything You are?

JANUARY 9

Ask, and it shall be given you; seek, and ye shall find; knock, and it shall be opened unto you:
MATTHEW 7:7

God wants us to come to Him with our requests and to ask Him for what we need: First we are to *confess* our sins, then we are to *worship* Him, and, finally, we are to *make petition* of Him.

Once we have confessed our sins and worshipped Him, we may present to Him our needs and desires. Instead of asking God for things, we should ask Him to do something *with* us rather than to do something *for* us. He has already promised to supply our every need if we seek the kingdom of God as our primary concern. With this goal in view, we should seek ways to bring about the kingdom rather than things in it. Make your request, "Lord use me and my experience to bring people closer to You." This attitude in prayer will also make it possible for us to pray for those who spitefully use us and for our enemies.

Father, help us to pray in the right spirit for the right things, always seeking a closer relationship to You.

JANUARY 10

I therefore, the prisoner of the Lord, beseech you that ye walk worthy of the vocation wherewith ye are called, With all lowliness and meekness, with longsuffering, forbearing one another in love;
EPHESIANS 4:1, 2

The Christian walk is a *worthy* walk, a *different* walk, but most of all it is a LOVING WALK.

When one walks in love, he actually walks in God, for God is love.

When one walks in love, he is no longer negative or neutral—he is a *positive* element of blessing in the world.

When one steps out of love, he steps *out* of the environment of God and into the environment of the Adversary. When one acts outside of love, he acts in harmony with the Enemy—he puts himself in a place where he has no defense, and the Adversary has the mastery.

As long as one walks *in* love, Satan has no dominion over him. When he acts *outside* of love, he weakens the faith element within himself. Our faith will unconsciously be measured by our love walk. When we walk by faith, we become independent of circumstances. When we walk in love, we walk in the realm of the Father's protection and we walk in HIS wisdom.

We have God's faith reproduced in us by His Living Word . . . by His nature, faith is imparted to us. We have more faith in the ability of God to heal, to give courage and strength to meet life's problems, than we have in the Adversary to thwart the purpose of God in us.

"I can do all things in him who strengthens me" (Philippians 4:13 RSV).

If we follow the law of love, we cannot fail!

> When we walk with the Lord,
>   In the light of His Word,
> What a glory He sheds on our way!
>   While we do His good will,
> He abides with us still
>   And with all who will trust and obey.
> JOHN H. SAMMIS

JANUARY 11

That they may teach the young women to be sober, to love their husbands, to love their children, To be discreet, chaste, keepers at home, good, obedient to their own husbands, that the word of God be not blasphemed. Young men likewise exhort to be sober minded. In all things shewing thyself a pattern of good works: in doctrine shewing uncorruptness, gravity, sincerity, Sound speech, that cannot be condemned; ...

TITUS 2:4–8

The greatest thing for a man and woman to remember throughout their married lives is that they have different roles to play. The woman is to be an inspiration to her husband. He in turn is to render honor and appreciation to her for all the wonderful things she does and is. In a good marriage each partner should care enough for the other to preserve each other's self-esteem. The husband should be aware of his wife's needs and feelings, and she should be aware of his. Both should be able to retain their own individuality without being threatened or censured by the other. In developing this situation, there will be a need to be honest in their relationship, but candid honesty can sometimes be cruel and harsh. We need to cushion honesty with sensitivity.

Father, make us sensitive to the needs of our mates and give us a greater love for one another.

JANUARY 12

I press toward the mark for the prize of the high calling of God in Christ Jesus.

PHILIPPIANS 3:14

Oh, how we need goals! Every person needs a goal. Women have to learn that they need goals in their lives, whether they are homemakers, business women, or whatever their lot in life.

Do you have a goal? You must! And then you must have a commitment to that goal. We are goal-oriented people. Our goal should be for excellence in whatever we do. Our goals should be definite—definable.

Many people are too vague in where they are going. They want "to make a lot of money," but how much is a lot? What is the plan? How do they intend to go about accomplishing this accumulation? They have no idea, they just know they "want to make a lot of money." That won't do it. Our goals must be definite, they must be specific.

So, set your goals—emotional goals, spiritual goals, physical goals, financial goals. Put a timetable on them and then reach for them, and you will be amazed at what you can accomplish.

Father, help us to reach for something—something good, something worthy, and then help us stretch our talents and abilities to achieve it.

JANUARY 13

Choose you this day whom ye will serve;... but as for me and my house, we will serve the Lord.

JOSHUA 24:15

Is the home we are creating a *haven* or a *hazard?*

A haven is a place of security against the storms of life ... a harbor ... a place of "refueling" ... of building and rebuilding ... a place where *confidence* is built up for each person in the home.

Love has a locale and it is called "home." Here love most deeply expresses itself. Here it most truly receives its nourishment. Here it most surely radiates its power.

HOUSES are made of wood and stone
but
Only LOVE can make a HOME.

A child psychologist says:
A mother's love should teach a child that he is *loved* ...
A father's love should teach a child that he is *competent.* A child needs both—to feel LOVED and to feel COMPETENT.

Dear God, in our homeland of America, help us to make our individual homes more of what You would want them to be.

JANUARY 14

If ye then be risen with Christ, seek those things which are above, where Christ sitteth on the right hand of God. Set your affection on things above, not on things on the earth.

COLOSSIANS 3:1, 2

Everything in your life will be influenced by your affections. Someone asked Tim LaHaye, who counsels with hundreds of married couples, what he would say was causing the most problems of the couples who came to him for counsel. The answer was "selfishness." "He or she does not make me happy—then I have to change him or her to make me happy, because 'Me' must be happy."

What did you give up to win? If you gave up some of your integrity, it is not worth it. With the goals and honors there must be integrity. Above all else, guard your affections!

One of the reasons so many people wanted to honor Roger Staubach, the great Dallas Cowboy quarterback, was that although Roger loved football, that was not where he put his first affection. His first affection was to God and to his family, then to football. He was greatly honored and respected. No one thought of Roger as a quitter when he left the game at the height of his fame and glory, because he had his affections in the right place. His concern was for his family, what risking serious injury in football might do to them.

> You're writing each day a record for men;
>   Be sure the writing is true,
> For the only record some people read
>   Is the Bible according to you.

Father, it is so easy for our heads to be turned by the praise of men. Help us to seek Your praise and Your approval—keep our heads on straight and our priorities in order.

JANUARY 15

For God so loved the world, that he gave his only begotten Son, that whosoever believeth in him should not perish, but have everlasting life.

JOHN 3:16

God created us for fellowship with Himself. Because He wanted us to love Him out of our own free choice, He gave to us a free will. Adam and Eve used it wrongly, and God devised a plan for His beloved Son to take on our form and to provide an expression of how much He loved us.

I have yet to meet anyone who—if given enough time—will not respond to genuine love. That is why God sent Jesus into the world, in order to reveal to us His overflowing, everlasting, all-encompassing love. God created us for fellowship with Himself, and He has provided everything needed for us to experience that fellowship throughout all eternity.

Lord, put Your arms around us and let us bask in the warmth of Your love as we learn more and more of Thee.

JANUARY 16

Who hath ascended up into heaven, or descended? who hath gathered the wind in his fists? who hath bound the waters in a garment? who hath established all the ends of the earth? what is his name, and what is his son's name, if thou canst tell? Every word of God is pure: he is a shield unto them that put their trust in him.

PROVERBS 30:4, 5

I have always been so grateful that I have the Lord God Himself guarding my pathway.

I once heard a missionary tell a strange and wonderful story. It happened in the Belgian Congo when Christians were being slaughtered and forced to leave the country. A missionary couple had been told that the authorities would probably come to their house on a particular night to either kill or imprison them. They gathered together with a little band of three or four other missionaries, and throughout the long night, they prayed and trusted the Lord for their deliverance. Even though their situation was desperate, they were unafraid because they knew God was in control of their destiny, and whatever it would be—whether they died or whether they lived—it was all right, because God would not leave them or forsake them. And so they prayed all night, and while they were praying, the authorities came almost to the front door, but they did not take them away; they did not kill them.

Morning dawned, and a leader of the village came and told them to get their belongings and leave—they were free to go. He urged them to hurry, saying, "We don't want you here anymore." Puzzled, the missionaries inquired as to why they had been spared. The man answered, "Last night when we came to get you, a host of men with guns stood guarding your house. We don't know where they came from, but we don't want you *or* them around here anymore."

Where *did* they come from? Were they a vision, an apparition, or were they God's heavenly host protecting His own?

Don't ever underestimate the Lord God Almighty! Don't ever underestimate prayer! It is the greatest defense! Miracles like this, if indeed it was a miracle, do not happen often, but that does not mean they cannot. God can do anything He wants to do. He is always our shield and protection—sometimes seen and sometimes unseen.

Lord, we thank You for protecting us from the assaults of our enemies. May we never doubt Your miraculous power, and may we ever be confident of Your eternal presence with us.

JANUARY 17

Those by the way side are they that hear; then cometh the devil, and taketh away the word out of their hearts, lest they

should believe and be saved. They on the rock are they, which,
when they hear, receive the word with joy; and these have no
root, which for a while believe, and in time of temptation fall
away. And that which fell among thorns are they, which, when
they have heard, go forth, and are choked with cares and
riches and pleasures of this life, and bring no fruit to perfec-
tion.

LUKE 8:12–14

There is something you will learn about the devil, if you have
not already. He always gives his best shot first. Everything else is
diminishing returns. God works the opposite way. He calls for
discipline, He calls for dedication, and sometimes deprivation.
Sometimes you have to surrender, you have to give up your will,
and it is very, very hard. But from then on everything gets better
and better and sweeter and sweeter. With Satan it is just the opposite.

Bill Glass, who used to play for the Cleveland Browns, made
the remark that if you don't think sin is fun, you have just not
been to the right places. Some sin *is* a lot of fun, but remember—it is that best shot coming first, and then will come all the
problems, difficulties, enslavement. Satan doesn't let you see the
difficulties or the ankle chains awaiting you when he's dangling
all the dazzle and the glitter trying to entice you. Oh no! He waits
until he has you going his way, and then he turns all the gold to
brass, the glitter to ashes, and the magic potion to hemlock.
Christians, beware! The pleasures for a season are not worth the
price you have to pay!

Lord, help us always to stay close to Thee so that we won't be
tempted to fall into the devil's snare. Help us always to resist
him, and then we will claim Your promise that he will flee
from us.

JANUARY 18

Seeing ye have purified your souls in obeying the truth through
the Spirit unto unfeigned love of the brethren, see that ye love

*one another with a pure heart fervently: Being born again, not
of corruptible seed, but of incorruptible, by the word of God,
which liveth and abideth for ever.*

1 PETER 1:22, 23

There is an old poem, "Tribute," that has been put to music
that has so much in it that is good:

I love you, not only for what you are
   But for what I am when I am with you.
I love you, not only for what you have made of yourself,
   But for what you are making of me.
I love you for the part of me that you bring out.

I love you for putting your hand into my heaped-up heart
   And passing over all my foolish, weak things
That you can't help dimly seeing there,
And for drawing out into the light all the beautiful belongings
That no one else had looked quite far enough to find.

I love you for ignoring the possibilities of the fool
   And weakling in me, and for laying firm hold
On the possibilities of good in me.

I love you for closing your eyes to the discords in me,
   And for adding to the music in me
By worshipful listening.

I love you because you are helping me to make the
   Lumber of my life not a tavern, but a temple
And the words of my every day, not a reproach,
   But a song.

I love you because you have done more than any
   Creed could have done to make me good,
More than any fate could have done to make me happy.
   You have done it just by being yourself.
Perhaps that is what being a friend means after all.

ROY CROFT

It is surely what being happily married means. Don't lose heart. Don't forget those silent, strong multitudes of women who wholeheartedly believe in marriage in its fullest and have given their lives happily to it, only to find themselves whole and complete, holding up a tottering world.

Quite a challenge! Quite a partnership! Quite amazing! Yes, and quite difficult! There are many women nonetheless who are doing just that, because they have a commitment—a commitment to duty, a commitment to excellence!

Lord, help us to be equal to our task to love as You would have us love and to freely express it.

JANUARY 19

And he said, Go forth, and stand upon the mount before the Lord. And, behold, the Lord passed by, and a great and strong wind rent the mountains, and brake in pieces the rocks before the Lord; but the Lord was not in the wind: and after the wind an earthquake; but the Lord was not in the earthquake: And after the earthquake a fire; but the Lord was not in the fire: and after the fire a still small voice. And it was so, when Elijah heard it, that he wrapped his face in his mantle, and went out, and stood in the entering in of the cave. And, behold, there came a voice unto him, and said, What doest thou here, Elijah?

1 KINGS 19:11–13

Don't look for Jesus among the dead teachers of the world. Don't look for Jesus among the good examples.

Don't look for Him among the heroes.

Where *do* we look for Jesus? We look for Him in His Living Word and in the hearts of believers where He dwells; we look for Him among the sinners who confess their need of a Savior; we look for Him among the lowly, the unlovely, unloved, unsung. Where do we look for happiness and joy? There's only one place—in Jesus. Where do we look for security? God is the *only* secure thing in our world. Where do we look for nourishment and growth? We need to find it among fellow believers in a church, and from feasting on His Word.

O God, help us to realize You won't be found in the obvious places but rather in the still, small voice that says, "Be still and know that I am God."

JANUARY 20

So Christ was once offered to bear the sins of many; and unto them that look for him shall he appear the second time without sin unto salvation.

HEBREWS 9:28

Where have you looked for identity? One of the major factors needed to find true happiness is a sense of identification. Some people seek their identity in other people. We must have someone with whom we can relate. It may be a hero, a teacher, or a friend. It seems as if the entire world is looking for a leader with whom they can identify. This is a universal need; you hear it on every hand. Jesus Christ is the person with whom you can identify. Unlike any other leader, He will abide when all others fail. The only Person who does not have feet of clay is the Lord Jesus Christ. Look to Him and seek your identity there. Look to others only when, and if, they in turn point you to Him.

Lord, help us to find our identity, our purpose, our reason for being—in You.

JANUARY 21

Wherefore seeing we also are compassed about with so great a cloud of witnesses, let us lay aside every weight, and the sin which doth so easily beset us, and let us run with patience the

*race that is set before us, Looking unto Jesus the author and
finisher of our faith; who for the joy that was set before him
endured the cross, despising the shame, and is set down at the
right hand of the throne of God.*

HEBREWS 12:1, 2

Sometimes we look around us and see wicked people pros-
pering, and we wonder why. We think we work hard and don't
have much to show for it, yet there is someone else who doesn't
love and honor God, and they seem to get by with everything.
We are all the time looking at others, instead of looking at God.
Instead of wasting time wondering where God is that He doesn't
see the terrible inequities about us, we should turn and look at
Him.

> Turn your eyes upon Jesus,
> Look full in His wonderful face,
> And the things of earth will grow strangely dim
> In the light of His glory and grace.
>
> HELEN H. LEMMEL

In the story of Jesus walking on the water, we find Peter wanting to do the same. Jesus tells Peter to come, and Peter does fine
until he takes his eyes away from Jesus. It is only when he looks
at himself instead of Jesus, he realizes that he is a mortal man in-
capable of walking on water, and he begins to fall. Jesus reaches
out and picks him up, and says, "Peter, Peter, *anyone* can walk
on water if I bid them come and if they keep their eyes on Me!"
If we could only realize that *that* is the secret—keeping our eyes
on Jesus!

*Precious Jesus, when the storms of life assail us and the waves
threaten to engulf us, help us to look steadfastly into Your
wonderful face, knowing the power and grace to rise above the
storm, to walk on the water, to rest in You and not ourselves.*

JANUARY 22

And we have known and believed the love that God hath to us.
God is love; and he that dwelleth in love dwelleth in God, and
God in him. Herein is our love made perfect, that we may have
boldness in the day of judgment: because as he is, so are we in
this world. There is no fear in love; but perfect love casteth out
fear: because fear hath torment. He that feareth is not made
perfect in love. We love him, because he first loved us.

1 JOHN 4:16–19

God loves us. If we could ever get that into our consciousness, life would change so much for us.

Have you ever received a love letter from someone who meant everything to you? Did you read it just once and put it away? No, you read it again and again, didn't you? The Bible is God's love letter to us, and we need to read and reread the portions that tell of His love for us.

We need to feel loved. Some people *are* loved, but they do not *feel* loved. Do you ever feel as though God doesn't love you? There is not one of us that has not at some time or another felt that nobody cares. We need to get out our love letter from God and read it and read it until we feel loved.

We must realize that God loves us just as we are—worthy or not. People who do not see that God loves them just as they are, are not free to love others just as *they* are.

We must know that God's love will endure. It has nothing to do with our feelings or our moods—nothing can separate us from the love of God. God's love is different from all other loves. It is human nature to love the people who love us. But it is God's nature to love, regardless, even when we have rejected Him and turned away.

We must respond to God's love by accepting it and loving Him back. The Bible is not a record of man's quest for God; it is a record of God's quest for man. God *first* loved us. Oh, that we might fathom just a little bit His wonderful, matchless love and let it flow freely through our lives to those around us who so desperately need it, who are totally unaware that they are loved at all.

Father, how could You love us so, unworthy creatures that we are? Thank You for that love; forgive us for ever doubting.

JANUARY 23

Forasmuch then as we are the offspring of God, we ought not to think that the Godhead is like unto gold, or silver, or stone, graven by art and man's device.

ACTS 17:29

We don't make any graven images, but we sometimes have distorted views of God. Sometimes we trust in the wrong things. No sooner do we find an experience or a doctrine in which we feel we can anchor our trust, than a great shaking comes, and we're left adrift again. This process must continue until all that can be shaken is removed and only those things which cannot be shaken remain. Often the answer to our most fervent prayers for deliverance comes in such a form that it seems that the very foundations of the hills at first moved and were shaken. We do not always see at first, but it is by means of this very shaking that the deliverance for which we have prayed is to be accomplished. We are to be brought forth into the larger place for which we long. This need for detachment is the secret of many of our shakings. We cannot follow the Lord fully as long as we remain tied to anything else, any more than a boat can make headway on a long journey as long as it is tied fast to the shore.

In what do we really trust? Do we trust in a doctrine? We have known fine, marvelous Christian people who trust in doctrine. Then they went away to school or they went here or there, and somebody shook it up. Maybe God is allowing that shaking up so that they might come to trust in Him and His Person, not in the doctrine. The doctrine is just a part of God—it is not God Himself.

We cannot afford to trust in our own faithfulness, our own goodness, our own good fortune. God can shake us apart from these things, but He does so with tender love that our false trust might be removed and that we might come to rest in the only true resting place—Himself.

Abraham had everything he thought he needed, then God came along and shook his foundation and told him to leave it all and come out on faith to a strange new life and way. It was only that God might bring him into a larger place.

Many of us have had our foundation shaken. Maybe it was a marriage that we counted on; maybe it was a home we thought was secure and right; maybe it was a job, a business. Oh, how God can shake us up! The beauty and joy come, though, when we remember that He does it with love, to bring us to that larger place where we rest only in Him.

Precious Jesus, help us not to put our trust and faith in people, doctrines, or things—but to trust only in You.

JANUARY 24

Ah Lord God! behold, thou hast made the heaven and the earth by thy great power and stretched out arm, and there is nothing too hard for thee.

JEREMIAH 32:17

These are difficult days. Inflation overwhelms us. Salaries do not meet our needs. The future seems uncertain, and we feel insecure. But God's promises are just as true today as they were to the widow and her mite, or to me struggling to raise two children. He still says, "Trust Me." If we do and act in faith, believing, He will do what He has promised: open the window of heaven and pour out a blessing so great that you will not be able to receive it (Malachi 3:10). Never doubt it. Failure leaves your vocabulary when you take God as your partner.

Lord, help us to truly make You our partner in all the areas of our lives, earnestly believing that You have unlimited blessings to pour out on us if we will just trust You.

JANUARY 25

Except the Lord build the house, they labour in vain that build it: except the Lord keep the city, the watchman waketh but in vain.

PSALMS 127:1

When we launch out to build a business, we should ask God for the plans. He will give them to us, and when we build according to His specifications and design, our business will be unique. It's not that we are so smart, but just that we have used a plan that has come straight off God's drawing board—His plan for economics, for people, for success. He is the architect.

It is important that we do this in the right order—request our plans from God first and then follow them, not decide on *our* plan first and then ask Him to bless it and make it His own.

It takes grit, grace, and gumption. God will furnish the grace, but we have to furnish the grit and the gumption.

Precious Jesus, teach us to seek You first and everything else will fall into place.

JANUARY 26

This then is the message which we have heard of him, and declare unto you, that God is light, and in him is no darkness at all. If we say that we have fellowship with him, and walk in darkness, we lie, and do not the truth: But if we walk in the light, as he is in the light, we have fellowship one with another, and the blood of Jesus Christ his Son cleanseth us from all sin.

1 JOHN 1:5, 7

Kim Wickes is a beautiful little Korean girl who lifts you close to heaven when she sings. Kim's eyes are no longer there, her eyeballs were removed when she was a little child. She has total blackness as far as visible, physical sight is concerned. But this girl walks with light more than most people with seeing eyes. She walks in God's love and God's light. God's love can overrule any kind of darkness, physical darkness, spiritual darkness. We *can* walk with light—GOD'S LIGHT!

Light gives us direction; light gives us guidance; light shows the way. If there is a certain area where you have to go, the lighting is so designed that it makes a pathway of light to follow so that you will arrive safely. God's love does that. It provides a pathway of light. So often as Christians we grope in darkness. "Oh, where do I go? Where do I turn? What do I do next?" Then it is time to get into that pathway of light, walk in His love and in His blessings. Light will come, *He* will light our path!

Dear Father, how I pray for light for all who grope in dark-ness of doubt or confusion or sin. Help me to be a light to someone today for You because of Jesus.

JANUARY 27

And I give unto them eternal life; and they shall never perish, neither shall any man pluck them out of my hand.

JOHN 10:28

When we come to Jesus and He forgives our sins, we can even repent and still not have salvation, because we must *repent,* and *believe,* and *accept.*

People can look at God and be sorry for their sins, but they often don't really want to give up their lives to Christ. They are sorry, and they might make a lot of New Year's resolutions, but until it becomes a personal relationship, their salvation is not complete.

It must be a *personal* relationship. God is a Person in the Per-son of Jesus Christ. He is the One we must seek in a personal relationship. It is not just being sorry for our sins, it is also accepting Jesus as our Lord and Master. When we do, the Holy Spirit changes our lives into this personal relationship and makes us joint heirs with Christ.

As you know, an adopted child cannot be disowned. We are adopted by the Spirit. We do not do it. We receive and repent and accept, but the Holy Spirit at that moment, *at that moment,* comes into our lives and joins us to the Body of Christ, joins us to the Person of Christ, joins us to the Family of God, and we can never be disjoined. We can never be cast out, and we can never be disowned. That is the assurance of the believer.

"Blessed assurance, Jesus is mine!"

Father, as is the love of a godly mother for the babe in her arms, so is Thy promise of love and assurance to us. Thank You for our safekeeping.

JANUARY 28

Brethren, I count not myself to have apprehended: but this one thing I do, forgetting those things which are behind, and reaching forth unto those things which are before.
PHILIPPIANS 3:13

We are prone to remember our past failures. Don't let your past failures haunt you and pull you down. Write down your fears, the things which are holding you back. Confess them to God and He will relieve you of them.

This is a quote from James Robison:

What is repentance? Well, we will first take up what repentance is *not.* It is not remorse, it is not regret, it is not reform, it is not religion, but repentance is "Turning your eyes to Jesus, and turning your back on everything God despises, on everything God says is despicable or destructive."

Repentance is trust in Jesus and turning toward Him.

Dear God, help us to know that every day is a new day and a new opportunity at life. Give us the courage to conquer new horizons but the wisdom to know when the conquest is right for us.

JANUARY 29

Now the God of peace, that brought again from the dead our Lord Jesus, that great shepherd of the sheep, through the blood of the everlasting covenant, Make you perfect in every good work to do his will, working in you that which is well-pleasing in his sight, through Jesus Christ; to whom be glory for ever and ever.

HEBREWS 13:20, 21

I am so grateful that God does not check us out in the "feelings" department. He checks out our "will" department, like checking the rudder of a ship. Today, I do not feel righteous. There are days when I do not feel spiritual. There are days when I do not even feel close to Him.

Your feelings can depend upon the loss of sleep, an upset stomach, a friend who put you down, but if you have purposed to do the will of God, then you are in His will and you will come out right, whether you "feel" like it or not.

Dear Lord, it is wonderful to "feel" spiritual and close to You, but it is even more wonderful to know that even when we feel the least faithful and worthy, You just go right on—guiding our lives—watching over us—loving us.

JANUARY 30

And when they looked, they saw that the stone was rolled away.

MARK 16:4

This is the story of two women, very close followers of Jesus, who were on their way to the tomb early in the morning that first day of the week. They were anxiously discussing who would be able to roll away the stone from the door of the sepulchre . . . FOR IT WAS GREAT!

How like these two women we all are, people throughout the centuries. We worry and fret over the obstacles that have to be rolled away—often they are "very great," far beyond our meager personal strength—only to find that when we finally come to those obstacles

they have been rolled away!

How foolish we are to fret and fear when we possess within us the OMNIPOTENT GOD OF THE UNIVERSE, going before us, fighting our battles, lifting our burdens—if we but bow our heads and ask.

Gracious Father, teach us to number our days that we may apply our hearts unto wisdom.

JANUARY 31

What promises did you make to God at the beginning of this month when the year was fresh and new? How many of them have you kept?

Refresh your memory and renew those vows by writing them on this page and earnestly contemplating them. Then pray that God will give you a new zeal to keep the ones which will draw you to a closer walk with Him or to a better understanding and relationship with the people whose lives you touch.

1. _____
2. _____
3. _____
4. _____

The woods are lovely, dark, and deep,
But I have promises to keep,
And miles to go before I sleep,
And miles to go before I sleep.

ROBERT FROST

February

FEBRUARY 1

Now therefore thus saith the Lord of hosts; Consider your ways. Ye have sown much, and bring in little; ye eat, but ye have not enough; ye drink, but ye are not filled with drink; ye clothe you, but there is none warm; and he that earneth wages earneth wages to put it into a bag with holes.

HAGGAI 1:5–8

Oh, in this cold, wintry weather we ofttimes have lots of time to think. We are kept inside by ice and sleet, perhaps, or put to bed with a cold or the flu. The forced solitude gives us time we don't ordinarily have for thinking and reflecting.

The fire in the hearth is a powerful symbol to me: It gives *warmth;* it is *alive;* it *dies down* and *burns up again;* it must be *stirred;* it must continually be *fed* with new wood—it is fascinating!

My uncle used to say, "A fire in the hearth is a happy thing, as long as it is controlled." It does symbolize a lot of things about living a good, productive life. We all have to be stirred up, we all have to be fed—and free—and yet disciplined and channeled in the right direction.

O God, control us, stir us, feed us, and help us to produce the warmth and zeal needed to get Your job done.

FEBRUARY 2

God is not a man, that he should lie; neither the son of man, that he should repent: hath he said, and shall he not do it? or hath he spoken, and shall he not make it good?

NUMBERS 23:19

43

PRAY frequently and read your Bible. This is the way you keep in touch with Christ. **Take time to read your Bible!** In this busy world we live in, we must take time out to do the important things. So it is also with our spiritual lives: We must take time to communicate with God. When we read the Bible, He speaks to us. When we pray, we speak to Him. Throughout the entire process, the Holy Spirit works in our hearts and directs us along the pathway of life.

Dear Lord, if we're too busy to read the Bible and pray, we're TOO BUSY! *May we never be too busy to spend time with Thee.*

FEBRUARY 3

And for their sakes I sanctify myself, that they also might be sanctified through the truth.

JOHN 17:19

Expect the Holy Spirit to work *in* you, *for* you, and *through* you. This is the promise of God to us if we follow the example of the Lord. If we will sanctify or consecrate ourselves to God, He will bring about the growth in our lives. If we say we believe in God, yet seek no other strength and guidance beyond our own, if we answer to no higher authority than our own stubborn will, then we give ourselves to hypocrisy. To give ourselves in love to no higher claim than our own vanity is sin. To say we believe in God yet go about as if we were the answer ourselves is the deadliest atheism. Christian perfection is not, and cannot be, human perfection. Christian perfection is the perfection of a relationship to God which shows itself amid the irrelevancies of human life. We are called to live in such a relationship to God that our lives produce a longing after God in other lives. God does not want us to be specimens in a showcase, He wants us where He can use us.

Father, help us to understand all these things which would make us more fit vessels for Thy use.

FEBRUARY 4

And thou shalt do that which is right and good in the sight of the Lord: that it may be well with thee . . .

DEUTERONOMY 6:18

We can tell when we are doing wrong by three things:

- First of all, we will be uneasy about it.
- Second, we will argue in defense of the wrongful thing we are doing.
- Third, we will try to find someone else who will tell us that the wrong thing is actually right.

So when you start to argue about something and you are a little uneasy—stop! Is it really right?

There is no need to be uneasy or defensive if it is right. If it's doubtful, it's wrong. The same principle applies to us in the decisions we have to make in life.

Lord, help us to "mind the stops," being sensitive to know those things that are wrong for us and turning always away from them.

FEBRUARY 5

All scripture is given by inspiration of God, and is profitable for doctrine, for reproof, for correction, for instruction in righteousness.

2 TIMOTHY 3:16

One of the ways God has revealed His Word to us is through the Person of Jesus Christ. Another way is through the pages of the Bible. The first of these is the Living Word of God; the second is the written Word of God. Although they are distinct, there are some things about them that show how closely they are related. Both are a unique blending of the human and the divine. In Jesus Christ, the eternal, preexistent Son of God became flesh and lived among men. He was the physical manifestation of the Triune God.

The Bible is likewise a unique combination of human and divine elements. Second Timothy 3:16 says that all scripture is "God-breathed." Second Peter 1:20, 21 indicates that holy men of God spoke as they were "borne along by the Holy Spirit." In short, both the Living and the written Word are the products of God operating through human agencies.

God, help us see You in all the ways You reveal Yourself to us, but especially may we love Your Holy Word and Your Living Word, the blessed Jesus.

FEBRUARY 6

And we know that all things work together for good to them that love God, to them who are the called according to his purpose.

ROMANS 8:28

Through the power of your creative imagination, you catch a vision . . . you dream a dream. You visualize yourself as the person you want to be! You see yourself as a triumphant personality, striding toward horizons of constructive accomplishment! You see yourself as a master servant of the race, ministering to human needs and radiating happiness. You strive to make the ideal in your mind become a reality on the canvas of time. You select and mix the positive colors of heart, mind, and spirit into the qualities of good living: patience, determination, endurance, self-discipline, work, love, and faith.

Each moment of time is a brush stroke on the painting of your unfolding life. There are the bold, sweeping strokes of dynamic purpose. There are the lights and shadows that make life deep and strong. There are the little touches that add the stamp of CHARACTER and WORTH. The "art of achievement" is the art of making life—your life—a MASTERPIECE.

O Master Painter, help us to truly paint a masterpiece.

FEBRUARY 7

For I reckon that the sufferings of this present time are not worthy to be compared with the glory which shall be revealed to us.

ROMANS 8:18

God will mend a broken heart if we give Him all the pieces . . . yet, how very difficult that is when we hurt so much. Through Him, though, we really can know peace. God *does* comfort! He *does* enable us! He *does* encourage us! God says, "I am your refuge and your strength" (*see* Psalms 46:1).

Holding us are the everlasting arms, but we must trust before we can experience their wonderful support.

You know, it is strange that there is no record in history, ever, of a missionary who committed suicide. And yet they are often in the most difficult places. Many people face situations that certainly are not comfortable or pleasant and really seem intolerable, but the people who commit suicide are the Hollywood or the existential people, the intellectual people who seemingly have everything—yet, they do not have God. They are not in the center of His will, so life for them is meaningless, it has no purpose.

But the missionary—on a foreign land, away from family and home, sometimes ill, often without sufficient comforts—has never committed suicide. For life holds purpose, oh, so much purpose, for him.

As Christians, we always have purpose, for we are called according to *His* purpose. And therein lies the power. Not the power just to endure, but to be triumphant. Jesus overcame, and now He offers that experience to us. He has been there! He understands! He is able to help!

And so He says, ". . . be of good cheer; I have overcome the world" (John 16:33).

God uses suffering to prepare us to be of service, to comfort others, to help people who are hurting, and then He gives the peace. . . . "Not as the world giveth, but I give you *My* Peace" (*see* John 14:27). It is a different kind of peace. It is an inner tranquility, not an absence of problems, but a presence of inner tranquility.

Father, may Your peace, which passeth all understanding, be ours this day and forevermore.

FEBRUARY 8

Whereas ye know not what shall be on the morrow. For what is your life? It is even a vapour, that appeareth for a little time, and then vanisheth away. For that ye ought to say, If the Lord will, we shall live, and do this, or that. But now ye rejoice in your boastings: all such rejoicing is evil. Therefore to him that knoweth to do good, and doeth it not, to him it is sin.

JAMES 4:14–17

God does not count success as we count it, nor does He count achievement by length of days.

Teenagers at the graveside of a friend who had died in an accident shared a beautiful experience, and many of them made commitments to the Lord in the tenderness of that moment. It would seem to us a life had been cut short, but God teaches us that there is no such thing as a life cut short. Every minute of every day in the lives of all His creation is granted or suspended according to His plans for each individual life.

He gave us minutes, hours, weeks, and years just so we would have a track to run on, but time to Him has no beginning and no end—it is ever the eternal *now*. His timing is always perfect and just, no life is ever over until it has fulfilled God's plans for it on earth.

Lord, Your mysteries are beyond knowing, but we do know that our very lives are in Your hands, and we must hasten to do the things whereunto You have sent us while there is still time.

FEBRUARY 9

The God of my rock; in him will I trust: he is my shield, and the horn of my salvation, my high tower, and my refuge, my saviour; thou savest me from violence.

2 SAMUEL 22:3

How can we fail if we have God as our partner?

Many years ago I worked for an insurance company at a time when people were paid very low salaries. Inflation had hit, and I was trying to rear two children. Teeth needed fixing; music lessons had to be paid for; food had to be bought. I thought I could not afford to tithe.

The money ran out before the month ran out. I would literally pace the floor, not knowing how I was going to pay the bills. Well, I talked to the Lord about it and read in Malachi 3:10 where God said, "Trust me." He told me I wasn't doing such a great job and asked me to let Him take care of everything, to take Him as my partner. I decided to give Him a try.

The following week, a city in which we insured the houses was hit by a hurricane. I worked overtime and made about $300 in overtime money. I am sure God sent that extra money to me. Even though He did not send the hurricane, He used it. Something wonderful happened in my life. I can't explain it, I just recommend it.

To tithe seemed impossible. I was paid twice a month. I began to put my tithe in first, because if I waited, there would not be enough left. There were times when we had only cereal and milk for a week or two, but we never went hungry. And God was as good as His Word. He *did* open the windows of Heaven and pour out His blessings.

FEBRUARY 10

Delight thyself also in the Lord; and he shall give thee the desires of thine heart.

PSALMS 37:4

What a wondrous revelation it was when I finally learned to delight in the Lord. When duty becomes delight, our relationship with God, Himself, changes into that of a joyous relationship with a friend in whom we delight.

To delight in the Lord we need to learn what delights Him, what makes Him happy. In Proverbs we find the things that the Lord hates, so of course the opposites would be what delights Him.

Many years ago when I was in the First Baptist Choir, we used to sing this song:

> My God and I go through the fields together,
> We walk and talk as good friends should and do;
> We clasp our hands, our voices ring with laughter,
> My God and I walk through the meadows hue.

Lord, may the desires of our hearts be to delight more and more in Thee.

FEBRUARY 11

Let love be your greatest aim; nevertheless, ask also for the special abilities the Holy Spirit gives, and especially the gift of prophecy, being able to preach the messages of God.
                                    1 CORINTHIANS 14:1 TLB

Your married life begins as most marriages do, romantic, exciting, compelling, new. Everything about it is wonderful during the first few weeks and months. Like most things in life, however, it begins to tarnish unless it is "polished" and treasured like sterling silver. When routineness begins to occur, a new sense of privilege and opportunity in daily tasks must appear. When the romance and dignity of daily life begins to pale and fade amid the pressures which seem to be common with daily duty, the mind must find a new excitement and fresh pleasure in duty to keep the wonder in living.

Lord, we know attitude is the mind's paint brush. It can color any situation gloomy or gray or happy and gay. May our attitudes be right.

FEBRUARY 12

For you were called to freedom, brethren; only do not use your freedom as an opportunity for the flesh, but through love be servants of one another.

GALATIANS 5:13 RSV

Today the nation remembers the everlasting influence of a great man—ABRAHAM LINCOLN. Many words will be said and written about this outstanding American, a boy who came from the humblest of homes, one without the benefit of good lighting, adequate plumbing, good schools, or even a balanced diet;—one who came from obscurity and failure, heartbreak and ridicule, to occupy the highest office in the land: **The Presidency of the United States.**

Let us study some of the things he said during some hard times in our country—and would still say to us today: "A house divided against itself cannot stand. Our cause must be entrusted to, and conducted by, its own undoubted friends, those whose hands are free, whose hearts are in the work, who do care for the results.

We are indeed going through a great trial, a fiery trial. In the very responsible position in which I happened to be placed, being a humble instrument in the hands of our Heavenly Father, as I am, and as we all are, to work out His great purposes . . . I have desired that all my works and acts may be according to His will. And that it might be so, I have sought His aid. But if, after endeavoring to do my best in the light which He affords me, I find my efforts fail, I must believe that for some purpose unknown to me, He wills it otherwise. Through our limited understanding we may not be able to comprehend His purpose . . . yet we cannot but believe that He who made the world still governs it. **The will of God prevails!"**

Thank you, Mr. Lincoln!

Dear Lord, help modern-day man to realize You made the world, You govern it even today, and that You will ultimately be exalted.

FEBRUARY 13

For God so loved the world, that he gave his only begotten Son, that whosoever believeth in him should not perish, but have everlasting life.

JOHN 3:16

God has been trying to show us how much He loves us from the beginning of time. He did it throughout the Old Testament by sending the prophets. They were all rejected, as Jesus indicated in His parable of the great husbandman who had sent his stewards to tend his vineyards. The stewards were all rejected. Finally, he sent his son, thinking they might respect him, but they didn't. Instead, they killed the son.

This is a picture of what God did through Jesus Christ. God loved us so much that He sent His Son, knowing full well that He, too, would be rejected. But Jesus was God's ultimate revelation that He loves us. Jesus showed the world through His willingness to die for us, and through His resurrection, that He had victory over death and over all the problems of life forever.

Father, forgive us for ever rejecting Your gift to us. Oh, that the whole world might receive Him gladly!

FEBRUARY 14

Finally, be ye all of one mind, having compassion one of another, love as brethren, be pitiful, be courteous.

1 PETER 3:8

Be good
  to your neighbor!
Tell your husband you love him
  at least twice a day!
Bring your willingness, warm heart and enthusiasm
  to every person you meet!
Do your best ...
  God will bless even the tiniest talent!

Dear Father, may each person we touch feel Your warmth in our touch, our smile, our love.

FEBRUARY 15

There is no fear in love; but perfect love casteth out fear: because fear hath torment. He that feareth is not made perfect in love.

1 JOHN 4:18

Human love is a response to divine love. It is not a product of the human heart, although we might think it is when we love our children, sweethearts, or others. The origin of this love is God. No matter how much we might distort it or misapply it, the fountainhead of human love is God. Even our parental love and the love between individuals is at its best when shared between two Christians. This is because God is the added dimension. He is the source of all love, and His dimension gives a depth to our relationships which is far beyond our limited capacities. The most treasured thing a man or woman can bring into a love relationship is the kind of love that is Christian. It is the selfless sharing of two lives in God, and because it begins and ends in Him, it is able to cast out all fear. What a deepening experience it is to share something without having to clutch it or cling to it for fear that someone may steal it away. In Christ we have the basis for perfect love which casts out fear because it rests in Him.

Lord, we desire to love as You love—unselfishly, fearlessly, holding nothing back. Such love can come only from You. May we reach a Christian maturity that will allow us in some measure to love like that.

FEBRUARY 16

But now, O Lord, thou art our father; we are the clay, and thou our potter; and we all are the work of thy hand. Be not wroth very sore, O Lord, neither remember iniquity for ever: behold, see, we beseech thee, we are all thy people.

ISAIAH 64:8, 9

Emerson once wrote, "We are bound up in the bundle of life together, and we affect each other mightily. Like soft clay, each molds the other until this home product that we are making together becomes either a model or a menace to all who see it." No couple can live to themselves alone. The serene quietness or the agitated upheaval of the morning breakfast table is carried over into the work-a-day world and influences all with whom we come in contact. Marriage is not a launching site for attacks upon the world; it is, rather, a place of refuge and strengthening for life. Marriage is that happy struggle where loved ones share the experiences of tears and laughter, defeat and victory, hardship and ease.

Lord, help us to work without ceasing to make our marriage the haven of love and security it ought to be.

FEBRUARY 17

Be still, and know that I am God.

PSALMS 46:10

BE STILL—when your car won't start and you're late already.
BE STILL—when the sticky orange juice has been spilled on the floor you've just mopped.

BE STILL—when you've discovered your new bedspread has just been decorated with red Magic Marker.

BE STILL—when your refrigerator breaks down just before you're leaving for your vacation.

BE STILL—when your husband finally arrives for dinner, forty-five minutes late!

BE STILL—when your baby's sick and causes you to miss a very important social luncheon.

BE STILL—when your washing machine breaks and you haven't a clean diaper in the house.

Dear Father, please calm our "frazzles" and help us to be still, resting in Your serenity.

FEBRUARY 18

Be still, and know that I am God: I will be exalted among the heathen, I will be exalted in the earth.

PSALMS 46:10

This morning I am again grateful that I have health enough to work and handle a lot of things that need to be done today.

Last night I was very, very weary, so, once again, I thought of this poem which means a great deal to me. It is called "For One Who Is Tired."

Dear Child,
God does not say today, "Be strong"—
　He knows your strength is spent—
He knows how long the road has been—
　How weary you've become, for

He who walked this earth alone—
　Each boggy lowland and each rugged hill, understands—
And so He simply says, "Be still,

　Be still and know that I am God."
The hour is late and you must rest awhile,—
　And you must wait

Until life's empty reservoirs fill up
  As slow rain fills an empty upturned cup.

Hold up your cup, dear child, for God to fill.
  He only asks that you be still.

GRACE NOLL CROWELL

And I think of that wonderful verse "Wait on the Lord, and He will renew your strength" (*see* Psalms 27:14).

There are days when we have to spend a little more time in waiting, and listening, and reading His Word, waiting for the presence of the Holy Spirit to somehow stir a numbed conscience. I have often said that ego is the greatest enemy of men, and fatigue is the greatest enemy of women. Fatigue clouds our minds and erodes our dispositions.

So, today, as the many duties that I can accomplish crowd in, I am grateful that last evening I spent a little time waiting on the Lord, and He has renewed my strength.

Father, help us when our human frailties overwhelm us to be still and wait for Your strength, for Your refreshment, and most of all, for Your blessed presence.

FEBRUARY 19

Wherefore be ye not unwise, but understanding what the will of the Lord is. And be not drunk with wine, wherein is excess; but be filled with the Spirit; Speaking to yourselves in psalms and hymns and spiritual songs, singing and making melody in your heart to the Lord. Giving thanks always for all things unto God and the Father in the name of our Lord Jesus Christ.

EPHESIANS 5:17–20

Oh, to be filled with the Spirit! We just pray that we will let the Spirit fill more of our lives day-by-day! And as we depend on

Him, as we study, as we learn, as we pray, He is there. He is *always* there!

But the filling is not always the same. Wouldn't it be wonderful if we would be so filled with His Spirit that we would overflow . . . be people of the overflow! You know, when a vessel overflows, we cease to see the vessel, we just see the overflow.

Oh, that we might do that! That we might let His Spirit so fill us that we would overflow, and people would see only the Lord and His Spirit and *not us!*

Give me a faithful heart, likeness to Thee
That each departing day henceforth may see
Some work of love begun, some deed of kindness done,
Some wanderer sought and won,
Something for Thee.

SYLVANUS D. PHELPS

O God, make us people of the overflow, that the filling might be so complete that we would know eternally what You have for us to do.

FEBRUARY 20

He that findeth his life shall lose it: and he that loseth his life for my sake shall find it.

MATTHEW 10:39

I remember the words of that wonderful missionary, Jim Elliott, who said, when told he was a fool to go to the Auca Indians, "No man is a fool to lose that which he cannot keep for that which he cannot lose."

Oh, a commitment to excellence, in a relationship with God! In relationship with home! In relationship with others!

And how many times as women we have to learn to say, "God, help me to live by the peace of God, instead of by the pressures of life."

Our Father, we know that each day we must make decisions. By our choices we determine what we are. May our judgments be made, not simply for our own convenience, or to suit a passing fancy, but with the purpose of doing that which is acceptable in Your sight, which is truly excellent. Keep us from going astray. May we say with the Psalmist, "You, O God, will keep on guiding me all of my life with Your wisdom and Your counsel."

FEBRUARY 21

Keep thy heart with all diligence; for out of it are the issues of life.

PROVERBS 4:23

Once I counseled with a young man who was the type who likes to fly in an airplane and keep one foot on the ground. He wanted to be in the world of movie stars and fantastic hit records, but success just kept eluding him. He was a fine young man, but he had his priorities mixed-up. He had put his love on fame and fortune, and it had not paid. My counsel to him was, "If the Lord wants you to serve as the minister of music in a little obscure church, do it. Then God will open the doors to bigger places. But you have to put your affection on Him and let Him lead." And He will do it! I know He will!

It is so hard for young people, because they have been brought up in a "now, instant-coffee society." Everything is instant; they want everything *now*. It is so hard for them to see that you have to pay your dues, you have to serve your apprenticeship, and you have to wait, and sometimes wait, and wait, and wait. But, if our affections are on the Lord, in His own time, in His own way, the thing He has for us will surely come to pass.

Dear Father, make us patient and willing to wait upon Thee, for that better thing that You have in store for us.

FEBRUARY 22

But ye, beloved, building up yourselves on your most holy faith, praying in the Holy Ghost, Keep yourselves in the love of God, looking for the mercy of our Lord Jesus Christ unto eternal life.

JUDE 20, 21

Exercise your faith. When you do, it develops its own ongoing strength, its own "spiritual muscles." So much of the growth of a Christian is like the growth of your body. You need to exercise, take in the right food, and do the right things to develop your body. To develop your soul and spirit, you need to exercise your faith, *use* it, nourish it with food from God's Word, build up your confidence in God.

Jesus said to His disciples, ". . . O ye of little faith" (Matthew 6:30), when He walked to them on the water, and they were scared to death. They needed to exercise their faith. Peter did, and, as a result, he was able to do something no mortal man had ever done before, or since—he walked on the water. But then his faith faded, his spiritual muscles grew weak, and he began to sink.

Peter found that faith is not a once-and-for-all proposition. We can be doing very well, and a distraction will come along and drag us down. It is then we need to get back on our "exercise program" and if we follow it faithfully, we will see our faith begin to develop and grow.

Lord, help us to grow stronger and stronger in our love for You and faith in Your love for us.

FEBRUARY 23

Whereby are given unto us exceeding great and precious promises: that by these ye might be partakers of the divine nature, having escaped the corruption that is in the world through lust. And beside this, giving all diligence, add to your faith virtue; and to virtue knowledge; And to knowledge temperance; and to temperance patience; and to patience godliness; And to godliness brotherly kindness; and to brotherly kindness charity. For if these things be in you, and abound, they make you that ye shall neither be barren nor unfruitful in the knowledge of our Lord Jesus Christ.

2 PETER 1:4–8

God keeps His promises so much better than we ever dream. My imagination was not big enough to fathom all the blessings He had in store for me. But that's God! He has so many good gifts He's just waiting to pour out on His children!

Honor Him! Try Him! Trust Him for the blessings He has promised!

> The windows of heaven are open,
>   Blessings are falling tonight
> There is joy, joy, joy in my soul
>   For God has made everything right.
>
> I gave Him my old tattered garments;
>   He gave me a robe of pure white;
> I'm feasting on manna from Heaven,
>   And that's why I'm happy tonight.

Lord, help us to honor Thee and expect great things from Thee; pour out Your bountiful blessings, and we will try to use them for Your glory.

FEBRUARY 24

I acknowledged my sin unto thee, and mine iniquity have I not hid. I said, I will confess my transgressions unto the Lord; and thou forgavest the iniquity of my sin.

PSALMS 32:5

Perhaps the most important reason for us to develop a prayer life is to provide a basis for us to confess our sins to God. God already knows all about our sins, so the benefit comes from the fact that we have an opportunity to acknowledge them ourselves. Unconfessed sins separate us from fellowship with God. Since God has not moved, we must acknowledge our erring to Him. When we do this, He immediately forgives us of our sins and restores us to fellowship. Confession of sins is simply naming them as sins, or acknowledging our sins to God specifically. There are three kinds of sins which we must acknowledge. First are our sins of *omission.* We often ask God to forgive us of sins of omission, but rarely do we specify what these sins are. They are the specific acts which God commends to us that we fail to carry out. Second are our sins of *commission,* our deliberate sins, our willful breaking of God's moral laws. Finally, there are the sins of *disposition.* These are the sins of the spirit or attitude. They are the heart attitudes such as that of the elder brother of the prodigal son. They express themselves in bitterness, negativism, fault-finding, resentment, and other critical attitudes. Oh, how we need to confess our sins to God!

> *God, how foolish we are to think we can hide a sin from You by failing to confess it. Help us to hold nothing back. "Create in us a clean heart and renew a right spirit within us."*

FEBRUARY 25

> *But I will sacrifice unto thee with the voice of thanksgiving; I will pay that that I have vowed. Salvation is of the Lord.*
>
> JONAH 2:9

You can't run away and hide from God, but the story of Jonah is about a man who tried. He went to the seacoast, bought a ticket to go the opposite direction from where God had told him to go, and climbed into the bottom of the ship to hide from the Lord. Aren't we just like that? When we begin to have feelings of bitterness, resentment, or frustration, we don't want to come to God's house because we're afraid He'll speak to us. So we stay away. We try to get as far away as we can. Somebody comes to talk to us about our responsibilities and obligations to the Lord and His house and His work, and we really resent them. We throw up all kinds of defenses.

When God tells us to do something, we cannot get away. Jonah found himself in the bottom of that ship, and what happened? A fierce storm built up, and the sailors couldn't figure out what was happening. They found Jonah sleeping and made him draw straws with them to see who had offended the gods. Jonah drew the short one. Do you think that was by chance? No, God had planned the whole thing. God's plans are *going* to be carried out. God does not coerce people and make them repent, but sometimes He has to shake them up. He sees all things, and somehow His plans are *going* to be carried out. How much better if we obey in the beginning and do not have to go through all the discomfort!

Well, Jonah "fessed up" and said the storm had come because of him, the first sign he had admitted even to himself the consequences of his disobedience, resentment, and rebellion. When the sailors prayed to Jonah's God, Jehovah, and threw Jonah into the sea, the storm stopped. They then stood in awe before God and vowed to serve Him. God can use any occasion or circumstance to bring people to Himself.

After three days and three nights in the depths of the great fish, Jonah repented and went back to Ninevah to do what God had told him to do, convinced that he could not run far enough to get away from God. Neither can we. He sees everything we do. He loves, He cares, He sees!

Heavenly Father, thank You for caring enough to confront us with our selfish ways. Cleanse me, show me, use me, today.

FEBRUARY 26

For God is not the author of confusion, but of peace, as in all churches of the saints.

1 CORINTHIANS 14:33

But the Comforter, which is the Holy Ghost, whom the Father will send in my name, he shall teach you all things, and bring all things to your remembrance, whatsoever I have said unto you.

JOHN 14:26

As we read our Bibles, the Holy Spirit teaches us the things of God. He was promised as the Guide who would lead us into all truth. Sometimes He pours so much out to us that every page seems to come alive. He prepares our hearts and minds so that we can understand the written Word. In addition, the Holy Spirit makes intercession for us. He leads us through our daily circumstances and protects us from our adversary, the devil. In 1 John we are informed that He bears witness with our spirit that we are indeed the children of God. This subjective experience operates within our lives, but it must always be consistent with what we have learned from Jesus Christ and from the Bible.

Lord, may Your Holy Spirit bear witness to our hearts of You and the blessed Son You sent to make us children of Thine.

FEBRUARY 27

As newborn babes, desire the sincere milk of the word, that ye may grow thereby: If so be ye have tasted that the Lord is gracious.

1 PETER 2:2, 3

God uses His written Word to bring people unto Himself. Through the centuries many have come to know Him merely by reading the Bible. The Scriptures are to be used both for revelation of Himself and as a means whereby we may grow spiritually.

When we read the Bible, we will receive nourishment, but we will also have our hearts and minds cleansed. In addition, we will have the most reliable textbook about God ever devised, and we can truly come to know Him.

Lord, cleanse us, renew us, immerse us in Your Word.

FEBRUARY 28

There is none like unto the God of Jeshurun, who rideth upon the heaven in thy help, and in his excellency on the sky. The eternal God is thy refuge, and underneath are the everlasting arms: and he shall thrust out the enemy from before thee; and shall say, Destroy them. Israel then shall dwell in safety alone: the fountain of Jacob shall be upon a land of corn and wine; also his heavens shall drop down dew. Happy art thou, O Israel: who is like unto thee, O people saved by the Lord, the shield of thy help, and who is the sword of thy excellency! and thine enemies shall be found liars unto thee; and thou shalt tread upon their high places.

DEUTERONOMY 33:26–29

Comfort and peace can never come from anything within ourselves. People look outside themselves for the meaning to their existence, for security, and for fulfillment. The only thing we will ever know about God we find from looking at Him and from reading His Word—not from looking at ourselves. We can never find the comfort, peace, joy, and the special meaning of living by looking within ourselves. These things come only by looking at God. Jesus said, "And I, if I be lifted up from the earth, will draw all men unto me" (John 12:32).

Our inheritance is comfort, peace, and joy. How many times do we fail to claim our inheritance? We go around with long faces, worrying, when all the time what we need is to know God better. If we ever see Him as He really is, we will fall in love with Him. We can look at ourselves, but we will see only inconsistencies and so many negative things. We must look rather at Jesus—He is our comfort, our peace, our joy.

> *O Lord, might we learn to look at You, to know You better. You have saved us, are saving us. You will keep us. All we have to do is continually and everlastingly get to know You better. Knowing about You is our life-time task.*

FEBRUARY 29

We have so much to learn of the wonders of God!

The many facets of our life in Him are too much for us to fathom in a month or two. We have touched on so many things this month—how God loves us, how the Holy Spirit will lead and empower us, how to have a happier home and a more effective prayer life.

Have *you* grown this month? Have you learned anything about God? about yourself?

Call upon the Lord that He will grant you wisdom and insight as we search out the riches of His truths together.

Your prayer:

Dear God, here at the end of the month, but really at the beginning of a fresh New Year, I earnestly pray that

_____

_____

_____

_____

_____

Next year, as you come to this page, it will be interesting for you to see if indeed God *has* accomplished the things in your life that you desire.

March

MARCH 1

Blessed are the poor in spirit: for theirs is the kingdom of heaven.

MATTHEW 5:3

Oh, the blessedness of the person who has realized his own utter helplessness and who has put his whole trust in God. Oh, the blessedness of the husband who has realized his own helplessness and has put his whole trust in God! Oh, the blessedness of the wife who has realized her own helplessness and has put her trust, her *whole* trust in God!

The man who is poor in spirit is the person who has realized that *things* mean nothing and that *God* means everything. Poverty is not a good thing. Jesus would never have called blessed a place where people live in slums and have not enough to eat and where health rots because conditions are all against it. That kind of poverty is what the Christian Gospel seeks to remove. But, the poverty which is blessed is the "poverty of spirit"—the spirit which realizes its own utter lack of resources to meet life and which clings to God for its health and strength is blessed.

Jesus says that to such a poverty as this belongs the Kingdom of Heaven. Why should this be so? From the Lord's Prayer we get the definition. The Kingdom of Heaven—the Kingdom of God—is a society where God's will is as perfectly done on earth as it is in heaven. This tells us then that only he who does the will of God is a citizen of the Kingdom, and that we can do God's will only when we realize our own utter helplessness. The Kingdom of God is the possession of the poor in spirit, because the

poor in spirit have realized their own utter helplessness without
God and have learned to trust and obey.

We think of the song,

> Trust and obey
>   For there's no other way
> To be happy in Jesus
>   But to trust and obey!
>   JOHN H. SAMMIS

How true that is! Our allegiance is claimed from many quar-
ters. A halfhearted commitment to God is usually no match for
these many demands. We need to make and maintain a firm and
decisive commitment to God to live under His Lordship.

*Father, give us the strength of determination, the realization
that we are utterly helpless to cope with the temptations and
the difficulties of life, unless we are completely committed to
You.*

MARCH 2

Blessed are they that mourn: for they shall be comforted.
          MATTHEW 5:4

There are three ways in which today's Beatitude has been
translated. It can be taken quite literally, "Blessed is the man
who has endured the bitter sorrow that life can bring." The
Arabs have a proverb, "All sunshine makes a desert." The land
on which the sun always shines will soon become an arid place
where no fruit will grow. There are certain things which only
rain can produce and certain experiences which only sorrow can
beget.

Sorrow can show us as nothing else can the comfort and compassion of God. When things go well, it is possible to live for
years on the surface of our emotions, but when sorrow comes, a
person is driven to examine the spiritual meaning of life, and if

he accepts it aright, a new strength and beauty enter his soul.
And so, we learn from sorrow.

> I walked a mile with Pleasure,
> She chattered all the way,
> But left me none the wiser
> For all she had to say.
> I walked a mile with Sorrow,
> And ne'er a word said she;
> But, oh, the things I learned from her
> When Sorrow walked with me.
>
> ROBERT BROWNING HAMILTON

The second meaning this verse can have is, "Blessed are those who are desperately sorry for the sorrow and the suffering of this world." From the first Beatitude we saw that it was all right to be detached from *things,* but it is never all right to be detached from *people.* The world would have been a much poorer place if it had not been for those who cared intensely about the sorrow and the sufferings of others.

The third meaning of this Beatitude could be, "Blessed is the person who is desperately sorry for his own sins and his own unworthiness." The very first word of Jesus was, "Repent." No person can repent unless he is sorry for his sins. I must repent and return to Jesus. Christianity begins with a sense of sin. Blessed is the person who is intensely sorry for that sin, a man who is heartbroken for what his sin has done to God and to Jesus Christ, a man who sees the cross and is appalled by the havoc brought by sin.

The way to the joy of forgiveness is through the desperate sorrow of the broken heart. So it could be that the real meaning of the second Beatitude is, "Oh, the bliss of the man whose heart is broken for the world's suffering and for his own sin, for out of his sorrow he will find the joy of God."

O Dear Father God, I repent of my daily sins. I am sorry that I have hurt Your loving heart. Thank You for giving me inner joy, and I pray I may never cease to be thankful. For Jesus' sake.

MARCH 3

Blessed are the meek: for they shall inherit the earth.

MATTHEW 5:5

Today's Beatitude is about what could be called the bliss of the God-controlled life. In our modern English the word *meek* carries with it an idea of spinelessness and subservience, and it paints the picture of a submissive and ineffective creature. The word *meek* in Greek was one of the great Greek ethical words. Aristotle defined *meekness* as the mean between excessive anger and excessive "angerlessness," and so the first classical translation of this Beatitude could be, "Blessed is the person who is always angry at the right time and never angry at the wrong time." If asked what the right and wrong times would be, we might say that it is never right to be angry for any insult or injury done to ourselves, but that it *is* right to be angry at injuries done to other people. Selfish anger is always a sin; selfless anger can be one of the great moral dynamics of the world.

The second possible translation of this Beatitude is "Blessed is the man who has every instinct, every impulse, every passion under control." This speaks not of self-control, but rather of the man who is completely God-controlled.

In the Book of Numbers, Moses was described as "meek above all men which were upon the face of the earth" (12:3). Certainly Moses was no milk-and-water character. He was no spineless creature. He could be blazingly angry. He dared the throne of Pharaoh, but he was a man whose anger was on the leash, only to be released when the time was right. So we see that it is the man who is God-controlled who will be blessed and inherit the earth, for only in His service do we find our perfect freedom and in doing His will, our peace.

Father, forgive me for the times I have been angry or hostile or peevish because I was thinking of myself and looking at the situation as to how it affected me. Thank You for showing me that this anger is SIN—*I confess it now and ask Your Spirit to control me today. In Jesus' Name.*

MARCH 4

Blessed are they which do hunger and thirst after righteousness: for they shall be filled.

Matthew 5:6

The hunger which this Beatitude describes is no genteel hunger which could be satisfied with a mid-morning snack. The thirst of which it speaks is no thirst which could be slaked by an ice-cold Coca-Cola. It is the hunger and thirst of a man who is starving for food—a man who will die unless he drinks. Since that is so, this Beatitude is in reality a question and a challenge. In effect, it demands to know how much you really want goodness. Do you want it as much as a starving man wants food? As much as a man dying of thirst wants water? How intense is our desire for goodness?

Most people have an instinctive desire for goodness. That desire is wistful and nebulous, rather than sharp and intense. When the moment of decision comes, they are not prepared to make the effort, the sacrifice, which real goodness demands.

The man who is blessed is not necessarily the man who attains goodness, but rather, the man who longs for it with his whole heart. If blessedness came only to the person who achieved goodness, then none would be blessed. But blessedness comes to the person who, in spite of failures and failings, still clutches to an impassioned love of the Highest.

The true wonder of man is not that he is a sinner, but that, even in his sin, he is haunted by goodness. Even in the mud, he can never wholly forget the stars.

In His mercy, God judges us not only by our achievements, but also by our dreams. Even if a person never obtains goodness, if at the end of the way he is still hungering and thirsting for it, he is not shut out from blessedness.

Dear Jesus, help us to seek first Your Kingdom and Your righteousness, and we know that then all these things shall be added unto us, for it is in our SEEKING *that You come to us and comfort us and even reward us.*

MARCH 5

Blessed are the merciful: for they shall obtain mercy.
                                          MATTHEW 5:7

"Mercy" is the ability to get right inside the other person's skin, and then we can see things with his eyes, think things with his mind, and feel things with his feelings.

Clearly, this is much more than an emotional wave of pity. It demands a deliberate effort of the mind and of the will. It denotes a sympathy that comes from the deliberate identification with the other person until we see things as he sees them and feel things as he feels them. Is that not what God did in Jesus Christ? In Jesus Christ, in the most literal sense, God got inside the skin of mankind. He came as a man; He came seeing things with man's eyes, feeling things with man's feelings, thinking things with man's mind. God knows what life is like because God came right inside life.

Queen Victoria was a close friend of Principal and Mrs. Tulloch of St. Andrews. Prince Albert died, and Victoria was left alone. Just at the same time, Principal Tulloch died, and Mrs. Tulloch was left alone. Unannounced, Queen Victoria came to call on Mrs. Tulloch, who was resting on a couch in her room. When the queen was announced, Mrs. Tulloch struggled to rise quickly from the couch and to curtsy. The queen stepped forward and said, "My Dear, don't rise. I am not coming to you today as a queen to a subject, but as one woman who has lost her husband to another."

That was just what God did. He came to us, not as a remote, detached, isolated, majestic God, but as a Person, the Supreme instance of mercy.

Dear Jesus—I'm glad I know You as a PERSON—How wonderful You are. I just want to praise You today, because You love me and have mercy on me.

MARCH 6

Blessed are the pure in heart: for they shall see God.
MATTHEW 5:8

This Beatitude demands from us the most exacting self-examination. Is our work done from motives of service or from motives of pay? Is our service given from selfless motives or from motives of self-display? Is the work we do in the church done for Christ or for our own prestige? Even our church-going, is it an attempt to meet God or to fulfill the role of habitual and conventional respectability? Is even our prayer life and our Bible reading engaged upon with a sincere desire to have company with God, or because it gives us a pleasant feeling of superiority that we do these things?

In our religion are we conscious of nothing so much as the need for God within our hearts, or are we made comfortable with thoughts of our own piety?

To examine our motives is a daunting and shameful thing, for there are few things in this world that even the best of us do with completely unmixed motives.

It is warming to remember that it is by God's grace we keep our hearts clean, or it is by human lust we soil them. We are either fitting or unfitting ourselves to someday see God.

So then, this Beatitude might read, "Oh, the bliss of the man whose motives are absolutely pure, for that man will someday be able to see God."

Father, on my own I could never be pure, so I would miss seeing You, but thanks to Jesus and His righteousness, I can come into Your presence. I'm so glad we are friends.

MARCH 7

Blessed are ye, when men shall revile you, and persecute you, and shall say all manner of evil against you falsely, for my sake. Rejoice and be exceeding glad: for great is your reward

in heaven: for so persecuted they the prophets which were be-
fore you.

MATTHEW 5:11, 12

People need to discover the lost radiance of the Christian faith. In a worried world, the Christian should be the only person who remains serene. In a depressed world, the Christian should be the only person who remains full of the joy of life. There should be a sheer sparkle about the Christian life, but too often the Christian dresses like the mourner at a funeral and talks like a specter at a feast.

He is to be the salt of the earth. The Christian must be the communicator of joy. If a Christian is not fulfilling his purpose as a Christian, then he is on his way to disaster. We are meant to be the salt of the earth, and if we do not bring to life the purity, the power, the radiance that we ought, then we invite disaster.

A man's Christianity should be perfectly visible to all men. Further, this Christianity should not be visible only in church. Jesus did not say, "Ye are the light of the church." He said, "Ye are the light of the *world*" (Matthew 5:14, italics added). A Christianity whose effects stop at the church doors is not much use to anyone. It should be even more visible than the ordinary activities of the world. Christianity should be visible in the way we treat a shop assistant across the counter, in the way we order a meal in a restaurant, the way we treat our employees, the way we serve our employer, in the way we play a game, or drive or park a motor car, in the language we use, and the daily literature we read. A Christian should be just as much Christian in the factory, the sales meeting, the shipyard, the schoolroom, the operating room, the kitchen, the golf course, or the playing field as he is in church.

When I was a youth growing up along the Oregon coast, I can remember seeing the lighthouses along the coasts which would guide the people through the fog and through the storm. So it is the Christian's duty to take a stand which the weaker brother will support, to give the lead which those with less courage will follow. The world needs our guiding light. There are people waiting in line for a leader to take the stand they would not dare to take themselves and to do the things they would not dare to do themselves. It is often difficult, but we need to be a lighthouse to young people and to others. Let your light so shine before men that they may see your good deeds and glorify your Father who is in heaven . . . **shine for God.**

Dear Jesus, You said, "If I be lifted up from among men, I will draw all men unto Me." Oh, if we can only live so that people can see You and want to know You better! That is our prayer.

MARCH 8

And whosoever shall compel thee to go a mile, go with him twain.

MATTHEW 5:41

It was the practice of the Roman soldiers to pick out a Jew and compel him to carry their burden, their armor, or whatever they wanted carried. It came from the Persian method of carrying a message—sort of like a relay race. You can imagine how the Jewish people hated being slaves to the Romans, and then to be compelled to carry the Roman burden a "Roman mile"—that was the ultimate humiliation. They would walk behind them and curse them, hating them and despising every part of it.

Then, here comes Jesus saying when you are compelled to do this, don't walk behind cursing, walk beside him, talk to him, ask about his family. And then, at the end of the first mile when you are released by law, ask him whether you can go farther, and tell him about Jesus.

No wonder they were astonished at His teachings! That is the Lord! Instead of harboring bitterness and hatred, go the second mile! Go with him the second mile. Don't be revengeful or curse him, but do good to him who despitefully uses you.

Instead of saying, "These are my rights!" and defending them to the death, how much better to say, "My Christian right is to give up my rights. My only Christian right is to love." A Christian thinks not of his rights, but of his duties, not of his privileges, but of his responsibilities. The Christian is the man who has forgotten that he has any rights at all. To fight to the legal death for rights, inside or outside the church, is far from the Christian way.

To love our enemies enough to go the second mile is a love not only of the heart, but of the will. It is a determination of the mind whereby we achieve unconquerable good will, even to those who hurt and injure us. Such love makes a person more like Jesus.

O Lord, we are just like those people who heard You. We are astonished at Your doctrine. We feel so unworthy. Our lives are so cluttered with confusion. We rerun movies of anger · and revenge, and we are sensitive and volatile. We make our own prisons of resentment and bitterness.

O Father, today may we all clear our minds of all vengeance, bitterness, resentment, and guilt and lay them at the foot of the cross.

May we walk out free. Help us to become more like You. Thank You, Dear Father, for loving us with such a love. May we become, daily, more like what You have planned for us to be, more like our Example, our Savior, our Lord—Jesus Christ.

MARCH 9

He that receiveth a prophet in the name of a prophet shall receive a prophet's reward; and he that receiveth a righteous man in the name of a righteous man shall receive a righteous man's reward. . . . Rejoice, and be exceeding glad, for great is your reward in heaven: for so persecuted they the prophets which were before you.

MATTHEW 10:41; 5:12

If we love a person deeply and passionately, humbly and selflessly, we will be quite sure that we will give that person all we have to give. We would give that person the sun and the moon and the stars if we could. He who is in love is always in debt. The last thing that enters his mind is that he has earned a reward.

If a man has a legalistic view of life, he may think in constant terms of the reward that he has won. If a man has a loving view of life, the day of reward will never enter his mind.

The great paradox of Christian reward is this: The person who looks for reward and who calculates that it is due him, does not receive it. The person whose only motive is love and who never thinks that he deserves a reward does, in fact, receive it. The strange fact is that the reward is the same kind of by-product and the ultimate end of the Christian life.

The Christian's reward is the reverse of the world's reward. The world's reward would be an easier time; the reward of the Christian is that God lays still more upon him to do for Him and his fellowman.

For the worldly man, who has never given a thought to God, to be confronted with God would be a terror and not a joy. If the man takes his own way, he drifts farther and farther from God. The gulf between him and God becomes even wider, until in the end, God becomes a grim stranger and one he only wishes to avoid. But if a man all his life has sought to walk with God, has sought to obey his Lord, if goodness and rightness of relationship have been drawing him closer and closer to God, until in the end he passes into God's nearer presence without fear, with radiant joy—that is the greatest reward of all.

Dear God, we know You are a rewarder of those who believe in You and who trust You. Thank You for the rewards of a job well done: the preciousness of Your presence here on this earth and the glorious vision of what is to come.

MARCH 10

Are not two sparrows sold for a farthing? and one of them shall not fall on the ground without your Father. But the very hairs of your head are numbered. Fear ye not therefore, ye are of more value than many sparrows.

MATTHEW 10:29–31

God the Creator, our Father, knows our needs and is more concerned about the things we care about than we ever could be. Sometimes we ask God to do particular things for individuals about whom we are concerned, without realizing that those very things would come between them and God. Sometimes the little burdens of life are given so that individuals will be kept close to God. As the Bible says, if an earthly father is asked to give bread to his children, he will surely not give them stones. Since this is the case, how much more can we expect from God who knows and cares more for us than our earthly fathers ever could!

Father, thank You for being far wiser than we and sometimes saying "No" when we ask amiss.

MARCH 11

When Jesus came into the coasts of Caesarea Philippi, he asked his disciples, saying, Whom do men say that I the Son of man am? And they said, Some say that thou art John the Baptist: some, Elias; and others, Jeremias, or one of the prophets. He saith unto them, But whom say ye that I am? And Simon Peter answered and said, Thou art the Christ, the Son of the living God.

MATTHEW 16:13–16

In the final analysis, every one of us must answer that question—"But whom say *Ye* that I am?" Someone put it this way: "Imagine that all the religious leaders of both cult and man-made flavors were gathered before God in heaven. God looked out among them and inquired, 'Whom do you say that I am?'"

One by one they responded with their names and descriptions of Him:

- The Source of divine energy.
- The Essence of all consciousness.
- The wholly Other.

- The Ground of being.
- The Infinite Transcendent.
- Emanation.
- Ad infinitum.

After all the words have been spoken and all the descriptions made, it comes down ultimately to what Jesus said to His disciples,

"But whom say *ye* that I am?"

Lord, we know that this is the greatest question with which we'll ever be confronted. May we answer with boldness, as did Simon Peter, "Thou art the Christ, the Son of the living God!"

MARCH 12

For the kingdom of heaven is as a man travelling into a far country, who called his own servants, and delivered unto them his goods. . . . His lord said unto him, Well done, good and faithful servant; thou hast been faithful over a few things, I will make thee ruler over many things: enter thou into the joy of thy lord.

MATTHEW 25:14, 23

I am thinking today of the story of the talents, as told in Matthew, and how important it is to *believe* God, believe our Master, to believe IN HIM, to believe in His goodness, to believe in His fairness.

If you will read again the story in Matthew, you will realize that the unprofitable servant saw God as unjust and demanding, so he did not multiply his talents, but simply buried them in the ground.

How you see God is so very, very important! Do you see Him as loving, kind, and just? Or do you see Him as some far-off dignitary, ready to pounce on you if you do wrong?

Oh, dear reader, please know that our God is *knowable* and that when we become one of His spiritual children and call Him

"Father," we can come to Him with boldness, yes, but also knowing that He will listen; He will hear!

My real Boss is never out. I think of Gladys Hunt when she said "Many a restless woman ought to go and sit on God's lap awhile." And as my dear friend, Corrie ten Boom, says, "Nestle, don't wrestle." I remember a woman who told me, when she had received a letter I had written to her on a day when she needed it, that it was like a little hug from God. How important it is that we see our God as loving, kind, just, fair, and a rewarder of those who believe Him.

I hope this message today will be a "little hug from God" to you.

Dear Father, help us to come to You as trusting children, realizing Your loving arms are ever outstretched to receive us, Your tender hands ever ready to comfort us and soothe our troubled brows.

MARCH 13

He shall have dominion also from sea to sea, and from the river unto the ends of the earth.

PSALMS 72:8

The fact that God is love is the explanation of providence. Because God is love, His creative act is followed by His constant care. He could have created the world and wound it up like some giant clock and just have let it run down, but He did not do that. Instead, He constantly broods over the universe. He constantly holds it and sustains it. Without His love, God would not be compelled to watch over His creation and to hold it together. If that were the case, we would simply fly out into space and be adrift. But God's love would not permit Him to be so capricious or careless about those He has placed in this earthly setting. It is God's love that explains His providential care for the universe.

Lord, only a fool could imagine that this marvelous, intricate universe could have just happened by chance. Thank You for creating it all—and keeping it in Your care.

MARCH 14

*Humble yourselves therefore under the mighty hand of God,
that he may exalt you in due time: Casting all your care upon
him; for he careth for you.*

1 PETER 5:6, 7

How do we find our security and make our peace with God? I
think we find it in the realization that we matter to God.

I once visited my father in the nursing home where he was
confined. When you see elderly people, some literally just exist-
ing, sometimes you ask, "Why, Lord. Why?"

I had gotten my father a stereo, and as I started to leave, I
heard him singing in his 87-year-old voice, "We should never be
discouraged; take it to the Lord in prayer." The tears were rolling
down his cheeks, and I thought, *This is the answer!* Even those in
almost intolerable situations can have Jesus in their hearts and
God in their lives. That is such a security, because, regardless of
our situation, we *matter* to God!

Remember the story of the widow and her two mites? Here
came the wealthy and they put in their money. Then came the
little widow, and she dropped in her two mites. The clink of the
coins fell on the ears of Jesus and He noticed her. Of all the people that passed by, He singled out this little widow to compliment
her and make comments about her that have been told down
through the years. He never mistakes you in the crowd. *You
matter to God.* When you realize that, then you don't have to go
out and prove to the world how much you matter. And you don't
have to feel alone and forgotten when your world falls around
you. You know that God *knows* you and that, no matter how little you might seem to have, it is much in God's eyes, and He
loves and cherishes it because He loves and cherishes you. YOU
MATTER TO GOD!

*Thank You, God, for making me somebody who matters to
You.*

MARCH 15

Remembering without ceasing your work of faith, and labour of love, and patience of hope in our Lord Jesus Christ, in the sight of God and our Father;

1 THESSALONIANS 1:3

Work was instigated by God. We must strive to please Him. There is a poem which says "Oh Lord of all the pots and pans . . . When I polish sandals, I polish them as if they were thine." We must seek to work so well that if Jesus sees it He will approve.

Work should be prompted by love. There is a story of a boy carrying an older boy on his shoulders. A man they pass says how heavy the bigger boy must be for the smaller boy to carry. The child answered, "He ain't heavy, mister, he's my brother." Our labors should be prompted by love.

Sometimes our labor is so daily, so routine. How can we find something special in it? Paul says the endurance is founded on hope. Our prisoners of war had hope. They sustained those difficult, lonely years only by hope. They had a faith that gave them hope—hope of someday being returned home. As long as a man has hope he is walking not to the night but to the dawn.

And so I go on not knowing
I would not know if I might,
For I'd rather walk with God by faith
Than walk alone by sight.

AUTHOR UNKNOWN

Dear Father, help us to have the hope and faith that will make our work a pleasure—may we do it as unto Thee.

MARCH 16

The Lord also will be a refuge for the oppressed, a refuge in times of trouble.

PSALMS 9:9

Dr. George W. Truett said something once which changed the whole thought pattern of my prayer life. In addition to the notion that God's will is always *right* for us, which we have all heard many times, and that God's will is always *best* for us, Dr. Truett added a third notion. He asserted that God's will is always *safe* for us. This adds another dimension to our prayer lives. Not only are we sure that God's will is correct and good, but we know it is also secure. By accepting God's will we are secure, and we can enter into a new dimension of joy in prayer.

Lord, may we find rest in the safety of Your will.

MARCH 17

Commit thy works unto the Lord, and thy thoughts shall be established.

PROVERBS 16:3

I have on my arm a diamond watch. It is special to me for two reasons. It was given to me by Ethel Waters in September of 1976. We were friends and she called me to her room and said, "I have something for you, Baby Girl" (that is what she called me and she wanted me to call her Mom), and she handed me her watch. I dissolved in tears and said, "Oh, I can't possibly take that." She said "Yes, you can, Baby Girl. Those are real diamonds, I bought them in my heyday." She said one of these days she was going where she did not need any more clocks. Sure enough, a little over a year later, I went out for her funeral at Forest Lawn. Wires came from around the world for this woman.

It tells me something else, too, for to God there is no such thing as an unwanted child. She was born to a thirteen-year-old victim of rape, outside of Philadelphia. By all the standards of the world, in today's society, she would be unwanted and probably aborted.

But you see, to God there is no such thing as an unwanted child. Somewhere along the line, God touched her life and she became a role model for many. She was featured on *Time* maga-

zine as the "Woman of the Year." She starred in broadway
shows, stage and screen, and sang the beloved song, "His Eye Is
on the Sparrow, and I Know He Watches Me," to literally thousands and thousands of people.

I was speaking in California at Robert Schuller's Garden
Grove Church to a seminar of 2,500 women. Della Reese was the
emcee. My subject was "Commitment to Excellence." (By the
way, that is a very important thing. Don't ever do slipshod work.)
As we were having lunch before the afternoon program, Della
noticed my watch and a ring that Ethel had given me. I was telling everybody that we were friends and I told her the story, and
she suggested that I tell it that day. I told her I had not intended
to, it really was not a part of that particular subject—Commitment to Excellence in Life and Business. But she insisted I tell it.
So I closed my talk with the story I have just shared with you.

As I was leaving, a woman stopped me. She was not very well
dressed, her hair was not groomed nicely and she was over-
weight. Obviously, she had a low self-image. She reached out her
hand, and stopped me, and said, "Oh, I want to thank you, thank
you." There was something about the intensity in her eyes that
arrested my attention and I just waited. I did not know for what
she was thanking me. Then she said, "All my life I have known I
was an unwanted child, but today you set me free. God loves
me."

I still get goose bumps when I remember that, and I hope
you will remember everywhere you go, that we must communicate to a hungry, hurting, rejected-feeling world the message
"God cares! God loves! He wants you for His own." That is our
message.

God help us to communicate it with excellence.

MARCH 18

*Commit thy way unto the Lord; trust also in him; and he shall
bring it to pass.*

                                                    PSALMS 37:5

Be somebody. God doesn't take time to make a nobody. "God does not love you because you are important, but you are important because God loves you." There is no such thing as an average person. Each one of us is a unique individual. Each one of us expresses humanity in some distinct way.

> The beauty and the bloom of each soul is a thing apart, a separate holy miracle unto God, never once repeated throughout all the millenniums of time.
>
> LAYNE WESTON

There are some people who have the quality of richness and joy in them and they communicate it to everything they touch. It is first of all a physical quality, then it is a quality of the spirit.

And so, I would pray that today I would communicate to each person I meet that special quality of richness, of joy, of genuine love, of caring. And more important, I would help each person I meet today to know that he, too, was created in the image of God, he can "be somebody," can have that bloom and that beauty of maturity and grace which God has hidden within each child of His creation.

Father, today, let each one of us help every other person we meet to know, through You, he is SOMEBODY.

MARCH 19

His name shall endure for ever: his name shall be continued as long as the sun: and men shall be blessed in him: all nations shall call him blessed. Blessed be the Lord God, the God of Israel, who only doeth wondrous things. And blessed be his glorious name for ever: and let the whole earth be filled with his glory.

PSALMS 72:17–19

"The Lord's blessing is our greatest wealth. All our work adds nothing to it."

This simply means **to give God the glory.** He is the source of all blessing; He is the source of all wisdom; He is the source of all skill; He is the source of everything we have! And that is the greatest blessing! Certainly we build and we work, but that does not add anything to what is really the whole story. It is a continuation, and we are to do it, but without His blessing the work would be of no value. To be plugged in to the right source is the most important thing.

Dear Lord, it is all Yours! How can we take credit and boast of one little thing we do, when nothing, nothing is our own? To God be the glory, great things He hath done!

MARCH 20

This is the day which the Lord hath made; we will rejoice and be glad in it.

PSALMS 118:24

That verse comes easily to my heart today. As I look out of my window this beautiful spring morning, I see a gorgeous cardinal in the bare tree branches, I see the azaleas with their beautiful full flowers, making the whole yard glow as the first early sunlight goes through them. And I see the new buds forming on the trees, and it is easy to be glad! It is easy to rejoice!

Then I think of my family and the wonderful blessings that we have had, and how precious they have been, and again it is easy to rejoice. Yet, my heart goes back to those whose lives are not as blessed this spring morning, to the northern part of our nation where snow still covers the grass, and where the trees are bare and stark, and where the icy winds still blow, and it doesn't even look as though spring is coming.

I think of the gray times of the mind, when weariness and heartache, or pain, keep the heart from having a lilt and make it hard to rejoice.

Once, I did a study of the times in the New Testament when Jesus said to people, "Cheer up, Rejoice, Cheer up." I found that every time He told somebody to cheer up, there wasn't really anything to cheer up over. So I studied that, and I was amazed to find that what He really meant was in that wonderful verse in John 16:33, ". . . In the world ye shall have tribulation: but be of good cheer; I have overcome the world."

So our *lasting cheer,* and our *lasting rejoicing,* comes only in this overcoming through Jesus Christ.

When I have our managers at the mountain (and what a glorious time that is) every morning before we eat breakfast, we join hands around the table and we sing. Usually the song we start with is "This is the day, this is the day, this is the day that the Lord hath made. We will rejoice, we will rejoice, we will rejoice and be glad in it."

And somehow that sets the tone as we share in our morning prayer. And it sets the tone of the day so that we will rejoice, we will find things to rejoice about. That doesn't mean that every heart is trouble-free, or every home is free from difficulties and problems. It doesn't mean that we will have no obstacles that day, but it does mean that we can lift up our hearts and rejoice, because we believe in a God that overcomes.

Father, how I pray today I will be able to carry this truth through the day with my co-workers. And in the frustrations and irritations of the day, the traffic, the interruptions of phone calls, and the many questions that have to be answered, help me today to remember that this is the day YOU *have made. Help me to continually rejoice in it.*

MARCH 21

Looking unto Jesus the author and finisher of our faith; who for the joy that was set before him endured the cross, despising the shame, and is set down at the right hand of the throne of God.

HEBREWS 12:2

The effectiveness of faith does not depend on how fervently we believe, but on the value of the object of our faith . . . THE

VALUE OF THE OBJECT OF OUR FAITH. "Faith" is a noun and "believing" is a verb.

If you have a project that you believe in strongly enough, you can accomplish almost anything. That is human achievement, and it is admirable. Human achievement depends upon having faith in something and the ability to keep it going, but spiritual faith depends upon the object, the *person,* in whom you have your faith.

Sometimes we think, *Oh, I just have to have more faith.* But *faith* is a noun, *believing* is the verb. *Believing* is the coming *to* the object, but *faith* is having arrived. It is the *value* of the object of our faith that determines whether or not it will be effective. Many people believed fervently in Hitler, yet they came to destruction and death because the object of their faith was invalid.

So, where is your faith placed? What do you believe in? *Whom* do you believe in? That is the thing! If you believe in Jesus Christ as Lord and Master, as the Son of the everlasting, omnipotent God, then your faith is in the right place.

> *Father, I thank You for Jesus, for His beautiful example, for His love for me, and for His presence with me. Because of Jesus, I can come to You, my Heavenly Father, with joy, with boldness, with humility. Help me to show my gratitude daily by loving You more and by serving You better.*

MARCH 22

And ye shall know the truth, and the truth shall make you free.
                                                    JOHN 8:32

The song "Amazing Grace" was written by John Newton. He was a young sea captain with a godly mother. When she died, he had very difficult times. He went to sea on a slave ship for many years.

Soon, he became master of his own slave ship. On a voyage from Brazil he suffered many hardships. He read the book by Thomas à Kempis called *The Imitation of Christ.* It began to convict his heart, and he wanted to know more about this Christ. When he docked the ship, as he walked down the gangplank, he vowed he would never again be the master of a slave ship. He became a land surveyor to finance his way through school, then he trained to become a pastor. It was while serving in a pastorate in a small town in England that he wrote the words to "Amazing Grace."

Father, thank You for touching this man so long ago, for the beautiful song he gave the world, and for the blessing it has been to so many.

MARCH 23

Charity suffereth long, and is kind; charity envieth not; charity vaunteth not itself, is not puffed up, doth not behave itself unseemly, seeketh not her own, is not easily provoked, thinketh no evil.

1 CORINTHIANS 13:4, 5

What is Charity?
   It is SILENCE . . . when your words would hurt.
   It is PATIENCE . . . when your neighbor's curt.
   It is DEAFNESS . . . when scandal flows.
   It is THOUGHTFULNESS . . . for others' woes.
   It is PROMPTNESS . . . when stern duty calls.
   It is COURAGE . . . when misfortune falls.
Paul, in his great dissertation on LOVE in 1 Corinthians, used the Greek word *agape,* a beautiful and meaningful word. In Latin it was *amore,* but the Latins had done to this word what America is doing to the word *love*—cheapened it in lustful stories and plays. So, when the scribe Jerome was translating the Scripture, he used the Latin word *caritas,* translated "charity," instead of the Latin word *amore,* translated "love." He used the word *caritas* to portray the deeper meaning of "esteem"—the whole reverential, tender-hearted affection that we share in the faith.

Dear God, we know that real love comes only from You. Help us to be so filled with agape *love that it will spill over from our lives to those around us, who so desperately need and want love.*

MARCH 24

Being confident of this very thing, that he which hath begun a good work in you will perform it until the day of Jesus Christ.
PHILIPPIANS 1:6

Chase out failure and bring in confidence. Make *achievement*—not activity—your goal.

You have to be risk-oriented if you would accomplish great things and brave new frontiers.

Arthur H. Compton, the Nobel prize winning physicist, said: "Every great discovery I ever made, I gambled that the truth was there, and then I acted on it in faith until I could prove its existence."

Father, give us confidence so that we will be willing to step out on faith in Thy name.

MARCH 25

Husbands, love your wives, even as Christ also loved the church, and gave himself for it. . . . and the wife see that she reverence her husband.

EPHESIANS 5:25, 33

Praise and pray and peg away!

Give more affection and praise than criticism . . . compliments instead of complaints! It is so easy to find things that are wrong. In working with women, I find they are happier in their work, more fulfilled, better women, and better wives when we give them praise and recognition and reassurance.

Husbands, realize that your wife needs a lot of *reassurance.* That is why she wants you to tell her every day that you love her. Tell her that you do! Praise and pray and peg away!

Change yourself, not your partner! Marriage is not a personal reformation crusade for your mate. Many times I would have liked to change Dave, but I found that I had to change *me.* When he retired recently, young and healthy, he began to sit around the house much of the time—oh, I resented that! I had to pray and pray and pray. I did more praying than I did praising. I pegged away, but I didn't praise him much. Finally, I had to come to grips with the fact that he was happy, and I just had to turn it over to the Lord. Only then was I able to praise and pray and peg away. You see, when I changed *myself*—my attitudes—then the Lord was able to give me the right attitude about Dave.

Dear Father, help us to be generous with our praise to those we love, remembering Your sweet generosity to us, even when we are least deserving.

MARCH 26

Behold, what manner of love the Father hath bestowed upon us, that we should be called the sons of God: therefore the world knoweth us not, because it knew him not. Beloved, now are we the sons of God, and it doth not yet appear what we shall be: but we know that, when he shall appear, we shall be like him; for we shall see him as he is.

1 JOHN 3:1, 2

I met a man and said, "How are you?" He said, "Oh, pretty good under the circumstances." I asked him, "What in the world are you doing *under* the circumstances? Get *over* those circumstances!"

God has a great plan for every day. The time that we have, really, is only today, for family tenderness, for doing what God wants us to do.

I have written in my Bible, "Don't ever be afraid of tomorrow.

God is already there." When we get hold of what it cost God to justify us and the love that made Him do it, our selfish view takes on a biblical perspective.

God offers us the freedom of knowing that our personal worth is bound up in His character. He believed that I was worth dying for. He declared that those who believe are justified. And so, I am *somebody!*

I have learned to submit to authority without surrendering my own identity, because I have learned to submit to God.

Dear Lord, thank You for loving me and counting me as somebody worth dying for.

MARCH 27

For this is the message that ye heard from the beginning, that we should love one another. . . . My little children, let us not love in word, neither in tongue: but in deed and in truth. And hereby we know that we are of the truth, and shall assure our hearts before him. For if our heart condemn us, God is greater than our heart, and knoweth all things. Beloved, if our heart condemn us not, then have we confidence toward God. And whatsoever we ask, we receive of him, because we keep his commandments, and do those things that are pleasing in his sight. And this is his commandment, That we should believe on the name of his Son Jesus Christ, and love one another, as he gave us commandment.

1 JOHN 3:11, 18–23

In our society, men and women are conditioned to equate love and sex so much that the terms are often used interchangeably. But love and sex are not the same thing. Sex is only one expression of love, and if it is not an expression of love it is lust. Marriage is love, and lovemaking is not confined to the bedroom. Lovemaking is that thoughtfulness, courtesy, and caring that expresses itself in such phrases as: "Let me help you." "I love you." "You are wonderful." "You must have had a hard day." "It is so good being married to you." You make love by doing little acts that only love would think to be worth doing. Sometimes love is saying nothing at all. Love is forgiving, and frequently, it is overlooking something. In a successful marriage, you will have to learn to overlook your partner's weaknesses.

Father, help us to be mindful of the little things, considering nothing too small or menial if it expresses love and appreciation.

MARCH 28

All the ways of a man are clean in his own eyes; but the Lord weigheth the spirits. Commit thy works unto the Lord, and thy thoughts shall be established.

PROVERBS 16:2, 3

Where have you looked for stimulus? Another aspect needed for us to find true happiness is a stimulus. Many people seek to find their stimulus in sports, education, popularity, politics, and various activities. They seek some answer to the boredom confronting them. They look to all manner of things to fill the void in their lives. The thrills and excitement of "running for your life" do not provide the real answer to this dilemma. There must be a day when the cheering stops, when one comes to the end of the thrill ride. There is a stopping place, and it is there that boredom and frustration set in again. The only genuine stimulus for life is to be found in the person and presence of Jesus Christ. Only when we have found true identity in Jesus can we do something for others and find lasting satisfaction for ourselves.

Dear Lord, there is no thrill like the thrill of knowing You, feeling Your touch, and hearing Your soft voice saying, "Well done." May this be the stimulus which we seek.

MARCH 29

Ye are our epistle written in our hearts, known and read of all men: Forasmuch as ye are manifestly declared to be the epistle of Christ ministered by us, written not with ink, but with the Spirit of the living God; not in tables of stone, but in fleshy tables of the heart.

2 CORINTHIANS 3:2, 3

We all, as Christians, should be "letters of recommendation" for Jesus Christ. What kind of letter are you? Witnessing is not a program to be carried out, it's a life to be lived!

You're writing today, a gospel for men. The only gospel some people read. What is being written to them?

Father, keep the pages of our lives free from anything that might prove a stumbling block to those who read what we write day by day.

MARCH 30

For the Son of man is come to seek and to save that which was lost.

LUKE 19:10

The fact that God is love is the explanation of redemption. This is at the very heart of John 3:16. It means that God had to seek a cure for our sins. He had to find a remedy for our anxiety, for our sin, our confusion, and our problems. He did this because He loved us.

Dear God, thank You for seeking and saving me.

MARCH 31

It really doesn't matter whether this month came in like a lamb and is going out like a lion, or came in like a lion and is going out like a lamb. We are learning that our peace and our joy do not depend on the weather or our circumstances. *Our* peace and our joy must come from within.

Are you looking *within,* to the Power working in you, for your strength and assurance and your sense of worth? Then are you letting that Power flow to the *outside* to make you a better husband or wife, a better employer or employee, a believer whose faith is strong and whose confidence in God's providential care gives a serenity that is obvious to those about you?

The year is one-fourth gone—the time to make it a good year is *now.* Avow this day to make April, and all the months that follow, days of growth and spiritual productivity.

APRIL 1

. . . One thing I know, that, whereas I was blind, now I see.
JOHN 9:25

"It is April . . . and I can see!"
There is the story of a poet in Italy. He is walking down a street where there are many beggars. He notices that one beggar gets far more people to stop and place money in his cup than do the other beggars around him. When the poet reaches the beggar, he sees this sign around the beggar's neck: "It is April . . . and I am BLIND."

How tragic to be blind in April . . . and what an April this should be for us . . . for WE CAN SEE!

Dear Father, open my eyes, my ears, and my heart that I may see, hear, and know—then accept—Thy will and Thy way.

APRIL 2

For as the earth bringeth forth her bud, and as the garden causeth the things that are sown in it to spring forth; so the Lord God will cause righteousness and praise to spring forth before all the nations.
ISAIAH 61:11

Spring is a very special time:
    there is a freshness,
    a newness,
    a hint of full blooms to come
        that creates
    an atmosphere of hope and expectation.

Somehow you want to stand tall,
   walk tall,
   think tall,
   and act tall!
This may be why
   when one walks taller
   and brisker
   and happier
They say there is *spring* in his step!

Father, may our bearing reflect our faith in You and Your bounteous blessings to us.

APRIL 3

. . . that like as Christ was raised up from the dead by the glory of the Father, even so we also should walk in newness of life.
                                            ROMANS 6:4

SPRING is more than a season . . .
   it is sometimes lazy "fever,"
   sometimes a housecleaning "fervor,"
   sometimes a thing called baseball,
   or a time for kite flying,
      but always
   it is a time for NEWNESS AND FRESHNESS.

SPRING is
   new green leaves on tired, bare wintry limbs,
   fresh perfumed air of honeysuckle and wisteria,
      or
   just the fresh smell of SPRING air,
   blowing through the musty rooms so recently vacated by winter.

Precious Jesus, thank You for this beautiful time and the new life and anticipation for all the good things this season promises.

APRIL 4

You know these things—now do them! That is the path of blessing.

JOHN 13:17 TLB

When we think about *service* and its deeper meaning, we read in *The Living Bible* that service "is the path of blessing."

It was the night of the Last Supper, and our Lord had looked forward to being with His close friends on that special evening.

They met in the Upper Room to share the meal together. The roads of Palestine were dusty and unpaved, and it was the custom for servants to wash the feet of guests when they arrived in a home. Since the group had no servant, they were accustomed to washing one another's feet, but this evening their minds were on "who would be greatest in the Kingdom," and not one volunteered to wash the dirty, dusty feet of the others. After the meal was over, Jesus arose and took a basin of water and a towel and washed the feet of His disciples. Then He said to them, "I have given you an example. You call me Lord and Master, and you are right—I am—but the one who will be greatest must be the servant. This is the way to greatness . . . and happiness" (*see* John 13:13–17).

Service is the path to blessing. Jesus had done for them what they were not willing to do for each other . . . and He gave us the greatest example and definition of *service*—Service to God through service to each other.

Father, that we might not be too proud to wash feet, forgive us for ever thinking we are "too good" to perform any service for others, no matter how menial.

APRIL 5

And about the ninth hour Jesus cried with a loud voice, saying Eli, Eli, lama sabachthani? that is to say, My God, my God, why hast thou forsaken me?

MATTHEW 27:46

Yes, Jesus suffered physical anguish during His Crucifixion, but He also suffered that total, ultimate separation that was demanded as a payment for man's sin. Jesus literally went down into hell, but the Psalms said that He would not be left there. His separation came as a result of man's disobedience. He suffered total separation into utter darkness and degradation. Here the sinless One was totally immersed in sin for us. He, the sinless One, became the means by which you and I can enter into the very presence of God. He purchased our salvation. The blameless One for sinners was slain. How could anyone resist that? How could anyone pass by and not want to partake of that gift? They who passed by railed at Him, wagging their heads. In sharp contrast, we ask, "Is it nothing to you who pass by?"

Lord, Jesus, thank You that You *suffered above that which we are able and thereby purchased our salvation.*

APRIL 6

Then said Jesus, Father, forgive them; for they know not what they do. . . .

LUKE 23:34

This is what is commonly called the first word from Jesus on the cross. The first word is a word of forgiveness. Isn't it precious to know that the first thought in the heart of Jesus was a thought of forgiveness? The entire act of salvation, the entire day of the Crucifixion was to be centered on forgiveness. It was an act of forgiveness toward us, for every one of us. Thus, it is appropriate that the first statement from His lips expressed the thought which was uppermost in His mind: "Father, forgive these people, for they do not know what they are doing." Forgive them! Oh, how beautiful to think that even in agony, in heartbreak and sorrow, Jesus wanted to grant forgiveness! This was His total purpose, His total dedication for that day. He wanted us to be forgiven!

Father, forgive us for being so unforgiving of others! How can we accept Your ultimate act of forgiveness and yet hold hatred and revenge in our hearts? Cleanse us and fill us with Your love so we can then love our fellowman as we should.

APRIL 7

When Jesus therefore saw his mother, and the disciple standing by, whom he loved, he saith unto his mother, Woman, behold thy son! Then saith he to the disciple, Behold thy mother! And from that hour that disciple took her unto his own home.
JOHN 19:26, 27

Here is the second significant act of Jesus on the cross. In His agony and grief, He thought first of the people He came to redeem, and He asked God to forgive them. Then, He thought of His mother and the fact that she would now be without the Son she loved so much. Since His brothers were either still unbelievers, or perhaps young believers at best, Jesus wished to have her cared for by the one who was closest to Him, the disciple whom Jesus loved most, John. In this crucial hour, He made certain that His mother was cared for. In the hour of His death, even though He was God, He revealed His humanity. He was a man just as if He were not God, and He was God just as if He were not a man. Jesus was uniquely born; He was the God-man.

Lord Jesus, even in the hour of Your death You showed Your concern for others. May we use the opportunities life affords us to follow the examples You gave us and show love and concern for those whose paths cross ours.

APRIL 8

After this, Jesus knowing that all things were now accomplished, that the scripture might be fulfilled, saith, I thirst.
JOHN 19:28

Quite some time later, knowing that the Scriptures were fulfilled, Jesus again spoke. On this occasion He simply said, "I
thirst." This is one of the most significant of the statements made
by Jesus while He was on the cross. In it Jesus shows the extent
of His physical suffering. But His physical suffering was accom-
panied by something that no other man has ever experienced: the
complete abandonment by God. Think back to Gethsemane
when Jesus prayed in such agony that He perspired great drops
of blood. He would have let the cup of suffering pass from Him
except that He knew that without it, man's salvation could never
be accomplished. Then, following that long night of agony, the
morning of anguish, and the hours He hung on the cross, it is no
wonder that He cried out, "I thirst."

*Dear Father, how comforting to know that we have a Savior
who suffered all the things we suffer, who knew all the anguish we have known and felt all the pain. No matter what
happens to us, we can know He understands! Thank You
Lord, for such love.*

APRIL 9

*... Father, into thy hands I commend my spirit: and having
said thus, he gave up the ghost.*

LUKE 23:46

His forgiveness is total, complete, and absolute. These words
indicate that Jesus was aware of the finality and completeness of
His sacrifice, for they imply that His death was voluntary rather
than a matter of deprivation. As He had said earlier, "I am the
good shepherd: the good shepherd giveth his life for the sheep"
(John 10:11). What a joyous thing He has provided for us! He
gave Himself to provide forgiveness for us. One of the most basic
needs of man is to be forgiven. When we experience it, we are
accepted by God. When that fact enters into our consciousness,
we don't have to go out and prove that we are important. Instead,
we have become important, because God has forgiven and ac-

cepted us. All of this was made possible because of the voluntary sacrifice of Jesus Christ in our behalf. When He had completed that sacrifice, He literally dismissed His spirit.

Blessed Lord, we know that no man took Your life from You. You voluntarily gave it up to provide forgiveness for us. Oh wonder of wonders—that we should be so blessed!

APRIL 10

When Jesus therefore had received the vinegar, he said, It is finished: and he bowed his head, and gave up the ghost.
JOHN 19:30

"It is finished." When every prophecy had been fulfilled, Jesus acknowledged the fact by asserting that His work was finished. What He had come to do, to complete—the work of salvation—had been wrought. That which had been planned from the beginning was now complete. The course of human history from Genesis in the Garden with Adam and Eve, through Abraham, Isaac, and Jacob, and on through the entire Old Testament in history and in prophecy had now come to its fruition. Everything had pointed toward this day and this event, and it was now complete. As far as God was concerned, the sacrifice for man's sin had now been made. The debt had been canceled. Christ had finished His work on our behalf. From the cross onward, individual men would have to experience that provision for themselves. By accepting that provision, we can experience the satisfying sense of peace that comes with forgiveness. By appropriating that sacrifice for our sins, we can be accepted as heirs of God and joint-heirs together with Christ. What a glorious thing is ours, all because Jesus did a complete work in our behalf. He made the sacrifice which was so complete that He could say, "It is finished."

Father, thank You for the finished work of Jesus on the cross. It is sufficient. We need none else.

APRIL 11

*And it came to pass, as they were much perplexed thereabout,
behold, two men stood by them in shining garments: And as
they were afraid, and bowed down their faces to the earth, they
said unto them, Why seek ye the living among the dead? He is
not here, but is risen. . . .*

LUKE 24:4–6

Easter is many things!

It is the furry bunny rabbit placed in the eager hands of little
children . . .
It is a thousand church bells in a thousand cities . . .
It is a new light in the eyes of a discouraged pastor as he sees
a full church before him . . .
It is a little girl, looking like an angel in her pale pink or-
gandy . . .
It is flowers—tulips and hyacinths and white lilies . . .
It is the time when even the skeptic and the unbeliever are
caught up in the miracle of spring . . .
It is a time of *revival,* of the spirit and of the land . . .
Easter is all of this—but oh, so much more. For **Easter is
Resurrection!**

It is truth! . . . and *it is hope!* The world needs hope more than
all else! "Is there hope?" is the constant cry of humanity, and
Easter is the answer to that cry. *"He is Risen!"* Christ the Lord is
Risen and Lives *today!* It was the Resurrection of Jesus Christ
from the dead that set off a chain reaction of HOPE in the world.
There *is* HOPE FOR THE HOPELESS; there *is* ENCOUR-
AGEMENT FOR THE DISCOURAGED; there *is* HELP FOR
THE HELPLESS; there *is* POWER THAT CAN TURN DE-
SPAIR INTO HOPE; there *is* PURPOSE FOR THE DE-
SPAIRING; there *is* STRENGTH FOR THE WEAK!

In the Gospel of John, the writer tells of the morning several
days after the Resurrection, when life for the disciples had as-
sumed more normal routine and food for the body had become a

necessity. The disciples had gone fishing and toiled the night long. In the early morning light they saw, to their wonder and amazement, a lone figure on the shore. It was their Risen Lord preparing the fire to cook the fish for their morning meal. The glorified risen Redeemer of men, triumphant over death and ready now to claim His Kingdom, prepared breakfast for His hungry disciples and shared the simple meal with them as a beloved comrade! No doubt John was moved to describe the incident, with all the little touches of detail in order that he might forever illustrate the tremendous truth that *Christ is present with His followers in the ordinary affairs of life,* that He is concerned for their daily necessities, and that He makes sacred their secular pursuits through His presence and blessings . . .

He is risen! He is risen indeed!!!
He is alive—He is alive! Is He alive in your heart?

Dear God, oh, how I pray that Jesus will be alive in the heart of every reader. Oh, Jesus, thank You for loving me, saving me, keeping me moment by moment. Jesus, I love You.

APRIL 12

Let not your heart be troubled: ye believe in God, believe also in me. In my Father's house are many mansions: if it were not so, I would have told you. I go to prepare a place for you. And if I go and prepare a place for you, I will come again, and receive you unto myself; that where I am, there ye may be also.
JOHN 14:1–3

The fact that God is love is the explanation of a life beyond the grave. If God were merely a Creator, man might live through a short lifetime and then die forever. Not so! God has a life for us after death. He has a great beyond. He has a place prepared for us, as Jesus said in John 14:1–6. We will have a place where we will live and worship and have a marvelous life for all eternity. The scales of life will be balanced there.

Lord, it is wonderful to know that this life, even at its best, is faded and drab, compared with that glorious place You have prepared for us.

APRIL 13

Now unto him that is able to do exceeding abundantly above all that we ask or think, according to the power that worketh in us.

EPHESIANS 3:20

God takes insignificant men and women and uses them beyond their wildest expectations and imaginations. The Jewish leaders were amazed at the boldness of Peter and John. What had changed these men who just seven to eight weeks earlier cringed and followed afar off and denied even knowing Jesus? They were amazed, but *we* should not be, for we know through the teaching of the Word that the indwelling of the Holy Spirit gives us power to live changed lives—from cringing, frightened cowards to bold, fearless witnesses for Christ.

When the Holy Spirit comes in power, we will see results. They might not be the results we expect or plan, but they will be God's results.

This is the message—**Jesus is alive!** His power and presence are real. That was the message in the day of Peter and John; it is the message now. Down through the centuries it will be the message until He comes again. He is the Lord and Master. He is God.

God of all the universe, oh, that we might appropriate the unlimited power You have made available for us. Help us to live changed lives, that people might know we've been with Thee.

APRIL 14

Then Jesus said unto them, Verily, verily, I say unto you, Moses gave you not that bread from heaven; but my Father giveth you the true bread from heaven. For the bread of God is he which cometh down from heaven, and giveth life unto the world. Then said they unto him, Lord, evermore give us this bread. And Jesus said unto them, I am the bread of life: he that cometh to me shall never hunger; and he that believeth on me shall never thirst.

JOHN 6:32–35

When we sing the song, "When I Survey The Wondrous Cross," it comes to my mind that there is a whole world out there that is hurting. The walking wounded, I call them. They have needs, even though you can't always see them. Many times I think of the girl whom Billy Graham said was all *Vogue* on the outside and *vague* on the inside. A lot of people are like that. They look so sophisticated and so in control, but they are hurting.

This brings to mind a poem that I copied in England out of a book written by Studdert Kennedy:

We are hungry Lord,
We are hungry for something Lord,
We have so much—rich food, cake and candy for ourselves,
But we are hungry.

People around us are so stiff and tight and hard to reach,
They make us that way, too.
But, Oh Lord, we are hungry for something more.

People we know keep talking about great ideas,
Questions, brilliant questions, in the problem of God's existence

But we are hungry for You, not ideas, not theories, not even theology.
We are hungry for You.

We want You to touch us,
To reach down inside us, and turn us on.
We want to know somebody who knows You.

There are many people who are willing to counsel us to death,
But we are hungry for someone who knows You.

And You can get so close to us that we will know You too,
That we can see You then,
We have so many things, but we are hungry.

Deep, deep down inside, we are hungry,
Oh, we may appear to be silly, lazy, or even unconcerned at
    times,

But we are hungry.

We are hungry for Your kind of power, for Your kind of love.
For Your kind of joy, for Your kind of peace.
Yes, the world is hungry.

O God, we are *hungry for You. Feed us, fill us, with Thyself.*

APRIL 15

*And whither I go ye know, and the way ye know. Thomas saith
unto him, Lord, we know not whither thou goest; and how can
we know the way? Jesus saith unto him, I am the way, the
truth, and the life: no man cometh unto the Father, but by me.*
                                        JOHN 14:4–6

God is love, therefore He has a plan for our future. Otherwise,
He would have just created the world and set it in motion. But
He did not do that; He created us to love and to respond to Him
by our own free will and to have a personal relationship with
Him. He seals us by the Holy Spirit unto that day when we will
join Him forever. In the days and years between now and then
we can experience a personal relationship with Him and have
confidence in Him, because of the presence of the indwelling
Holy Spirit in our lives.
HE IS THE WAY!

Lord, thank You for sending Jesus to bring us to Yourself.

APRIL 16

For the life of the flesh is in the blood: and I have given it to you upon the altar to make an atonement for your souls; for it is the blood that maketh an atonement for the soul.

LEVITICUS 17:11

There are some people who want a cross without a Christ. They would like to have the symbol without being identified with the Person who gave His life upon it. When we hesitate to speak about Jesus, we reflect this attitude. Many who would like to have a Christ without a cross would prefer Him as a great teacher or moralist without the stigma of His sacrificial offering for sin. Finally, there are those who would prefer to have neither Christ nor His cross. They are completely untouched by Calvary or the Resurrection. These individuals think they can get along without Him altogether. Praise God, there are those who believe in both Christ *and* His cross. He was the sacrifice who took our sin penalty and provided a way for us to enter into the presence of the Father as forgiven, accepted children. Don't let anyone rob you of that joy and eternal happiness which can be yours through faith in Jesus Christ.

Lord, make us willing to take up the cross and boldly bear witness that we belong to Jesus.

APRIL 17

Love is very patient and kind, never jealous or envious, never boastful or proud, never haughty or selfish or rude. Love does not demand its own way. . . .

1 CORINTHIANS 13:4, 5 TLB

This is the time of year, during this Easter season, that we turn our thoughts inward to examine our *motives*—the heart and soul of our actions. When we were children we learned the story of Sir Galahad and his search for the "Holy Grail," and this description of this gallant knight was engraved on our memory: "His strength was as the strength of ten because his heart was pure."

His goal was *worthy* and his heart was *right,* so marvelous strength was given to him. It is equally true of us, for our lives should be a continual outpouring of *loving, living,* and *serving—* to the extent that our town or community or church or home will be the better for our being there. A heart comes closer to being pure if its *motives* are right. Action may be bungling, stumbling, and awkward, but right motives will eventually bring love and rewards to the individual who continually practices them.

Dear Lord, the desire of our hearts is to be filled with Your knowledge and understanding so that we may walk worthy of Your love.

APRIL 18

Ye also, as lively stones, are built up a spiritual house, an holy priesthood, to offer up spiritual sacrifices, acceptable to God by Jesus Christ.

1 PETER 2:5

"Take us the foxes, the little foxes that spoil the vines: for our vines have tender grapes" (Song of Solomon 2:15). Little foxes . . . those unsuspected, unwatched, insignificant little causes that nibble away domestic happiness and make our homes less noble than they should be.

Harriet Beecher Stowe wrote a long time ago:

You may build beautiful, convenient, attractive houses. You may hang the walls with lovely pictures and stud them with gems of art. There may be living there together persons bound by blood and affection in one common interest, leading a life common to themselves, apart from others. And these persons may each of them be possessed of good and noble traits. There may be a common base of affection, of generosity, of good principles of religion. And yet, through the influence of some of these perverse, nibbling, insignificant little foxes, half the clusters of happiness of these so promising vines may fail to come to maturity.

Yes, the home may hold a little community of people, all of whom may be willing to die for each other. And yet they cannot live happily together, or they achieve far less happiness than their circumstances and their fine traits entitle them to expect.

The reason for this is that the home is the place not only of strong affections, but also of entire unreserve. It is like "undress" rehearsal. It is back room . . . dressing room. From there we go forth to more careful and guarded relationships, leaving behind us debris of hurt feelings and wounded pride like so much cast-off clothing.

O God, help us to make our homes a refuge, a place of peace, a place of harmony, a place of beauty, where love is expressed.

APRIL 19

I am come that they might have life, and that they might have it more abundantly.

JOHN 10:10

Oh, how important for us as women to know that God our Father listens. He never says, "There you go, talking like a woman." He always understands us. Jesus liberated every woman with whom He came in contact—He made them free. *He made them free!*

A. W. Tozer, in his fabulous book, *That Incredible Christian,* said,

In seeking to know God better, we must keep firmly in mind that we need not try to persuade God. He is already persuaded in our favor, not by our prayers but by the generous goodness of His own heart. "It is God's nature to give Himself to every virtuous soul," says Meister Eckhart. "Know then that God is bound to act, to pour Himself out into thee as soon as ever He shall find thee ready."

Oh, how I would like for this to be the definition of my life, that of the Incredible Christian, as he puts into practice the teachings of Christ and His apostles. That is a life full of paradoxes. Speaking as a woman to women, I would say, "In Christ she has died, yet she is alive evermore. She loses her life to save it. She is strongest when she is weak, and weakest when she is strong. She fears God, but is not afraid of Him. She knows that she has been cleansed from her sin, yet is conscious that in her flesh dwells no good thing. She knows that only in Christ Jesus can she become her whole self."

Lord, when people look at us, may what they see be incredible, amazing, wonderful, strengthening, and may they realize that the source of any good in us is Your life in us.

APRIL 20

And now abideth faith, hope, charity, these three; but the greatest of these is charity.

1 CORINTHIANS 13:13

Once when I was speaking with a group of wives and mothers, the subject of how to get along with husbands came up. I would not want to imply that husbands are hard to get along with, but this is a subject that often comes up! A wife must love her husband as God does, otherwise she only sees him as a human creature who leaves the bathroom in a mess, procrastinates about mowing the lawn, doesn't pick up his clothes, and on and on and on. The secret, though, is to see him as God sees him—then you can overlook all of these things.

To be lovable and sweet to your husband when he is lovable

and sweet to you is not really giving—that's trading. So often we make trades in life. We're sweet and kind to the people who are sweet and kind to us. To really love, we must go beyond that, with the grace of God and His love. We get to know God better and better when we begin to do this. The closer we come to God, the easier it is to love others.

There was a couple driving down the road. It was their twenty-fifth wedding anniversary. They were sitting far apart. She said, "You know, when we were first married, we snuggled up close together." He just kept on driving and said, "I haven't moved."

God hasn't moved, but if we move away, even just for a moment, we begin to look at others critically. We begin to feel that we have not been treated fairly. But, if we "snuggle up" to God, stay close to Him, we will find it easy to love others—overlook their faults and really love them.

Dear Jesus, I want to stay close to You. Forgive me when I wander off. I need You. I love You. Help me today.

APRIL 21

... for we shall all stand before the judgment seat of Christ. ... So then every one of us shall give account of himself to God.

ROMANS 14:10, 12

Man is God's creation. We must first acknowledge and recognize that God is the Creator of the world, the heavens, the entire solar system. It is really not so important *how* He did it. It really doesn't matter whether He did it over ten billion years or whether He did it in a snap of His fingers. That was *His* decision. I learned a long time ago that I'm not going to stew and fret over something God has already decided. It is already done, and the important thing is to recognize that *He did it!*

In the beginning God reached down and scooped up the earth

and He breathed the breath of God into the being that He
created. That is something very, very special. Man is something
very special.

A man was speaking allegorically, describing how it was when
God decided to make man. He created this creature and gave
him consciousness. He also gave him free will to make a choice
between God and Satan, between good and evil, between God
and self. One of the angels said to God, "Oh, what a risk you are
taking to make a creature like that—with free will. He might decide he is so smart that he can save himself, that he is so great
that he can do everything himself, that he does not need You."
God answered, "Yes, I am taking a risk. I have created a being
with a capacity for choosing wrong, but I have put an emptiness
inside him that cannot be filled until it is filled with Me, and so
he can choose Me or reject Me, but the responsibility is his."

In this permissive society of ours, people blame everything
they do wrong on their parents or something or someone else.
This started away back in Genesis. When God found Adam and
Eve hiding because they were naked, Adam blamed it all on Eve.
And what did Eve say? "The *serpent* did it!" We read the same
thing about the men being tried in Germany for the killing of
millions of Jews. Each man would say, "My superior told me to
do it." Today in America, we call that "passing the buck," and
don't we all do it? From the time we are children, all the way to
adulthood, we try to find someone else to blame for what is not
right. Now the classic statement is, "The devil made me do it,"
but the truth is *we* are responsible for our own lives, for our own
responses to God.

Many times we hear people say, "My life is my own. I can do
as I please. What I do doesn't bother anybody else." What a
misconception! Every life you touch is influenced by how you act
and what you believe. God will hold you accountable. Somebody is watching you. Everyone of us has an influence on someone else, and we are responsible.

In 1953, Billy Graham held a crusade in Dallas. He had each
person hold a candle. All the lights were turned off, and each
person lit his candle with his match. The resulting illumination
was not a huge glow of light, but rather, you could see every indi-

vidual light. They did not blend together; each light counted. So it is that every person is an individual before God. We are responsible to Him. We are responsible for our families, for every person we touch. God help us to so choose that, "they may see our good works and glorify our Father which is in Heaven."

Father, I am only one, but I AM *one—help me to make the light entrusted to me count for Thee.*

APRIL 22

And Jesus called a little child unto him, and set him in the midst of them, And said, Verily I say unto you, Except ye be converted, and become as little children, ye shall not enter into the kingdom of heaven. Whosoever therefore shall humble himself as this little child, the same is greatest in the kingdom of heaven. And whoso shall receive one such little child in my name receiveth me. But whoso shall offend one of these little ones which believe in me, it were better for him that a millstone were hanged about his neck, and that he were drowned in the depth of the sea.

MATTHEW 18:2–6

A newspaper story showed a little boy sitting in front of what had been his house before it was leveled by a devastating tornado. He said so touchingly, "Home didn't seem like much until it wasn't there."

How callous and casual we are with the essentials of our lives. Every woman, when she seriously thinks of what she still knows, still knows the value and intrinsic treasure of her home, for it is truly her most comfortable, natural habitat. She was born equipped to know more about this than any other creature.

Priorities are primary. In the home you are influencing all the time—for excellence or mediocrity. There is no room for guilt when you are rightfully placing people above things and household procedures and food preparation and all the other pressing demands. There was a little boy whose mother was a perfectionist, and she was constantly scrubbing and cleaning. Finally, he said to her pleadingly, "Mommy, please leave me a dirty place to play."

We all need a comfortable place to play. Mothers do not deal primarily with things like detergents, toothpaste, shining wax on the floor, and hairspray, as TV commercials would have you think; MOTHERS DEAL IN HUMAN BEINGS, and everything they do affects the mind, the spirit, and the emotional makeup of their children. You are a mother every moment of your life, either bad, good, or indifferent. Yes, we are influencing all the time—for excellence or mediocrity—for eternity!

Lord, may the marks we leave on our children be enobling and uplifting—we know they are enduring.

APRIL 23

Therefore, my beloved brethren, be ye stedfast, unmoveable, always abounding in the work of the Lord, forasmuch as ye know that your labour is not in vain in the Lord.

1 Corinthians 15:58

In the midst of the hustle and bustle of life, we all have to have "safety valves" to keep our nerves, emotions, and minds on a fairly even keel.

It is very important to keep a good *sense of humor*—and a good *center of gravity.* The center of gravity, perfectly balanced in a tightrope walker, is what keeps him from falling off.

For my personal helps, I have poems, quotes, sayings, Bible verses, which I have collected to remind me of the basic values in life. One of my favorites is this poem, entitled, "Don't Lose Desire," by James J. Metcalfe.

Don't lose desire in this life . . . do not decide to quit . . .
When everything goes wrong for you . . . just make the best of
    it . . .
Have faith in God, appeal to Him . . . and never give up hope . . .

However dark the corridors . . . where you may have to grope . . .
Let not your heart surrender to the demon of despair . . .
God knows your troubles and He hears—the slightest, whispered
     prayer . . .
There is no wrong that you have done that cannot be ab-
     solved . . .
Nor any frightful problem that somehow cannot be solved.

The ability to go on when ordinary men say the battle is lost,
the faith one has when no one else can see a reason for it, the vision to see the rainbow before the storm is over, the willpower to
go on struggling after strength is gone—*that* is genius!

*Dear Father, I pray for our young people today. I pray espe-
cially for my grandchildren. If it be possible, let nothing happen to them that will damage them physically or spiritually.
Help them through temptations. Send them a melody of
song—a word from Your Book—a memory of a prayer in the
moment of temptation. O Dear God, help me to be a better
model for all young people to know and to follow. Forgive me
when I've failed. Thank You for the resource of Your love
and Word.*

APRIL 24

*For thou, Lord, art good, and ready to forgive; and plenteous
in mercy unto all them that call upon thee.*

PSALMS 86:5

The hardest thing for people to do is to let go of a hurtful
memory, a time when somebody hurt them.

"But somebody did this or that, I can forgive them—but I can
never forget it." Yes, you want to keep it, resenting it over and
over and over, let it go on creating turmoil and pain. How harm-
ful this is to you and to the other person, but the worst thing
about it is that it will keep you from having a perfect relationship
with the Lord and with other people. It surfaces again and again.

Only God's love can master that; human love cannot. My mother died when I was a year and a half old. I lived with my grandparents on a farm and was wonderfully and warmly loved. Then, when I was six, I went to live with my father who had re-married. Unfortunately, my stepmother was a cruel woman, and my father allowed her to be. In time, the Juvenile Court declared her unfit to rear children, and removed me from their home. I went back to my grandmother and then made my own life. Many years later, my father and his wife moved nearby me. He was getting old, and they needed help—someone to take care of them. I was near, and I was elected. At first, it bothered me. I resented it a lot, you know, "Where were you when I needed you?" Then it seemed as though God said to me, "Mary, I didn't ask you where *you* were when *I* needed *you.*" So the Lord really mastered that and gave me the grace to do for them and take care of them until they both passed away—and to really enjoy it! You and I, human effort, human love, could never achieve it.

Heavenly Father, I want to be a good child today. Thank You for helping me to let go of a "hurtful memory." Give me strength and joy to serve others who might be hurting.

APRIL 25

And the glory which thou gavest me I have given them; that they may be one, even as we are one: I in them, and thou in me, that they may be made perfect in one; and that the world may know that thou hast sent me, and hast loved them, as thou hast loved me. Father, I will that they also, whom thou hast given me, be with me where I am; that they may behold my glory, which thou hast given me: for thou lovedst me before the foundation of the world. O righteous Father, the world hath not known thee: but I have known thee, and these have known that thou hast sent me. And I have declared unto them thy name, and will declare it: that the love wherewith thou hast loved me may be in them, and I in them.

JOHN 17:22–26

The best demonstration of God comes not from argument, but from a life of love. God's love is demonstrated to us in the Person of Jesus Christ. He is the supreme example. In Him we actually see two things about the love of God. First, there is the fact that love holds nothing back. As John 3:16 says, "For God so loved the world, that he gave his only begotten Son . . ." It is difficult to understand just how much love that took. Although I cannot understand the extent of God's love, I can understand the motive for His sending His Son into the world. That motive was *love*. Second, there is the fact that such love is truly undeserved. We did not deserve it in the least, but God freely gave it to us, nonetheless. We are never worthy of God's love, yet He views us as being of such great worth to Him that He freely gave His only Son in our behalf.

Blessed Father, we are so unworthy, but we are grateful that You loved us so much. Thank You for that love. Thank You for Jesus, His life, His death, the salvation He provides for us.

APRIL 26

For, brethren, ye have been called unto liberty; only use not liberty for an occasion to the flesh, but by love serve one another. For all the law is fulfilled in one word, even in this; Thou shalt love thy neighbour as thyself. . . . Bear ye one another's burdens, and so fulfil the law of Christ.

GALATIANS 5:13, 14; 6:2

Are you developing a "serving heart?" When God calls us to serve, we automatically say no to a lot of other things. There is a big price to pay if we would serve.

First, it will cost in *time*. I have found that there is no way that I can be both at the lake on Sunday morning and at the church teaching my Sunday school class. There must be a ruthless cutting out of secondary things to spend time with first things—priorities—priorities of time. It takes time to listen, but listening is my business, and so I listen. When you talk to God, *He* listens.

I can call Him any time, anywhere, person-to-person, collect. He *listens!* So we, too, must listen . . . it's part of the price we pay.

The second thing it is going to cost us in personal peace is *ease of mind*. You will have problems of others to pray about, to agonize over, to walk through. They will wake you up in the middle of the night and gnaw at you in the daytime, but this is just part of what it costs, if you would serve.

The third thing that it is going to cost is some of *yourself*. You will get involved with people, and sometimes you will be hurt, and chances are you won't even be appreciated. If you get appreciation, then that is the bonus, but don't expect it or you will be disappointed. So it will cost you a lot of yourself.

And the fourth thing it is going to cost is *convenience*. People do not seem to have problems at convenient times. Most seem to choose the most inconvenient times. It would be nice if you could have certain set "office hours" for dealing with people's problems or situations, but it doesn't happen that way.

There was a man in the inner city of London who had given many years working in a very discouraging task. A friend came to him one day and said, "Why don't you leave this job before you are broken by its inhuman burden? Why don't you run away from it all?" "I would like very much to leave it all," the man replied. "But there is a strange, loving man on a cross who won't let me."

Yes, when we see the cross with love and agony streaming down, all humanity takes on a new color; every person becomes a possibility for redemption; every wanderer can come home; every burden can be lifted. And I become excited again over the wonder of God's grace to me, and I am ready to serve again and again.

Dear God, we know that You have a task for us that only we can do. You do not have anybody else waiting in the wings to do it. You have designed it for us. God help us to do Your work, Your way, in this day . . . regardless of the cost.

APRIL 27

*But sanctify the Lord God in your hearts: and be ready always
to give an answer to every man that asketh you a reason of the
hope that is in you with meekness and fear.*

1 PETER 3:15

People, Christian and non-Christian, try to find meaning in
life. Modern existentialists, atheists, agnostics, and even a few
people who call themselves Christians, are trying to find this
meaning within man himself.

The true answer to this quest is found in the Westminster Cat-
echism: "The chief end of man is to glorify God and to enjoy
Him forever."

In other words, the reason for man's creation, and the whole
purpose of his living, is to express praise of God with his lips and
with his life.

Then again we find in the Scriptures, "In every thing, give
thanks" (1 Thessalonians 5:18). That has sometimes been difficult for me to learn. It has been difficult for me to understand,
but it took me a lifetime to understand that I did not have to understand everything, for God's thoughts are higher than my
thoughts.

And so today, I just sing with my heart:

> To God be the glory,
>   Great things He hath done!
> So loved He the world
>   that He gave us His Son,
> Who yielded His life an atonement for sin
>   And opened the Lifegate that all may go in.
>   FANNY J. CROSBY

*Dear Jesus, You said: "I am the life, and no man cometh
unto the Father except by Me. And again, "I have come that
ye might have life, and have it more abundantly!" How
thankful we are that You love us in such an abundant and
abounding way.*

APRIL 28

Let your light so shine before men, that they may see your good works, and glorify your Father which is in heaven.

MATTHEW 5:16

God still makes Himself known to man. One of the ways that He reveals Himself to us today is through other people. We often make the mistake of looking to some other believer as a pattern for life instead of looking through them unto Jesus Christ Himself. This is our woeful mistake. We are told that we are supposed to live in such a manner that people may see Jesus through our lives. We are to look to God, but once we have come to know Him, we are to act as witnesses to let others know Him whom we love and worship, and "whom to know aright is life eternal." *We* are the means God chose to communicate His message to the world.

Lord, we know we disappoint You time and again when we fail to carry the message. Forgive us and give us a sense of urgency that would keep us always at the task.

APRIL 29

My little children, let us not love in word, neither in tongue; but in deed and in truth. And hereby we know that we are of the truth, and shall assure our hearts before him.

1 JOHN 3:18, 19

I am grateful that John's writings gave encouragement and assurance. The Gospel of John was written so that we might know that Jesus Christ is the Son of God. He wanted us to realize His humanity, His pain and His sorrow, His work, His winsomeness, and His triumph.

I think it is also one of the greatest Gospels to teach us how to live as God's people. Becoming a Christian is a matter of repentance and faith. It stems from faith in Christ alone as Personal Savior.

But, living as a child of God involves more than faith. As James put it, "Faith without works is dead" (*see* James 2:17).

And so how do we live as a Child of God? How can we know how to live in such a way that will please God?

I am everlastingly grateful that I live in a day and a time when we have the Scriptures, and we can know what God wants us to do as His children, how He wants us to live, how He wants us to worship Him, and how He wants us to relate to other people.

O God, how I pray that as we study the Book of John—like the two on the road to Emmaus—our hearts will be stirred within us, burning within us, and we will come closer to the One who said, "I am the Way, the Truth, the Light."

APRIL 30

It is April and I can see!

Oh, how blind we often are to the beautiful miracles of nature all around us! How can we live through spring and experience the awakening of new life and not see the parallel in the Resurrection of our Blessed Lord?

Pause now to make a list of things you have noticed in recent days that herald the joyful fact that spring is indeed here, new life is bursting forth all around us, and balmy summer days are just around the corner.

1. _____
2. _____
3. _____
4. _____
5. _____
6. _____
7. _____
8. _____

Lord, thank You for these beautiful gifts of nature and for this breathtaking season of new life and resurrection. Give us a sense of expectation, a zest for life, and a tremendous sense of awe and gratitude for the Resurrection of our wonderful, beautiful, precious Savior, Jesus.

May

MAY 1

But God, who is rich in mercy, for his great love wherewith he loved us, Even when we were dead in sins, hath quickened us together with Christ, (by grace ye are saved;) And hath raised us up together, and made us sit together in heavenly places in Christ Jesus; That in the ages to come he might shew the exceeding riches of his grace in his kindness toward us through Christ Jesus. For by grace are ye saved through faith; and that not of yourselves: it is the gift of God: Not of works, lest any man should boast. For we are his workmanship, created in Christ Jesus unto good works, which God hath before ordained that we should walk in them.

EPHESIANS 2:4–10

Christ has never betrayed a confidence placed in Him.

Preachers and teachers may prove to be less than perfect.

The support and friendship of other Christians may play us false.

The liturgy, or social function of the church may go flat, and since we, ourselves, are part of all of this, the spiritual soil of our lives is soon seen to be shallow.

Basically, all of this happens because our hope, our trust, our confidence was not in Christ, but in the church. Place your confidence in Jesus Christ. HE NEVER FAILS!

O God, we never cease to be amazed that WE *can be participants in Your matchless, marvelous love.*

MAY 2

*For Moses had said, Consecrate yourselves today to the Lord,
even every man upon his son, and upon his brother; that he
may bestow upon you a blessing this day.*

EXODUS 32:29

Until you make a definite consecration of your life to Jesus
Christ, you cannot begin to live victoriously, or have a life
guided by God's promises. When we are converted, we accept
Christ and are saved by His power, by His blood, from eternal
damnation and guilt. In addition to this initial conversion experience, we are continually transformed into what He wants us to
be. As the Bible says in Romans 5:1–5, because of our faith in
Him we have been lifted to the place of highest privilege where
we now stand, and we look confidently and joyfully toward becoming all that He has in mind for us to be.

Our salvation is a once-and-for-all act of conversion, but all
that happens to us thereafter is a process of transformation. To
experience this later process, we must consecrate our lives to
Him. Consecration is a decision, it is not a matter of emotion. It
is a matter of the will. Our emotions will be in it, but consecration is not merely feeling like it, it is a matter of turning our wills
over to God.

Lord, may we DECIDE *for Thee, consecrating ourselves to
truly make You Lord of our lives.*

MAY 3

*For I know that in me (that is, in my flesh,) dwelleth no good
thing: for to will is present with me; but how to perform that
which is good I find not.*

ROMANS 7:18

When God gave Adam and Eve free choice, He didn't go
wrong. So must we give our children free choice, whether we

want to or not. We do not determine the will of another individual. We can set the atmosphere, and we can try to show God to our children through our lives and forgiveness, but each person has a free will.

God created us in His image and that includes our children. Because He wanted it to be of our own free will to love Him, He gave us free choice. Knowing that we would fail, He had a plan to send Jesus to show how much He loved us. The song says, "Oh, how I love Jesus, because He *first* loved me!" No matter how rebellious or contrary our children seem to be, genuine love will eventually win them over. They need to be convinced that God is a God they can talk to at anytime, person-to-person, regardless of their sins and their rebelliousness. **God is always available.**

Precious Lord, thank You for giving me a choice, but leaving nothing to chance!

MAY 4

For a dream cometh through the multitude of business; and a fool's voice is known by multitude of words. When thou vowest a vow unto God, defer not to pay it; for he hath no pleasure in fools: pay that which thou hast vowed. Better is it that thou shouldest not vow, than that thou shouldest vow and not pay.
ECCLESIASTES 5:3–5

A lot of people have gotten away from keeping their word—they're saying they will do a thing but not doing it. Pay what you owe when you say you will pay it, and you will have a credit rating as good as a millionaire, for that is all they can do.

We must learn to be just. We must be honest with the other person, giving them the right to be honest with us and keep their own word. We must have a standard that is unshakable, that is sure, that you can count on. We must have absolutes.

Everybody has to build his life around something or someone stable. God Himself is the only thing that meets all these requirements—He is the firm foundation, the great "I AM," the same yesterday, today, and forever.

> *"On Christ the solid rock I stand, all other ground is sinking sand. . . ."*

MAY 5

And they shall teach no more every man his neighbour, and every man his brother, saying, Know the Lord: for they shall all know me, from the least of them unto the greatest of them, saith the Lord: for I will forgive their iniquity, and I will remember their sin no more.

JEREMIAH 31:34

Oh, how we all long to be forgiven! What can wash away my sin? Nothing but the blood of Jesus. It is said that at least seventy-five percent of all the people in the hospitals are there because of guilt.

So many people carry guilt around. Corrie ten Boom said, "When we come to Jesus and repent of our sins, He takes them and buries them in the sea, and then He puts up a sign, 'No Fishing.' " Once God forgives our sins and buries them, we dishonor Him and indicate we don't really believe what He says, if we drag them out again and carry them around. God says He not only forgives our sins but He remembers them no more. Oh, that we might graciously accept His forgiveness and go on, believing our slate is wiped clean, rather than dragging around, full of guilt, over something God says He has already forgotten. Satan would keep us guilty and ineffective, Jesus would have us victorious and triumphant that we have a God who can forgive sins and make us clean.

> *Lord, it is much easier to confess our sins to You than it is to forget them. When we honestly confess, help us to know we are honestly forgiven.*

MAY 6

But my God shall supply all your need according to his riches in glory by Christ Jesus.

PHILIPPIANS 4:19

A friend in Bethlehem really loves Jesus. She delights in the Lord. I know others who also love God, but they don't have a burning zeal for Jesus. Israelites witnessed God's miracles in Egypt and the parting of the Red Sea, but their faith in God was not strong enough. They wanted more and more.

They didn't feel God was able to help them overcome. They saw themselves as grasshoppers and lacked confidence. God expects us to be confident. He did not give us an insect-sized personality. He gave us a giant personality to look over the obstacles. Because the Israelites saw God as being too little, they also saw themselves as too little.

God is responsible for our basic needs. He provides us with the power to take care of those needs. There are many needs other than the tangible needs, such as food and clothing. There are also the needs for fulfillment and achievement, these too are basic. God is honor-bound to provide all these basic needs if we trust in Him.

Father, we do trust Thee and know that You will supply our every need according to Your riches in Christ Jesus.

MAY 7

But sanctify the Lord God in your hearts: and be ready always to give an answer to every man that asketh you a reason of the hope that is in you with meekness and fear.

1 PETER 3:15

We live in a negative, hostile, and suspicious world. Sometimes we have to defend the faith that we hold and the faith by which we live.

Our Christian defense must be reasonable; it must be intelligent; it must be given with gentleness. Some people try to force their Christian views on unwilling listeners and succeed only in turning them away. People must be *wooed* into the Christian faith, not *nagged* into it.

Our defense of our faith must begin with reverence. It must be carried on in a way that would be pleasing to God. If you have a difference of opinion, it must be discussed in a tone and atmosphere that God can honor. The language of God is love. It is a language of the heart, not of the tongue. We are saved because we are loved. **God is love.**

Father, may we share Your love, Your salvation, in a gentle, Christ-like way that will attract people rather than turn them away.

MAY 8

Yea doubtless, and I count all things but loss for the excellency of the knowledge of Christ Jesus my Lord: for whom I suffered the loss of all things, and do count them but dung, that I may win Christ.

PHILIPPIANS 3:8

Let's take a commitment of excellence into our work, whatever our work might be. We can use it in the work in our homes, in making the home a beautiful place, a place where love is communicated. Everything in life tends to tarnish. Silver has to be polished; chrome has to be continually polished to keep it clean; brass has to be polished; gold has to be rubbed to remove the accumulation of particles from the air. Everything in life has to be kept up. Our relationships have to be kept up.

I remember hearing Tom Landry say one time, "The ultimate in life is not in achieving and winning, but in giving God first priority." How easy it is to get off the track, especially in today's complex world.

Take time each morning to pray. When problems tumble

around you, ask for His guidance. The Bible tells us to ask, seek, and knock. *Don't forget to pray.*

The commitment to excellence starts the very first thing in the morning, every day—getting plugged into the source of all excellence, the source of all power, the source of all resources. I am called to live a perfect relationship to God so that my life produces a longing after God in other lives, not an admiration for myself.

O precious Jesus, this is my prayer and goal.

MAY 9

For the husband is the head of the wife, even as Christ is the head of the church: and he is the saviour of the body. Therefore as the church is subject unto Christ, so let the wives be to their own husbands in every thing. Husbands, love your wives, even as Christ also loved the church and gave himself for it.
EPHESIANS 5:23–25

Who has the last word? How many times you have heard this! In the Christian home, the man is responsible directly unto God, but he never has the last word—*God does!*

God will deal with that man if he speaks indirectly. That is why the woman in a godly household has a phenomenal amount of freedom, if that home functions properly. She knows that God is going to deal with her husband, which frees her from the responsibility of ever trying to make him good or kind or wise. Only God can do that, and he carries a tremendous burden to be always attuned to the will of God in order to use his God-given authority in God's way. The majority of decisions in the home should be made mutually, but ultimately the husband will be held responsible for the outcome.

Dear Father, give us the grace to take our proper place in Your order of responsibility, never assuming roles that are not rightfully ours.

MAY 10

Her children arise up, and call her blessed; her husband also, and he praiseth her.

PROVERBS 31:28

Much will be said and written this season about mothers, for we are near the day designated as **Mother's Day.** It's a day to pause in our rushing about and give extra special thought and appreciation to mothers throughout the world and then, of course, to that one special mother who means the most to us.

We so often picture Mother with graying hair and the maturity of years of experience, with the children already reared and taking their place out in the community and the world. And it *is* good to remember and honor mothers of grown-up children.

But, also, we should not neglect to pay the proper homage and tribute to that growing number in today's society—the mothers of young children. What a task these young mothers have, and how well they are doing it!

Within this century, we have seen revolutionary changes in American families and in the role of a mother. From the days when Father was the autocrat and ruled the home and business with an iron hand, and Mother stayed at home and tended the children, we have come to the day when many mothers are having to work outside the home, and we have had to take a new look at things. We have to work harder to strengthen family life, and, in today's economic society, much of this burden falls upon the mother. To her falls the task of using her time not only in the work force but also to guide her children wisely and well. Time, however, is a quality rather than a quantity: It is not *how much* time we spend with our children, but *how well* we spend it, that will reap the dividends of character and strength.

"A mother is *truth* with a map in her hand ... *beauty* with a cake in the oven ... *wisdom* with a confused bank account ... and a *miracle of love* with a sick child in her arms."

Lord, bless all mothers everywhere this season—the older saints, with gray hair and years of experience and memories;

*the young saints, with little ones pulling on their skirts, and
the ones in-between who still don't know if their job has been
well-done. Fashion a special blessing for them and grant
them the wisdom, grace, and patience they so desperately
need to fulfill the task to which You have called them.*

MAY 11

*Then were there brought unto him little children, that he
should put his hands on them, and pray: and the disciples re-
buked them. But Jesus said, Suffer little children, and forbid
them not, to come unto me: for of such is the kingdom of
heaven.*

MATTHEW 19:13, 14

Every woman should know that there is still no place on earth
where she is more innately gifted and equipped to comprehend
the meaning of life than in the home.

A woman can confidently select that sphere as her only one
and be assured that there is a majesty about it, or she can make
whatever length of time she is able to be at home remarkably
productive in quality all the way, for she knows **she must not fail
here at any cost!**

She knows that any other successes bought at the cost of her
home and family are strangely and surely tarnished.

*Lord, may this be our most shining triumph—our jobs well-
done, lovingly and wisely done, in our homes.*

MAY 12

*Then shalt thou say in thine heart, Who hath begotten me
these, seeing I have lost my children, and am desolate, a cap-
tive, and removing to and fro? and who hath brought up these?
Behold, I was left alone; these, where had they been? Thus
saith the Lord God, Behold, I will lift up mine hand to the*

Gentiles, and set up my standard to the people: and they shall bring thy sons in their arms, and thy daughters shall be carried upon their shoulders.

ISAIAH 49:21, 22

Not long ago, Ann Landers said in her column, "Someday the liberated woman will discover that her most important job, the one with the greatest rewards, was right under her nose—and she blew it!"

I say, "Thank God" for the women who have not blown this wonderful opportunity at home, because all through the land we hear so many things that seem to demean those values which most women deeply cherish—marriage, home, children. The spotlight of truth is incredibly bright, totally revealing, and a sure guide to the right path. We believe that every woman who knows God really wants to follow this right path, and a lot of women who do not know Him also instinctively want the things that give value to life, that give comfort to heart, that make them feel loved, and that give meaning to their future. This is true particularly in a woman's marriage, in her home, which is so much "her." Anything that causes tremendous extremes in reaction can cause problems, and anyone who deliberately weakens the home and family and reduces them to anything less than God intended them to be, will someday have to face His judgment for tampering with the very heart of His plan for mankind.

Lord, help us not to "blow it." If we can succeed at only one thing, let it be in this most precious of all relationships—our families.

MAY 13

That their hearts might be comforted, being knit together in love, and unto all riches of the full assurance of understanding, to the acknowledgement of the mystery of God, and of the Father, and of Christ. . . . As ye have therefore received Christ Jesus the Lord, so walk ye in him.

COLOSSIANS 2:2, 6

Here on earth, love has a locale. It is called *home!* Here love receives its power and most assuredly radiates its power. Life's most complete, continually enriching experience is a good marriage. Marriage offers the opportunity for the greatest expression of human potential or the greatest potential for destruction. Your choice of a marriage partner is your second greatest decision in life.

Is your home a haven or is it havoc?

O God, help us to make our homes havens of love and warmth and security in the midst of an uncertain world.

MAY 14

If so be that ye have heard him, and have been taught by him, as the truth is in Jesus: That ye put off concerning the former conversation the old man, which is corrupt according to the deceitful lusts; And be renewed in the spirit of your mind; And that ye put on the new man, which after God is created in righteousness and true holiness. Wherefore putting away lying, speak every man truth with his neighbour: for we are members one of another. Be ye angry, and sin not: let not the sun go down upon your wrath: Neither give place to the devil.

EPHESIANS 4:21–27

The "glue" which cements a home together is the will of God. Every Christian home should seek the Lordship of Jesus Christ above all else. In practical terms this means not to let a single day go by without asking God's blessing on the particulars in it. It also means that a couple will find time to be alone together in seeking the face of God, such as in prayer together in the evening. Third, it means that a couple will join together in public worship where God's Word is faithfully preached and taught. As Billy Graham has put it, there are three ways for a person to be rid of anxiety and to have a full and happy life: (1) stop seeking the trivial, transient things to which modern man has become accustomed; (2) get your eyes off yourself and focused onto Christ; (3) commit yourself fully to Him.

Father, make us partners in perfecting the union to which we have pledged our lives and loyalty. May we do the things to make our marriages strong and full of joy and pleasing to Thee.

MAY 15

. . . and let every woman have her own husband. Let the husband render unto the wife due benevolence: and likewise also the wife unto the husband. The wife hath not power of her own body, but the husband: and likewise also the husband hath not power of his own body, but the wife.

1 CORINTHIANS 7:2–4

The best way to insure mental health is to marry well. Life's most complete continuing and enriching experience is a good marriage. In fact, a good marriage is the nearest thing to heaven we can experience on earth. It offers the greatest opportunity for us to realize the wholeness of our personalities. In order to develop a good marriage and an enduring relationship, we must set our hearts and minds on attitudes which keep love aglow, open lines of communication, enrich mutual respect, build toleration, consideration, and appreciation.

Father, give us right attitudes regarding this lifetime commitment of marriage, and may it bring strength and fulfillment to our lives and to the one You have given us.

MAY 16

Who can find a virtuous woman? for her price is far above rubies. The heart of her husband doth safely trust in her, so that he shall have no need of spoil. She will do him good and not evil all the days of her life. . . . She looketh well to the ways of her household, and eateth not the bread of idleness. Her children arise up, and call her blessed; her husband also, and he praiseth her. Many daughters have done virtuously, but thou excellest them all.

PROVERBS 31:10–12, 27–29

"A wise woman builds her house, while a foolish woman tears hers down by her own efforts" (Proverbs 14:1 TLB). This is a description of what is happening in America today. Foolish women are tearing down their houses. A wise woman builds her house. If you build your house, you build the people in it. If you build a company, you build the people in it. To build a nation, you build the people in it. You build up your family, you build up your husband, build up your children. Tell them they are going to be great, tell them they are going to be special, make them believe it, and they will be great, they will be special. People spend so much time destroying, tearing down, criticizing, emphasizing the negative, when if they would just spend that time passing out praise and encouragement, they could really make an investment in the success and self-esteem of the person they are vocally evaluating. Often, it's the person who means the most to them, and then it's even sadder. Oh, that we might cease this moment from ever having a part in destroying the confidence and self-esteem of *anybody,* much less the people we love!

O Lord, make us sensitive to the influence You have given us, either to build or destroy, and may we use it only to lift up and encourage.

MAY 17

For they being ignorant of God's righteousness, and going about to establish their own righteousness, have not submitted themselves unto the righteousness of God. For Christ is the end of the law for righteousness to every one that believeth.

ROMANS 10:3, 4

Giving thanks always for all things unto God and the Father in the name of our Lord Jesus Christ; Submitting yourselves one to another in the fear of God.

EPHESIANS 5:20, 21

I learned a long time ago in an incredible way that we are to be submissive to our husband's needs, not his will. We are to be submissive only to the will of God.

All throughout the Scriptures, and especially the ones picked out of context and quoted, it is made totally clear that a strong, vertical relationship to God comes first, before human horizontal relationships.

We cannot begin to know ourselves and what kind of folks we are to live with until we let God, who made us, reveal this to us, lovingly and strongly. We need that first—then, and only then, can we relate to someone honestly.

Since all human relationships are predicated on mutual submission to the Lord first, all of our human relationships are transformed, specifically the relationship of husband and wife. If our being able to relate nobly even to a total stranger is dependent upon a strong vertical relationship with our Lord, how much more important would this be in the close togetherness of marriage!

Lord, help us to approach this most important relationship first of all, being rightly related to You.

MAY 18

But if any have caused grief, he hath not grieved me, but in part: that I may not overcharge you all. Sufficient to such a man is this punishment, which was inflicted of many. So that contrariwise ye ought rather to forgive him, and comfort him, lest perhaps such a one should be swallowed up with overmuch sorrow. Wherefore I beseech you that ye would confirm your love toward him.

2 CORINTHIANS 2:5–8

Satan loves to take advantage of the breaks in our relationships. We are to forgive the one who has wronged us and lift him up in prayer. Confirm to him the fact that you love him. Don't harbor hate—it corrodes. It robs you of your beauty, sparkle, and enthusiasm. Always forgive your enemies, nothing annoys them so much.

Father, teach us to forgive others as You have forgiven us— unconditionally, no strings attached.

MAY 19

For this cause shall a man leave his father and mother, and shall be joined unto his wife, and they two shall be one flesh.
EPHESIANS 5:31

People often say marriage is a 50-50 proposition. Don't you believe it! It is really a 100-100 proposition. When you marry you do not become half a person, and you do not bring half of yourself into marriage. Instead, you must bring 100 percent of your devotion, your dedication, your love, your talent, your ability, and everything you have into a marriage to make it work. The relationship is 100-100. It is two complete, total people in a relationship moving toward a common goal—the worship, love, and service of God.

Dear Father, help us not to keep score but to be willing to give whatever is required, even 100 percent, if necessary, to make our marriage the partnership You intend it to be.

MAY 20

Likewise, ye wives, be in subjection to your own husbands; that, if any obey not the word, they also may without the word be won by the conversation of the wives; While they behold your chaste conversation coupled with fear. Whose adorning let it not be that outward adorning of plaiting the hair, and of wearing of gold, or of putting on of apparel; But let it be the hidden man of the heart, in that which is not corruptible, even the ornament of a meek and quiet spirit, which is in the sight of God of great price. For after this manner in the old time the holy women also, who trusted in God, adorned themselves, being in subjection unto their own husbands: Even as Sara obeyed Abraham, calling him lord: whose daughters ye are, as long as ye do well, and are not afraid with any amazement. Likewise, ye husbands, dwell with them according to knowledge, giving honour unto the wife, as unto the weaker vessel, and as being heirs together of the grace of life; that your prayers be not hindered. Finally, be ye all of one mind, having compassion one of another, love as brethren, be pitiful, be courteous.

1 PETER 3:1–8

If men had been wise enough to make women feel that what they did was important, they would not have the problem with women fighting for liberation today. But we women also need to be wise. God made us different, so our approach is different. Little girls wind their arms around Daddy's neck and get what they want, but little boys just butt head-on. God gave us better sensitivity there, and we must have sense enough to use it.

Sit down with your husband when he comes home, have a cup of coffee or a glass of tea with him, and listen to him. Pay attention to him. Let that be first. It is important.

We have to realize what he is saying is, "Please make me feel important, more important than the other things in your life." If you don't, he might begin to resent that thing that claims your attention, the fact that it is fulfilling a lot of your needs.

Often, when husbands begin to complain, they are really saying, "Please make me feel that I am more important than those other things you're involved in." Before my husband retired, he did not like to come home and find me on the telephone. So I would tell people ahead of time that if he should drive in, I would hang up in the middle of the conversation and greet him at the door, for that was important to him.

Then, after I had spent a little time with him, I could get back to the phone, make my calls, or whatever I needed to do. But the important thing was to give him *his* time first. That is what I call "answering the first tug."

Dear Lord, please help us to "answer the first tug," being sensitive enough in the first place to feel the tugging.

MAY 21

Bring ye all the tithes into the storehouse, that there may be meat in mine house, and prove me now herewith, saith the Lord of hosts, if I will not open you the windows of heaven, and pour you out a blessing, that there shall not be room enough to receive it.

MALACHI 3:10

When you trust God with your finances and return a tenth to Him, you are saying, "You are the owner of all my material things—my money, my houses, my land, my cars—everything I possess." Once God has the ownership, they are His responsibility, and you can trust Him to see they are used for good. You are the steward; He is the owner. When you own something, you want it to be kept up, kept in good shape, multiplied, if it is an investment. God does that. He can take what you have, no matter how small, and multiply it if you'll dedicate it to Him. So when you tithe, you are acknowledging not only your stewardship, but also God's ownership. If you do your part, you will see that He is bigger than you are!

The blessing keeps going on and on—like a pebble thrown in the water. It reaches out to a lot of people. You don't provide just for yourself, you provide for lots of people. This is God's way.

Lord, help us to trust You. Sometimes we settle for little blessings, when You would give us so much more if we would just trust You.

MAY 22

Dearly beloved, avenge not yourselves, but rather give place unto wrath: for it is written, Vengeance is mine; I will repay, saith the Lord. Therefore if thine enemy hunger, feed him; if he thirst, give him drink: for in so doing thou shalt heap coals of fire on his head. Be not overcome of evil, but overcome evil with good.

ROMANS 12:19–21

If you want spiritual strength and you want competence and you want to be in control of situations, you have to have God's strength. You just have to; there is no other way. His is the only grace that can deal with unloving, unlovable people, but He will help you; He can handle it.

People bear scars from the way they were treated when they were children. Children growing up don't always have loving parents, and they end up bitter and resentful. But when they say to me, "They did this and this to me; you just don't understand," I can tell them *God* understands, and if they will give it to Him, He can handle it. You can't! It will make you sick; it will make you mad; it will make you unhappy. Who needs these things? Who can afford them?

Jesus came, lived, died, and rose again that we might not have to carry guilt, resentment, hostility, bitterness—these are baggage that we cannot afford to carry. I am just grateful He will take it and handle it. What a blessing to put the heavy burden down after years of staggering under its weight, and let God carry it for me!

Put it down. Whatever the grievance you carry—*put it down!* Take your burden to the Lord and leave it there.

Lord, thank You for carrying our burdens. Help us to be willing to relinquish them to Thee.

MAY 23

And I will wait upon the Lord, that hideth his face from the house of Jacob, and I will look for him. Behold, I and the children whom the Lord hath given me are for signs and for wonders in Israel from the Lord of hosts, which dwelleth in mount Zion.

ISAIAH 8:17, 18

In her book, *The Gift from the Sea,* Anne Lindbergh used a wheel as the symbol of a woman's life, noting that the wheel is circular, as is the pattern of a woman's life. There are many forces that are pressuring her and, yet, many forces pulling on her. There is home, family, children, husband, church, PTA, women's committees, civic organizations. All of these things are constantly pulling on us as women, and when we add career and inflation, truly, we have many pressures pulling at our wheel.

It is very, very important that we have a hub at the center of our wheel that is strong, that is sure. Only God is sure enough and strong enough for this place in our lives, only He could be the hub. Unless a woman's relationship with Him is sure and strong, unless He is central in her life, her wheel will be lopsided, making her journey rough and inconsistent.

Yet, even if the hub is constant, the rim can become "out of round," and that is what we must guard against. We must keep our rim rightly positioned to the hub and in perfect balance, and then we'll find harmony, a smoothness as we travel. There may be rough spots in the road, but our perfectly balanced wheel will help us glide over them with ease and grace.

Lord, thank You for being the hub of our lives, around which all our interest and activities revolve. Help us always to stay rightly related to You.

MAY 24

*We will not hide them from their children, shewing to the gen-
eration to come the praises of the Lord, and his strength, and
his wonderful works that he hath done. . . . That the generation to come might know them, even the children which should
be born; who should arise and declare them to their children:
That they might set their hope in God, and not forget the
works of God, but keep his commandments:*

PSALMS 78:4, 6, 7

When I was six and a half, I was rudely taken from the only
home I had ever known and sent across the country to live with
people I didn't know—with a stepmother who did not love me
and was not good to me. But, thank the Lord, those precious
early years with my grandmother were so very, very dear and
gave me a firm foundation upon which to build my life: the
strong and sure knowledge that Jesus was my friend.

Even when things were at their worst, I could go out into the
woods, walk up and down among the trees, and talk to Jesus as if
He were there. And He *was!*

One of the greatest blessings you can give your children is to
help them know that Jesus loves them, Jesus is their friend. If
they have *Him*, then they have everything they will ever really
need.

My grandmother also taught me that the Bible was God's
Word, that it was the source of wisdom. And so it has been the
source of wisdom for me through the years, a model for my life. I
have found my role models for women within its pages. Its words
of comfort have sustained and encouraged me, its strength has
uplifted me, its counsel has directed my path.

Never underestimate the influence on your children of their
early years—they will have a profound effect on them to the end
of their days.

*Dear Father, thank You for my blessed grandmother and the
impact she made upon my life. Thank You for being my
friend and seeing me through all the difficult times in my life,
and for the abundant joy You have given me.*

MAY 25

For I say, through the grace given unto me, to every man that is among you, not to think of himself more highly than he ought to think; but to think soberly, according as God hath dealt to every man the measure of faith. . . . Be kindly affectioned one to another with brotherly love; in honour preferring one another.

ROMANS 12:3, 10

Sometimes the pendulum swings so far to the right or to the left.

The serious use of the kind of philosophy that "I will not compete with my husband; so I will be a doormat for him," came first as a reaction to the most extreme element of the Women's Liberation Movement. Unfortunately, it has turned into the strangest of all situations. The woman now is competing by using another of her gifts or wiles to get her way, still under the guise of sacrifice and subservience. Incredible! No wonder men throw up their hands in disbelief. Most women we know do too. We feel so earnestly the need to tell women who have felt defeated at both extremes that there are multitudes of women who have used their finest gift of sensing and have found satisfaction in dealing with real relationships rather than manufactured ones.

God is the Lord of reality, and "make believe" is a children's game, a childish thing. The Bible tells us to put away childish things when we become adults. Marriage is not basically a contract, but a relationship, and it takes two people to relate. We have heard the word *submission* so many times that we weary of it. But we have seen many wives whose marriages are in trouble who try to fake submission, only to feel less self-esteem than ever before. This manufactured approach avoids honest relationships, rather than fortressing them. We know that this approach was originally born out of a sincerity we can all understand, but when women feel their credibility is being compromised, they usually try to do something about it. Often, if they are honest, they see that they have not kept the sparkle of marriage intact. They have not bolstered their husbands as they know they can and should. They have either let themselves go physically, emotionally, spiritually, mentally, or they have become naggers—and maybe all of these.

We women understand ourselves well enough to know how wily we can be. To lift this to a Christian absolute is unsound and damaging, indeed. We know of very few men who would not recognize and resent that they were being controlled and very few women who would not own up to the selfishness of their feigned unselfishness.

We are seeing many marriages hurt by adhering to these extremes in the woman's world today. Marriage is delicate, yet can withstand much. We need to be always aware of destructive influences that would make our tasks as wives more difficult.

Father, help us to avoid the extremes and look to Your Word for the true way to a happy, healthy marriage.

MAY 26

For God is not the author of confusion, but of peace, as in all churches of the saints.

1 CORINTHIANS 14:33

We must not mix things up—and oh, how we do today! We confuse sex with love, we confuse loudness with importance, we confuse playacting with reality, we confuse license with liberty, we confuse activity with accomplishment, we confuse noise with courage, we confuse power with authority, and we confuse selfish manipulation with Godly submission.

A whole nation can go down thinking it is progressing upward. William Blake said it in a poem:

> This life's dim windows of the soul
>   Distorts the heavens from pole to pole,
> And leads you to believe a lie
>   When you see 'with', not 'through' the eye.

What does that mean? We women ought to know. That is our gift—to see soulfully. It takes looking at things with your heart and soul, thoughtfully, with God's wisdom and guidance, and much prayer, to discern. We are all vulnerable in this tricky world and, yet, so needy.

And Jesus promises to supply our needs.

Lord, thank You for the order in Your plan for us. Help us to see things as they are—with our hearts.

MAY 27

Beloved, let us love one another: for love is of God; and every one that loveth is born of God, and knoweth God. He that loveth not knoweth not God; for God is love.

1 John 4:7, 8

The fact that God is love is the key to the riddle of creation. Sometimes we wonder just why God bothered to create a world that has been nothing but grief and trouble from its beginning. But it is not the problems or their absence that caused God to create the world. God's nature is love, and love cannot exist in a vacuum or in isolation. His very nature demanded that He create something to love, and that His creation be something that could love Him in return. This is why He created mankind. When God had created the universe, He still had nothing to love Him in return. After He created plant and animal life, He still had nothing to love Him in return. So He scooped up some earth and breathed into it the breath of life and created man. He *now* had something to love and something capable of loving Him in return. And so, man, God's crowning creation, is in all creation unique—God loves him, and he, in turn, can love God.

O God, help us to "love back." How could we fail to respond to the love You demonstrated when You made us in Your image!

MAY 28

As the hart panteth after the water brooks, so panteth my soul after thee, O God. My soul thirsteth for God, for the living God: when shall I come and appear before God? My tears have been my meat day and night, while they continually say unto me, Where is thy God? When I remember these things, I pour out my soul in me: for I had gone with the multitude, I went with them to the house of God, with the voice of joy and praise, with a multitude that kept holyday. Why art thou cast down, O my soul? and why art thou disquieted in me? hope thou in God: for I shall yet praise him for the help of his countenance. O my God, my soul is cast down within me: therefore will I remember thee from the land of Jordan, and of the Hermonites, from the hill Mizar. Deep calleth unto deep at the noise of thy waterspouts: all thy waves and thy billows are gone over me. Yet the Lord will command his lovingkindness in the daytime, and in the night his song shall be with me, and my prayer unto the God of my life. I will say unto God my rock, Why hast thou forgotten me? why go I mourning because of the oppression of the enemy? As with a sword in my bones, mine enemies reproach me; while they say daily unto me, Where is thy God? Why art thou cast down, O my soul? and why art thou disquieted within me? hope thou in God: for I shall yet praise him, who is the health of my countenance, and my God.

PSALMS 42

Is there something within man himself that longs for God? Is he capable of knowing God? The Bible says he is.

We have all wondered where God is sometimes. Does man seek God, or does God seek man? Man seeks God, because He has created man with the capability of seeking Him and knowing Him. When man seeks God, he finds God has already been seeking him.

Man's longing and search for God is a response to God's own searching for man.

What is a *soul?* This soul of yours is *you.* It is *me. I* am my soul. Man is more like God than anything else God has made. He is not just another animal in a line that has progressed, as evolution teaches. Man is never at rest until he rests in God.

God is not a doctrine. He is a Person, a Person to enjoy. Many ancient people thought of God as some angry tyrant who was going to take out His wrath on people, but it is not true. We love God because He first loved us.

To say we believe in God and then answer to no higher authority than our own stubborn will is hypocrisy. To seek no strength and guidance beyond our own and to give ourselves to no higher claim than our own vanity is the deadliest atheism. God is our comfort. He is enough. He is sufficient.

Both atheism and distorted ideas about God can render one person a major threat to others. Then, as a group, these people are a threat to the nations and people of the land. We don't make these rules, God does, and we have no choice but to abide by them.

We have had a few distorted ideas of our own in our nation's history. You can go into the New England states and see where witches were burned at the stake. Although religion is a personal thing, it is never an individual matter.

How do we seek God? A great many books tell us if we will simply look within ourselves, we will find the answers. Although it is important for us to know ourselves, if we want to see and know the Lord, we will never find Him by looking inside ourselves. We'll only find Him by opening ourselves to His light and looking at *Him.* We can never truly understand ourselves until we have looked at Him and seen ourselves as He sees us. Our aim then must be to see Him as He really is and to see ourselves in relation to Him.

Father, help us to ever "look unto Jesus, the author and finisher of our faith."

MAY 29

If ye then, being evil, know how to give good gifts unto your
children, how much more shall your Father which is in heaven
give good things to them that ask him?

MATTHEW 7:11

When love comes, fear goes. If you really love someone, you
are not afraid of him. This is true on the divine plane as well as
on the human level. The Lord Himself said that natural parents
would not give bad gifts to their children. He went on to say that
by comparison God would give even better gifts. God has good
gifts for those of us who are His children. When we come to Him
in prayer, we should enter into His presence as the children that
we are. He asks us to make our requests known to Him and as-
sures us that He will respond from His unlimited resources in
love.

Dear Father, help us to come to You as little children, trust-
ing You to supply our every need.

MAY 30

So Christ was once offered to bear the sins of many; and unto
them that look for him shall he appear the second time without
sin unto salvation.

HEBREWS 9:28

The Lord does not expect us all to be famous, brilliant, rich, or
beautiful, but He does demand from us our *best!*

We cannot change yesterday, that is quite clear,
    Nor begin tomorrow until it is here . . .
So all that is left for you and for me,
    Is to make TODAY the BEST that can be.

Today, **Memorial Day,** we pause for a little while to remember
that war and death and victory are a vital part of our American

heritage. Memorial Day is intended to keep the torch of freedom burning in our hearts and minds, placed in our hands from the still hands of thousands who lie buried under the green grasses of Gettysburg, 'neath the white crosses of Flanders Field, the sandy beaches of Anzio, the blue waters of Pearl Harbor, and the far eastern villages of Korea and Viet Nam.

We, the living, the ones for whom freedom was so dearly bought, have an obligation to the honored dead, an obligation to *keep* that freedom for their families and loved ones—and for ours.

What can we do to help secure freedom for our country, for ourselves, and for all who follow after?

- We can *think*—for ourselves—think and read and study.
- We can resolve to *eliminate prejudice* from our thinking.
- We can *worship God* regularly and keep alive the freedom of worship, which is our most precious gift.
- We can consider the small spot where God has planted us as a platform from which to *further understanding* between all people with whom we come in contact.
- We can *strive to be goodwill ambassadors* daily as we touch lives unavailable to diplomats, government heads, and others in high places.

Today, Dear Lord, with humble hearts, we thank Thee for our Christian and American heritage. May Thy will be done through us to preserve our freedom.

MAY 31

We sing, "God, Give Us Christian Homes," and, while it is true that our homes *are* a gift from God, it is also true that it takes constant work, infinite patience, and immeasurable love to make them Christian in the true sense of the word.

"God, give us Christian homes, homes where the mother in queenly quest, strives to show others Thy way is best. . . ." Does *your* family see you behaving in a queenly manner, full of grace and worthy of emulation? Is this the picture your children carry with them as they go off to school each day? Is this what comes to mind when your husband, or wife, thinks of you as he or she go about their daily routine?

Retrace this month in your mind and think of times when you have behaved in an "unqueenly" manner—have lashed out, lost your temper and lost your patience with the people you love the very most, bruised tender little feelings by a harsh or a cross, thoughtless word, behaved in a way for which you are now so ashamed. Be honest—write them all down.

1. _____
2. _____
3. _____
4. _____
5. _____
6. _____

Now, ask God to forgive you for each one and beg of Him to mold you into the kind of parent, wife, husband, or child He'd have you be and that you truly want to be. Now, go back and mark a big "X" through each wrongful act, and from this moment, *act* as a person who has been forgiven, whose sin has been forgotten by God, and who possesses every attribute through the Holy Spirit who indwells and empowers you, to live a radiant, triumphant, "queenly" life before your loved ones in the precious circle of your home.

June

JUNE 1

The Lord is nigh unto them that are of a broken heart; and saveth such as be of a contrite spirit.

PSALMS 34:18

There are none of us who can escape the broken heart somewhere, sometime in our life. We can be heartbroken over a circumstance, something that happened beyond our control. We can be heartbroken with the disappointment in a friend or loved one or an associate whom we have trusted and loved and counted on. We can be of a broken heart through grief and loss of a loved one.

So it is very comforting to know that the Lord is nigh unto them that are of a broken heart. I have a little saying in my office: "God will mend a broken heart if we give him *all* the pieces."

Giving him *all* the pieces would certainly mean that we would be a humble and contrite spirit, saying "Lord, I cannot do it myself. I am sorry for my failures. I need You. I want You. I love You."

Someone else has said that character is not made in a crisis, but is is *revealed* in a crisis. How true!

Our prayer today would be that we would love the Lord our God with all our hearts, with all our minds, with all our strength, with all our souls, so that our characters would be molded and fashioned after the spirit of the Lord, and He would be our natural resource in time of crisis.

JUNE 2

*Moreover, brethren, we do you to wit of the grace of God be-
stowed on the churches of Macedonia; How that in a great
trial of affliction the abundance of their joy and their deep poverty abounded unto the riches of their liberality. For to their
power, I bear record, yea, and beyond their power they were
willing of themselves; Praying us with much intreaty that we
would receive the gift, and take upon us the fellowship of the
ministering to the saints. And this they did, not as we hoped,
but first gave their own selves to the Lord, and unto us by the
will of God.*

2 CORINTHIANS 8:1–5

God sees. He never mistakes you in the crowd. The two coins
the little widow gave were very small in value, but Jesus heard
their tinkle as she dropped them in the collection and said she
had given more than all the rest—she had given all she had. This
is true down through history. God never overlooks you in whatever you give. He sees.

He saw Ananias and Sapphira and knew they lied about what
they gave. You remember Ananias was struck dead, not because
of the amount but because he was dishonest about what he gave.
The widow gave all that she had, while Ananias only pretended
to. The widow's mite was blessed by Jesus, but Ananias' large
gift was an abomination in God's sight.

Never make the mistake of thinking you can fool God, and
certainly not that you can impress him by a deceitful deed. **He
sees. He knows.**

*Lord, help us to be honest in our dealings with You, and may
our gifts be a true reflection of Your goodness to us.*

JUNE 3

*Let us therefore come boldly unto the throne of grace, that we
may obtain mercy, and find grace to help in time of need.*

HEBREWS 4:16

There are many excellent things we can read about prayer, but until we develop a prayer life of our own, we cannot begin to understand its reality. We cannot be consistent Christians, nor can we be Christ-like in our behavior, if we do not first develop a prayer life. Prayer is as essential to the Christian's spiritual life as oxygen is to his physical life. How can we expect to have the traits and attributes of Christ if we spend little or no time with Him? When we pray and spend time conversing with Jesus, we come into closer relationship with Him. Then He will begin to take comtrol of our lives with His personality and attitudes. Ephesians 3:12 tells us that we can come fearlessly into God's presence, assured of His welcome. It is by this means that we can actually claim part of God's power which far exceeds our highest desires or thoughts. Oh, how unlimited are the potentials and possibilities of God's resources which He places at our disposal!

Father, may prayer—communion with Thee—become the most important part of our day.

JUNE 4

Looking for that blessed hope, and the glorious appearing of the great God and our Saviour Jesus Christ;... That being justified by his grace, we should be made heirs according to the hope of eternal life.

TITUS 2:13; 3:7

When we look at the headlines in current magazines and papers, listen to the radio, and watch television, we must all agree the world needs a dose of hope.

There is a ship called Project Hope which carries doctors and nurses to different parts of the world where medical attention is needed. It is fitly named, as everyone needs hope—hope for health, hope for tomorrow, hope for eternity.

If millions of people in this world suffered from a crippling disease, and we had the antidote for it, we would surely rush to tell them the good news. And wouldn't we be foolish not to use it ourselves? *Our* good news as Christians is that we have the anti-dote for man's sins, a prescription for hope—His name is Jesus. We as Christians can give the world Jesus by letting His hope shine through our daily frustrations to all those hungry, search-ing, hopeless people in the world who so desperately seek it.

Lord Jesus, help us to be Your messenger of hope to a lost and dying world.

JUNE 5

Professing themselves to be wise, they became fools, And changed the glory of the uncorruptible God into an image made like to corruptible man, and to birds, and fourfooted beasts, and creeping things.

ROMANS 1:22, 23

Every age, every culture, and every land gives evidence that people think about God. They look beyond themselves for meaning to their existence, for security, for fulfillment. In the ancient world of the Roman Empire there was a great building, the Pantheon, in which all the gods of all the conquered peoples were placed. A place was offered to the Christians so they could put an idol of their God in a niche as did everyone else. They re-fused, and a great wave of persecution began.

This same tendency appears in our world today. Unbelieving men would make Jesus Christ just like any of the other gods of the world's religions. Like our ancient forebears, however, Christians refuse to permit this to come to pass. All the world wants to place our Lord in a nice little niche, but He wants to enter into the human heart and take up His residence there.

Lord Jesus, may we never try to display You in a niche to im-press the passerby, but rather grant You full access to every room of our lives and make You a vital part of everything we do.

JUNE 6

I thank my God upon every remembrance of you.
PHILIPPIANS 1:3

How precious it is when I hear from a dear friend and find the message closed with the precious words of Philippians 1:3. I believe if I know the true heart of most of our readers, each of us would want to become the kind of person who would bring to mind thankfulness and joy and, most of all, gratitude to God.

Gratitude is the heart's memory. How it grieves my heart when I think of the times when I have been unlovely, thoughtless, and careless and have left an unhappy memory rather than a pleasant one.

And so, today, I pray, Heavenly Father, as I think of the many people whose lives have been intertwined with mine, and the precious people that I thank You for letting me know and love and work with and be associated with. I honestly pray that today I will be the kind of person who will make them glad they knew me, glad they worked with me, glad they associated with me. Forgive me when I have failed to be the kind of person who would bring a happy memory. Help me to become more like You, O God, so that others will be the better for having known me. This I truly pray in Your name.

JUNE 7

Trust in the Lord and do good; so shalt thou dwell in the land; and verily thou shalt be fed.
PSALMS 37:3

When I was a teenager I remember a Sunday school teacher making this comment " 'Jesus went about doing good.' So many people are content with 'just going about.' " Among many other things in my growing mind, that found a niche, and I remembered it, and I have fervently prayed that I would never be guilty of "just going about," but that I could truly do some good in life, and leave something worthwhile behind. I think all of us would really like to make our lives count for something worthwhile. Yet our doubts are traitors; they make us feel that we cannot do anything worthwhile. They make us lose confidence. So, truly, we have to trust in the Lord—and then we are much more capable of doing good.

It is rather exciting to me to realize that I can be partners with God in doing some great things for people here on earth, that He has no hands but our hands to do His work today.

Today, O Lord, we pray for those who do not know that they can rest and trust in You, and who might be unable spiritually and physically, and we pray that You will give us an opportunity each day to do good in Your name.

JUNE 8

Because the foolishness of God is wiser than men; and the weakness of God is stronger than men. For ye see your calling, brethren, how that not many wise men after the flesh, not many mighty, not many noble, are called: But God hath chosen the foolish things of the world to confound the wise; and God hath chosen the weak things of the world to confound the things which are mighty; And base things of the world, and things which are despised, hath God chosen, yea, and things which are not, to bring to nought things that are: That no flesh should glory in his presence. But of him are ye in Christ Jesus, who of God is made unto us wisdom, and righteousness, and sanctification, and redemption: That, according as it is written, He that glorieth, let him glory in the Lord.

1 CORINTHIANS 1:25–31

Do you know what men have done to God's plan? They have complicated it! Certain size temple, certain kind of church, certain kind of garment, certain kind of ritual—things done in just a certain way. Man has complicated God's basics the same way the courts have complicated our laws. So we must cut through and come back to the basics. Reverence and fear of the Lord are basic! The reverence of God is the beginning, and that brings us to the reality of who God *is!* Once we realize who God is, then we can begin to know who *we* are. But let God be God.

A lot of women expect their husbands to be everything to them that only God can be. There are people who expect you to be everything to them that only God can be. Let *God* be God!

Lord, help us to turn to You in simple, childlike faith, knowing that when we strip away all the complicated trappings with which we have surrounded You, we will find You allsufficient.

JUNE 9

For he is our peace, who hath made both one, and hath broken down the middle wall of partition between us; . . . For through him we both have access by one Spirit unto the Father. Now therefore ye are no more strangers and foreigners, but fellowcitizens with the saints, and of the household of God.
EPHESIANS 2:14, 18, 19

Unresolved resentment builds brick walls.

Walls build up a brick at a time between you and your children, especially teenagers, if you are not careful to keep the lines of communication open.

The blame for lack of communication is on the communicator. If I am not communicating to my children, that is my fault. That is very hard for me to accept. I had rather think that they just don't listen, or they hear what they *want* to hear. But when you boil it all down, the burden rests on me. I have to figure out how to get through to them. Only then can I keep the wall of misunderstanding from going up.

You can build a wall
   Or you can build a bridge,
It all depends on the love you give,
   But if you build a wall,
Your world is small—small
   But the bridge of love will conquer all.

AUTHOR UNKNOWN

Lord, help us build bridges, not walls, for there are already too many things separating us from one another in today's world.

JUNE 10

And what is the exceeding greatness of his power to us-ward who believe, according to the working of his mighty power, Which he wrought in Christ, when he raised him from the dead, and set him at his own right hand in the heavenly places, Far above all principality, and power, and might, and dominion, and every name that is named, not only in this world, but also in that which is to come: And hath put all things under his feet, and gave him to be the head over all things to the church, Which is his body, the fulness of him that filleth all in all.

EPHESIANS 1:19–23

The disciples were discouraged and frustrated men when Jesus left them. He told them to wait. There are a lot of things we earn and develop in the Christian life. We work at being nice, sweet, forgiving, patient. These things are like muscles. The more you develop them, the more able you are to use them.

The power of the Holy Spirit, however, is not something we work up. To receive it, we simply must *wait,* and often waiting is the hardest thing to do.

It is vital that we wait, for the power for which we wait is the same power that raised Christ from the dead—and it is available to us if we will patiently wait for it, earnestly long for it.

The source of the power is the presence of Jesus. We need to be willing to carry out the "acts" of Jesus, as did the disciples after Pentecost—then we would see anew and afresh our relationship to Him and see and know Him as He really is.

Lord, we long for the power to live a life explainable only in terms of God. May we have the patience to wait for it and then use it for Your glory when it comes.

JUNE 11

Now unto him that is able to do exceeding abundantly above all that we ask or think, according to the power that worketh in us.

EPHESIANS 3:20

Attitudes are far more important than facts. When you struggle with difficult facts, look at your *attitude*. Christianity is having Christ's power. It is the indwelling of the Holy Spirit that gives that power.

Take a room that is dark. When you switch on the light, you can see. This is what happens when we come to Jesus and accept His gift of salvation. He is the Light of the World. He becomes the Light of our life. Like the dark room, there are corners and shadows. Only as we let God's Holy Spirit come in and fill all the nooks and crannies do we really have maximum power. It grows and takes over the dark places as we let it come in.

Father, may we open our lives to Your Spirit, that we may truly know the power of Your Resurrection which You would make available to us to empower us for Your glory.

JUNE 12

Therefore being justified by faith, we have peace with God through our Lord Jesus Christ: By whom also we have access by faith into this grace wherein we stand, and rejoice in hope of the glory of God.

ROMANS 5:1, 2

Power is one of the great words of the Christian religion. It ranks with faith and love and joy.

We must confidently and joyfully look forward to becoming all that God has in mind for us to be. We must constantly work toward this goal. We are confronted with problems and temptations that beset us as humans. It is only through Jesus that we can gain the confidence to become what He has in mind for us to be.

We can rejoice when we run into trials for we know they are good for us and teach us patience. Patience develops strength of character in us and makes us trust God more fully until our hope and faith are strong and steady. We can then hold our heads high, no matter what happens, and know that all is well. We know how dearly God loves us. The Holy Spirit fills our hearts with His love.

Lord, grant us patience and help us to trust You to love us and make us into the mature Christians You would have us be.

JUNE 13

And he said unto me, My grace is sufficient for thee: for my strength is made perfect in weakness. Most gladly therefore will I rather glory in my infirmities, that the power of Christ may rest upon me.

2 CORINTHIANS 12:9

In *Pilgrim's Progress,* the pilgrim is warming himself by a fire. Satan is trying and trying to put the fire out. There is a wall behind the pilgrim, and the fire keeps burning and cannot be put out. Behind the wall is a figure which represents the grace of God. There is a funnel of oil coming through to the fire, and God's grace is continually feeding the fire, which is the reason Satan cannot put it out.

God's grace has never been exhausted by any person. No one can ask too much. The Lord says, "Lo, I am with you, even to the end of this age. Fear not. Never doubt my love and power. Your heights of success will be won by the daily prudent doing of what I have said. Your daily persistence in trusting me will wear away all the difficulties and bring success for you. Never falter. Go forward boldly, go unafraid. I, the Lord, am with you. I go before you." These are nuggets of truth gleaned from His Word.

Though the world faces shortages of oil and natural gas and fuels, isn't it wonderful that as Christians we never have to worry about a shortage of fuel? It will never run out. God's grace is always sufficient.

Father, thank You for Your inexhaustible resources of love and grace, continually poured out on us, Your children.

JUNE 14

Thou has given a banner to them that fear thee, that it may be displayed because of the truth.

PSALMS 60:4

Today is **Flag Day.** Oftentimes we become remiss in remembering just what our flag means to all of us.

The year was 1777; the Continental Congress of the United States adopted the "Stars and Stripes" as the official flag of our country . . . the thirteen alternating red and white stripes representing the original thirteen colonies, and the thirteen stars representing the thirteen original states.

Many years have gone by. The president proclaims June 14 as Flag Day and as a day of public observance. We still have the thirteen alternating red and white stripes to symbolize the thirteen original colonies which valiantly displayed courage, bravery, and persistence.

Our stars have increased to fifty, a growing representation of our America. But the symbolism and stature and meaning of "Old Glory" remain as described by the Continental Congress:

"White signifies Purity and Innocence; Red . . . Hardiness and Valor; Blue . . . Vigilance, Perseverance, and Justice."

Fly your flag proudly! Teach your children its meaning! Remember its symbol of courage, purity, honor, and freedom!

Lord, to hold Thy banner high in honor and truth would be our prayer today.

JUNE 15

Blessed is that man that maketh the Lord his trust, and respecteth not the proud, nor such as turn aside to lies.

PSALMS 40:4

Many times people refuse Jesus because of something that one of His disciples has done. I have heard people say, "Oh, don't talk to me about being a Christian. I was cheated once by a Christian in business, and I want no part of them."

Many times we have lost blessings because we blame Jesus for the imperfections of some of His followers. Isn't it sad! We look at other people and expect them to be perfect and blame it on Jesus when they are not.

Don't put your faith in a person, don't put your faith in the church, don't put your faith in a teacher—because they will all let you down. Put your faith, rather, in *Jesus Christ,* and He will make things right and will never let you down. Never! A friend might; a friend might disappoint you in some unguarded moment. Your teachers might disappoint you, perhaps a well-known preacher or television personality you've heard talking about Christ—any person you have your eyes on could disappoint you or let you down. But Jesus never will! He never, never will! Keep your eyes on Him.

May we look only to Thee, O Lord, and not place our hopes on mortal men who, just like we, are subject to frailties and sin.

JUNE 16

And call no man your father upon the earth: for one is your Father, which is in heaven.

MATTHEW 23:9

We are told to keep God's name holy. The Bible says, "Our Father ... *hallowed* be Thy name."

In Hebrew, a person's name is given according to his character. Jesus gave new names to Simon Peter and to Paul in keeping with their new nature, their new character. If this is true of a human name, think how much more important it is to God's name.

Our names are very important to us. We don't like them to be misspelled or mispronounced. They are uniquely ours. God's name is very personally His.

Hallowed means unique, holy, different. Jesus says it is the name above every other name. You can ask anything in His name and it will be done. The name of God is of utmost importance. There is no other name under heaven, given among men, whereby we must be saved (*see* Acts 4:12).

His name shall be called Wonderful, Counselor, Prince of Peace. He is our friend, He is just, He is mighty, He is *love!*

Our most precious, Omnipotent, Holy Father, oh how we love Your name and how grateful we are that we have the privilege of calling You "Father."

JUNE 17

And Jesus answering saith unto them, Have faith in God.

MARK 11:22

God's contract is from God to us. It is initiated from Him— from the Ruler, the King, the Master. He says He will give us life, He will love us, He will give us salvation. It all comes from God. We are to receive and accept and obey.

Don't try to make it so technical, so difficult. It will permeate the intellect. Love is the great transformer.

Love transforms selfishness into service, ambition into aspiration, greed into gratitude, getting into giving, demands into dedication.

Love will come through into the heart. The essence of the new covenant by faith is forgiveness of sins and fellowship with the saints in love and fullness of the spirit.

Lord, help us not to complicate the beautiful simplicity of our contract with You—all the deep complexities involved in reconciling us to Yourself were on Your part—all we must do in childlike faith is RECEIVE. *Thank You for making it so simple that no one had to miss it.*

JUNE 18

And Jesus came and spake unto them, saying, All power is given unto me in heaven and in earth. Go ye therefore, and teach all nations, baptizing them in the name of the Father, and of the Son, and of the Holy Ghost.

MATTHEW 28:18, 19

Jesus told His disciples to wait for the power. Notice it was not a thing to be earned, they simply had to *wait*—wait for the Spirit to fill them with His Power.

On the day of Pentecost, the wait was over. The Spirit of God came to make the church His dwelling place. Jesus achieved salvation through His atonement—the Holy Spirit applies it. Jesus produced His church—the Holy Spirit fills it and causes it to realize its mission. Christ was the founder—the Spirit is the builder.

Christ provides the atonement. The Holy Spirit provides the power through which we are able to do things we never even thought of.

Father, help us to be patient and wait upon Thee for that good thing You have in store for us. May Thy Holy Spirit have access in our lives to do Your work through us.

JUNE 19

Study to shew thyself approved unto God, a workman that needeth not to be ashamed, rightly dividing the word of truth.
2 TIMOTHY 2:15

Where have you looked for nourishment, growth, and fellowship? If the institutional church is going to be a meaningful place where our people can have their needs met, it is going to have to come to grips with relevant issues and offer some realistic solutions to our problems. We get our nourishment from God's Word. Get into the Bible, into a study group where the Bible is taught, and into a church which teaches and preaches the Bible. It is the source of our nourishment. For fellowship we need to get into an evangelical church and make it our home church. There we can share in God's Word, meet and love other Christians, and reach out in a meaningful ministry. No man is an island unto himself, and no Christian can separate himself from other Christians and prosper spiritually.

Look around until you find an evangelical church, a church home where Christ is preached, His Word is taught, and there is a concern for the lost.

SEEK GOD'S GUIDANCE IN IT ALL!

Lord, lead us to find that place where we will find nourishment for our souls.

JUNE 20

I am he that liveth, and was dead; and, behold, I am alive for evermore, Amen; and have the keys of hell and of death.
REVELATION 1:18

". . . Why seek ye the living among the dead?" (Luke 24:5). There are some people who go about looking for Jesus among the great dead teachers of mankind. Although psychologically and intellectually Jesus taught an abundance of good and great things, He was not merely a great teacher. As the officers said, ". . . Never man spake like this man" (John 7:46). Others look for Jesus among the great men of history. Surely He was our example. If He were only an example, even a perfect one, how frustrating it would be for us. We would finally give up in despair, saying, "I cannot make it, His demands are too severe, I cannot be perfect." Still others look for Jesus among dead heroes. He is the greatest figure in history, but He is not dead. He is alive! The great message of the New Testament and Christianity is that Jesus Christ is indeed alive. He is not to be found among the great teachers, the great men, or the great heroes of history. They are all dead, but He is *alive!*

Blessed Jesus, we need no greater assurance to know that You are indeed alive than the warmth of Your love that fills our hearts.

JUNE 21

Blessed be God, even the Father of our Lord Jesus Christ, the Father of mercies, and the God of all comfort; Who comforteth us in all our tribulation, that we may be able to comfort them which are in any trouble, by the comfort wherewith we ourselves are comforted of God.

2 CORINTHIANS 1:3, 4

This is the time of the year when we give our thoughts to Fathers and set aside a day to honor them—**Father's Day.** I am reminded of a girl who went to see a young man who had attempted suicide. He had been on drugs and had a lot of problems. He was lamenting the fact that he was an orphan . . . had no father and no one to talk to. She wanted me to advise her what to say to him. I said to tell him that nobody is an orphan if he believes in the Lord. We have a Heavenly Father, and none of us ever need be without a father ... all of us have a father, a perfect Father.

A young friend of mine once said that when she hears some lecturer speaking on fatherhood, she always feels sort of lost because her father was not the type that you would want to love, was not easy to love. Earthly fathers are sometimes like that. But our Heavenly Father is a perfect, loving Father, and He cares for us in every detail of our lives. This is one of the greatest assurances and confidences—to know that we have a Heavenly Father who loves and cares for us. He sees to every detail of our lives. We can trust Him ... we can relax in His arms, like the song:

> Safe and secure from all alarms; ...
> Leaning on the everlasting arms.

God is your Father, call Home.

Dear Father, God, live in me and create within me a serving heart. Thank You for being that perfect Father, upon whom we can all depend.

JUNE 22

For we wrestle not against flesh and blood, but against principalities, against powers, against rulers of the darkness of this world, against spiritual wickedness in high places. Wherefore take unto you the whole armour of God, that ye may be able to withstand in the evil day, and having done all, to stand. Stand therefore, having your loins girt about with truth, and having on the breastplate of righteousness; And your feet shod with the preparation of the gospel of peace; Above all, taking the shield of faith, wherewith ye shall be able to quench all the fiery darts of the wicked. And take the helmet of salvation, and the sword of the Spirit, which is the word of God. Praying always with all prayer and supplication in the Spirit, and watching thereunto with all perseverance and supplication for all saints.

EPHESIANS 6:12–18

I have listed thirteen ways in which you can battle the devil:

- *Realize* the existence of a personal and powerful antagonist. The devil's cleverest wile is to convince us that he is nonexistent.
- *Learn* to recognize his wiles and then learn to get an advantage of him. We must not be ignorant of his devices. "Lest Satan should get an advantage of us: for we are not ignorant of his devices" (2 Corinthians 2:11).
- *Discern* what is of Satan. "To another the working of miracles; to another prophecy; to another discerning of spirits; to another divers kinds of tongues; to another the interpretation of tongues" (1 Corinthians 12:10).
- *Run.* "Flee also youthful lusts: but follow righteousness, faith, charity, peace, with them that call on the Lord out of a pure heart" (2 Timothy 2:22).
- *Resist.* "Submit yourselves therefore to God. Resist the devil, and he will flee from you" (James 4:7).
- *Refortify* yourself—study God's Word daily.
- *Renew* your strength through prayer. (Ephesians 6:18).
- *Rebuke* the devil—Even well-meaning people can be mouthpieces of the devil.
- *Respond* with Scripture. "Thy word have I hid in mine heart, that I might not sin against thee" (Psalms 119:11).
- *Reject* the popular disregard of the blood of Jesus. There is power in the blood!
- *Recognize* yourself to be dead to sin. "Likewise reckon ye also yourselves to be dead indeed unto sin, but alive unto God through Jesus Christ our Lord" (Romans 6:11).
- *Resort* to God's grace. "There hath no temptation taken you but such as is common to man: but God is faithful, who will not suffer you to be tempted above that ye are able; but will with the temptation also make a way to escape, that ye may be able to bear it" (1 Corinthians 10:13).
- *Receive* victory by faith through Christ. "He that committeth sin is of the devil; for the devil sinneth from the beginning. For this purpose the Son of God was manifested, that he might destroy the works of the devil" (1 John 3:8).

You cannot deal with the devil. Do not stop to reason with him. Dealings with the devil are going on today in the occult. We as Christians make two major errors concerning the devil: We *underestimate* him, or we *overestimate* him.

John Wesley says, "There is no evil done or spoken or thought without the assistance of the devil who worketh with strong, though secret, power. All the works of our evil nature are the works of the devil."

Dear Lord, keep us from evil and the power of Satan. May we so cover ourselves with Your armor that his attacks cannot harm us.

JUNE 23

Now then we are ambassadors for Christ, as though God did beseech you by us: we pray you in Christ's stead, be ye reconciled to God.

2 CORINTHIANS 5:20

Most of life's difficulties are caused by misunderstanding. Reconciliation is the means to change a relationship from one of conflict, enmity, or estrangement to one of friendship and togetherness.

Until we are reconciled with God, we are not able to be reconciled with others. We rejoice when there is reconciliation in families or marriages. We are lifted up by knowing that when we are reconciled to God, it is complete. How wonderful is the feeling of peace when you are reconciled with your fellowman and God!

Conflict produces ineffectiveness. The moment there is misunderstanding or conflict, start immediately to make amends.

Dear Father, may we always be open to reconciliation when misunderstandings arise in our relationships with one another.

JUNE 24

But he that is married careth for the things that are of the world, how he may please his wife. There is a difference also between a wife and a virgin. The unmarried woman careth for the things of the Lord, that she may be holy both in body and in spirit: but she that is married careth for the things of the world, how she may please her husband.

1 CORINTHIANS 7:33, 34

The bonds of matrimony are not worth much unless the interest is kept alive. In order to keep the interest alive, you must pay attention to each other. To handle ourselves we must use our heads, but to handle others we must use our hearts. We win them by tenderness, and we conquer them by forgiveness. It is important for women to set aside some time for their husbands each day, and for husbands to set aside some time for their wives each day. No matter how tired or weary you are, take a little time out just to be with each other. Be aware of each other.

Precious Lord, thank You for that one You have given me. May I never miss a day letting him know how important he is to me and what his love means to me.

JUNE 25

So ought men to love their wives as their own bodies. He that loveth his wife loveth himself. For no man ever yet hated his own flesh; but nourisheth and cherisheth it, even as the Lord the church: For we are members of his body, of his flesh, and of his bones. For this cause shall a man leaves his father and mother, and shall be joined unto his wife, and they two shall be one flesh.

EPHESIANS 5:28–31

Shifting values and expectations have made life difficult for everyone living in our generation. The situation is especially hard for men, since they are being challenged on every hand by women seeking to be on an equal footing. What a wonderful, glorious situation that leaves for those of us who do not have to go out into the world and prove we are men. You see, God created woman differently from man. He created woman to have a sense of insight and a need for appreciation which must be acknowledged and constantly demonstrated if she is to retain her proper self-esteem. He created man with a sense of pride which must not be injured or destroyed if he is to retain his proper self-respect. By keeping these two characteristics in perspective, the husband will spontaneously give of himself to his wife, and she will be unable to do anything but respond in kind, sweet devotion.

Dear Father, thank You for creating us as You did. Help us not to compete, but to love one another.

JUNE 26

That ye might walk worthy of the Lord unto all pleasing, being fruitful in every good work, and increasing in the knowledge of God.

COLOSSIANS 1:10

Followers of the Lord Jesus Christ will walk a different walk. We will not be like everybody else. I remember a fine Christian couple who always told their children to walk differently. When they were growing up the children would say that the kids down the block got to do so-and-so, and the parents would answer, "Maybe they do, but we are different. Our family is different. Our purpose is different. We walk differently, but with delight."

And that is it! We walk differently! We do not walk to the same places—do not walk in the same way—as those who are unbelievers, as those who do not know Christ as Lord.

Dear Lord, help us to be different, to "stand out"—if necessary, "stand alone," remembering that we are never really alone: You will always stand with us in the lonely places.

JUNE 27

For by one Spirit are we all baptized into one body, whether we be Jews or Gentiles, whether we be bond or free; and have been all made to drink into one Spirit.

1 CORINTHIANS 12:13

The "filling of the Spirit" is something that is done many, many times. God has set His seal of ownership on us. He has put His Spirit in us, and the presence of this Spirit never goes away. The presence of God, His Spirit, stays with us forever, but we do not always feel Him. We do not always acknowledge His ownership. We do not always let His guidance be in control. But He never leaves us. That is the "baptism of the Spirit," and it is a one-time thing.

There are, however, many *fillings* by the Holy Spirit. We can have a revival and have a filling; we can have a high moment during a service or at a spiritual retreat and have a filling. But so many times we place our trust in our feelings, and when they are gone we think, *Oh, the Lord has departed from me; He has gone away; I do not feel Him anymore!*

A new Christian once told me, "Oh, I am so afraid I am going to lose this feeling." I said, "You probably will, and if you are trusting in feeling, you will be disappointed. But—the fact that you have trusted God and He has come to live within you *remains.*" Feeling might depend upon health, situations, fatigue; so don't count on the feeling. Our salvation is a *fact* of the Spirit of God—it is an act of the Holy Spirit, and its continued presence in our lives does not depend on health, situations, fatigue, moods or any of those things. It depends on the trustworthiness of the Holy Spirit. He said He would never leave us nor forsake us, and *He never will!*

O God, fill me, control me, moment by moment, with your Holy Spirit—that I might become what You want me to be.

JUNE 28

And his father Zacharias was filled with the Holy Ghost, and prophesied, saying Blessed be the Lord God of Israel; for he hath visited and redeemed his people, And hath raised up an horn of salvation for us in the house of his servant David; As he spake by the mouth of his holy prophets, which have been since the world began: That we should be saved from our enemies, and from the hand of all that hate us; To perform the mercy promised to our fathers, and to remember his holy covenant; The oath which he sware to our father Abraham, That he would grant unto us, that we being delivered out of the hand of our enemies might serve him without fear, In holiness and righteousness before him, all the days of our life.

LUKE 1:67–75

Always God says, "fear not." He came to deliver us from fear. We all have enemies of doubt, anxiety, fear of anything that man can do to us. But God grants us the privilege of serving Him fearlessly, free from our enemies. He makes us holy, acceptable, ready to stand in His presence forever. How do you become holy? Only through Jesus Christ. *Our* righteousness is as filthy rags, but through the deliverance of Jesus, the Messiah, we can be accepted by God, as we all strive to be.

The Jewish people did not listen carefully. Why didn't they accept Jesus as their Messiah? They looked for a different way, a way more acceptable to them. It is true that hundreds of years had gone by between God's first promise of a deliverer and Jesus' actual appearing. Can you see why many of the people had given up, after looking so long? Of John the Baptist's pronouncement of His coming, they would say, "We have heard that for years and years, and nothing has happened." A few were still looking and believing, but most had quit believing so that they didn't recognize the Messiah when He finally came. But, mark it down—God always comes through with His promises, though it may take a long, long time.

Dear God, we know You keep Your promises. Help us to be patient and steadfast when the answers seem long in coming.

JUNE 29

For I am now ready to be offered, and the time of my departure is at hand. I have fought a good fight, I have finished my course, I have kept the faith: Henceforth there is laid up for me a crown of righteousness, which the Lord, the righteous judge, shall give me at that day: and not to me only, but unto all them also that love his appearing.

2 TIMOTHY 4:6–9

Life is very fleeting and often death sweeps down swiftly to close the earthly career of someone dear to us and opens the doors for them to a new "life" in a city not made with hands, where the streets are paved with gold and the decorations are done with the artistic Hand of the Almighty—the Hand that flung the flaming sun into orbit and hung the vibrant colors of the rainbow in the sky!

Our imagination fails us when we think of the sights that our loved one sees when he enters that celestial land—unbelievable beauty, the source of all that is lovely, pure, and beautiful!

Buckner Fanning, a pastor friend, mentioned in a sermon once that if we could only know of the beauties of heaven that await us, we wouldn't be worth a plugged nickel down here! No more pain, no more heartaches, no more sorrow, no more separation from loved ones, and no more loneliness.

From a favorite book of devotions *Streams in the Desert,* this prayer for one who is alone, speaks for us all:

O Thou who has promised never to leave nor forsake Thine own, give me a sense of Thy presence every passing hour. Push back the walls that surround me and open the doors that forbid me, so that I may go in and out unto others, walking confidently by Thy side. And, day after day, open the windows of my soul to new thoughts and the distant horizons of new affections, through Jesus Christ the Beloved Companion.

MRS. CHARLES COWMAN

JUNE 30

The year is half gone—how quickly our lives are rushing by! Let's do a little personal evaluation today—take a spiritual inventory, if you will:

1. You started the year with such high expectations, have you lived up to them? Are your dreams and plans coming to fruition, or are you disappointed in the progress you've made?
2. How about your prayer life? Are you spending time each day with the Lord, expressing your love for Him and seeking His will for your life?
3. Do you open your Bible every day, at least to the daily Scriptures in these devotionals (but we hope to a much more extensive study), in order to learn the great truths of God and let His Word speak to you?
4. Are you active and happy in your church? Do you pray for your pastor? Does he know you love and appreciate him?
5. Could the people you work with describe you as an "Incredible Christian?"
6. Are your neighbors blessed because you live next door?
7. Does the person driving the car in the lane next to you feel the warmth of your courtesy?

What kind of a Christian *are* you so far this year?

Don't be discouraged if you are missing the mark in any or all of these areas—God doesn't expect perfection. He does, however, expect devotion, and in all probability, that's where the trouble lies—you are not putting first things first. So, get back on the track, turn your eyes upon Jesus, look full in *His* wonderful face, and *all* of these things will come to pass, for He has promised that "He Who hath begun a good work in you will continue it until the day of Christ Jesus."

July

JULY 1

These things I have spoken unto you, that in me ye might have peace. In the world ye shall have tribulation: but be of good cheer; I have overcome the world.

JOHN 16:33

> FEAR has a thousand faces
> Each one is gaunt and pale . . .
> Each one screams "You Cannot!
> For 'tis certain you will fail!"
>
> COURAGE has many faces
> Though it needs but only one . . .
> And this one says—"Keep Trying,
> For YOU KNOW IT CAN BE DONE!"
> AUTHOR UNKNOWN

Dear Father, our Provider and Protector, give us courage in the face of failure and fearful circumstances. Help us to be strong and brave.

JULY 2

Stand fast therefore in the liberty wherewith Christ hath made us free, and be not entangled again with the yoke of bondage.

GALATIANS 5:1

It is time again to celebrate July 4th—**Independence Day!** We should all pause in deepest gratitude for our own beloved land

and the independence which was bought so dearly over two hundred years ago.

It took vision and determination for our forefathers to come to a new land, a bleak and rock-bound coast, and to build **America**—the "land of the free" and the "home of the brave." The foundation of belief in our land is beautifully expressed in the words of a song that has become so familiar to us that we may sing it without really hearing the words. Read them here and ponder on their meaning:

> My country, 'tis of thee, sweet land of liberty
> > Of thee I sing. Land where my fathers died,
> Land of the pilgrims' pride,
> > From every mountain-side, let freedom ring.
>
> My native country, thee, land of the noble free,
> > Thy name I love; I love thy rocks and rills,
> Thy woods and templed hills;
> > My heart with rapture thrills, like that above.
>
> Let music swell the breeze, and ring from all the trees
> > Sweet freedom's song. Let mortal tongues awake;
> Let all that breathe partake;
> > Let rocks their silence break, the sound prolong.
>
> Our father's God, to thee, author of liberty,
> > To thee we sing; long may our land be bright,
> With freedom's holy light;
> > Protect us by thy might, Great God, our King.
> > > SAMUEL FRANCIS SMITH

Let us join in working toward a better America . . . protected by the might of the Almighty.

Lord Jesus, help us to put on the whole armor of God and accept Thee as our Commander-in-Chief.

JULY 3

. . . With a great sum obtained I this freedom. . . .

ACTS 22:28

Courageous men came long ago to this land, and it blossomed under their hands. They contended with the greatest tasks of human society and government, and a great republic was born. They cherished noble ideals, and their country reached out to lead and influence the world.

They built upon supreme, universal, eternal principles. They saw weaknesses in their small country, but they turned them into goodness. They beheld enemies without fear, opposition without despair, problems without evasion, and sacrifices without cowardice.

As long as the principles of our forefathers remain, no storms of destruction will prevail. Out of every strife we have grown stronger, until we are welded into one secure, unbreakable nation.

We celebrate the ideals of our great republic, ideals of freedom and justice and equality of opportunity, to which the founders dedicated our nation. These are the thoughts that should come to our minds on **Independence Day.**

Through Thee, precious Lord, may we have the strength to remain noble, true, and faithful.

JULY 4

How the king rejoices in your strength, O Lord! How he exults in your salvation. . . . You have given him fame and honor. You have clothed him with splendor and majesty. . . . And because the king trusts in the Lord, he will never stumble, never fall; for he depends upon the steadfast love of God who is above all gods.

PSALMS 21:1, 5, 7 TLB

LORD, I BELIEVE IN AMERICA!

A nation is only as good as its people, and we should ever be:

- People who respect its laws and its flag
- People who appreciate its heritage;
- People who honor God and respect the rights of others.

During the July 4th holiday, we think about many things—

- We think of flags, firecrackers, picnics . . .
- We think of watermelon and fried chicken . . .
- We think of days spent on lakes, or beaches, or parks . . . with family and friends . . .
- We think of traffic and gasoline shortages . . .
- We think of July 4, 1776, the birth of our nation . . .
- We think of July 4, *this* year, and we try *not* to think of corruption in high places, inflation, and the uneasy peace in a confused and bewildered world.

We read and hear so many things we wish were not true. In the United States of America, we have a government of elected officials. *We* elect them. They are our *representatives.* If then, there are problems of honor, integrity, or right priority of values among our representatives—and there are—it stands to reason there are similar problems among us, the people.

We stretch the law all we can—even break it—as long as we don't get caught. A recent survey of high school students were asked the question, "Is it all right to cheat if you don't get caught?" A large majority indicated they thought it was all right. Where did they get that idea? They got it from adults, of course!

Integrity is the cement that holds the building blocks of ability and opportunity *together;* that cement is cracking severely in America; it is only natural that it would reach into high places.

Am I discouraged? NO!

We, who name the name of Jesus Christ have a great responsibility and challenge to do something to help change the climate of America.

Just as cities build "corridors of green" to keep the concrete and pollution from taking over, so we can build corridors of *honesty,* of *uprightness,* of *fellowship,* of *love,* of *free enterprise*— and it will be contagious!

> I pledge allegiance to the flag
> of the United States of America
> and to the republic for which it stands . . .
> one nation, under God, indivisible
> with liberty and justice for all.

Dear God, may we join in spreading these "corridors" this season of celebration of our nation's birthday.

JULY 5

For though I be free from all men, yet have I made myself servant unto all. . . .

1 CORINTHIANS 9:19

Independence means freedom and responsibility!

- It means the "American way of life."
- It is liberty without license.
- It is the right to *live* where we will.
- It is the right to *say* what we think.
- It is the right to *work* where we desire, as little or as much.
- It is the right—no, the *privilege*—to work for ourselves, to build a business, to make a profit and spend the bulk of it as we please.
- It is the right to associate with whom we like.
- It is the right to worship God as we please. Our way of life is precious to us. It must not be taken for granted. It has been purchased by blood, sweat, and tears—it is priceless!
- It is our responsibility as caring citizens to be mentally alert and constantly aware of national and international conditions. Our way of life is truly threatened on all sides today, and we, as American citizens, need to be thinking,

voting, and participating in matters that will greatly influence our destiny.

Keep the light of freedom burning! "All the darkness in the world cannot put out a single light."

Dear Lord, may our light so shine before men that we will glorify our Father in heaven.

JULY 6

There is no fear in love; but perfect love casteth out fear: because fear hath torment. He that feareth is not made perfect in love. We love him, because he first loved us.

1 JOHN 4:18, 19

The fact that God is love is the explanation of man's free will. Unless love is a freely given response, it is not love. Love cannot be legislated. Had God been merely law, He could have created a world filled with automatons. These would have been constantly obedient to the laws of nature and of God because they could not have made a choice. But God is love, and He made men who are capable of returning His love. We must respond to God because we love Him, not because we respond to some abstract law. Had God *made* men like automatons, there would have been no possibility of their having a personal relationship with Him. Our response is not a creed, nor a denomination, nor being baptized in a given church. These are the *effects* of a personal relationship with God. This personal relationship is possible and can come about only because God is love. His very nature demanded that He give to man a free will, and from the free will arose the possibility of having a free response to God in love.

Lord, thank You for the freedom You give us. Help us to use it to love You more.

JULY 7

Greed causes fighting; trusting God leads to prosperity.
PROVERBS 28:25 TLB

In my lifetime I have observed that what the Bible told us about the love of money being the root of all evil, is so very true. Most of the problems that humanity brings upon itself are caused by greed.

Recently, I was in Las Vegas, Nevada, for the Billy Graham Crusade and a meeting of our company people. We had flown in the day a great hotel had caught fire. As we flew into the city, we saw helicopters circling the roof, landing, and rescuing people; the rescue operations had been going all day.

It was speculated that the hotel management had failed to install sufficient safety precautions; the safety precautions already installed were not in adequate working conditions. As we gathered together that evening for the crusade, Mr. Graham and the team told us of the day's events. They had ministered to the people being brought over to the convention center and to the grief-stricken families. A somber mood had fallen on the whole city because of the terrible tragedy. The fire marshalls had disclosed how they had pleaded with the officials of the hotel to install safety precautions, but they had not done so because it "cost so much money." Yet the profits from the gambling casino were tremendous.

As I thought of the many people who lost their lives, and the families who had lost loved ones, children who had lost parents, mothers and fathers who had lost children—I remembered again how the love of money begets greed, which is behind so much of the hurt, the evil, and the problems that befall us.

> LOVE transforms—
> Ambition into aspiration,
> Greed into gratitude,
> Selfishness into service,
> Getting into giving,
> Demands into dedication
> FROM *Be Somebody*

O Dear God, help us to trust in You and Your providential care, believe that You have our best interests at heart, and the best plan for our lives, and, O God, help us never, never to fall victim to greed.

JULY 8

Be kindly affectioned one to another with brotherly love; in honour preferring one another.

ROMANS 12:10

Self gets in the way of love. The Bible tells us there are three kinds of people:

- the *natural* man, one who has not received Christ;
- the *spiritual* man, one who is controlled and empowered by the Holy Spirit;
- the *carnal* man, one who has received Christ, but who lives in defeat because of his own efforts to live the Christian life.

The carnal man is ignorant of his spiritual heritage; he is disobedient; he has lost his love for God and others; he has a poor prayer life; he has lost his desire for Bible study; he is jealous; he is full of worry, discouragement, a critical spirit, and frustrations.

What a contrast are the fruits of the spiritual man: *love* and *joy.* Joy is the flag that's flying when the King is on the throne. There are, of course, problems, but we should let the King reign on the throne. Love is the fruit of the Spirit expressed in *peace, patience, kindness, goodness, faithfulness, gentleness, self-control.* These are the things we as Christians *truly* want, and they will gradually become part of us, if we let the Spirit have full reign in our lives.

Dear Lord, how difficult it is for us to give up our selfishness. Please help us today to give Your Spirit full control, so that we may become what YOU *want us to be.*

JULY 9

Fear thou not; for I am with thee: be not dismayed; for I am thy God: I will strengthen thee; yea, I will help thee; yea, I will uphold thee with the right hand of my righteousness.

ISAIAH 41:10

In times of anxious strain we are told to have faith and all our troubles will magically disappear. That is simply not true. Jesus had faith, but He also knew the meaning of a heavy burden. Some of the greatest saints have cried out for "penicillin for despair," yet they also had faith.

We are told that our fears are imaginary. That is not true—*all fears are real,* none are imaginary. It may be that imagination causes our fears, or that we react in the wrong way to some circumstances of life, but fears are not imaginary. We are told to pull ourselves together, but we are not sure what that means. Many do not feel that they have strength enough to pull, even if they knew what to pull on.

When you feel despair, or deep anxiety, or trembling fear, or nervous strain, what attitude should you take toward it? Examine the experience of Christ when He felt "very heavy" (Mark 14:32–36). In His moment of despair, Christ did these three things:

1. *He got away from the crowd.* That night in Gethsemane, He moved a distance from the crowd and took with Him His three closest friends. There are times when it is good for us to be in crowds. There are other times when we need to be with trusted and close friends. Jesus, no doubt, talked with these friends about His troubles, and often that helps. It is wonderful to have a friend with whom to share our deepest thoughts. Often it helps to talk with a minister or a competent counselor. But then Jesus went further on *alone.* When one is in some dark valley, his first impulse is to tell his troubles to every person who will listen, but the more we talk about our troubles, the worse they become. Speech has a much greater effect on the emotions than we think. We can talk ourselves into almost anything.

2. *Jesus looked up to God.* He said, "Father, all things are possible unto Thee."

3. *He took His mind off Himself,* and that does much to relieve one of anxiety and fear. But often, this is hard to do because part of the mind wants to hold on to its worries and despair. That is the easiest way out. To despair is to lose hope, and to lose hope is to be able to give up and to quit. But, when one looks into the Face of God, he has hope, because he knows that "all things are possible unto Him."

Father, thank You for this day. Help me to live it thinking of others more than myself. Bless those for whom today is going to be a difficult day. Surround them with people who will minister to them in the way they need. Give me a serving heart today.

JULY 10

And I saw no temple therein: for the Lord God Almighty and the Lamb are the temple of it. And the city had no need of the sun, neither of the moon, to shine in it: for the glory of God did lighten it, and the Lamb is the light thereof. And the nations of them which are saved shall walk in the light of it: and the kings of the earth do bring their glory and honour into it. And the gates of it shall not be shut at all by day: for there shall be no night there.

REVELATION 21:22–25

One evening I jetted on a new 727 from Denver to Salt Lake City. What an incredibly beautiful sight as we came over the continental divide just as the flaming red sun was setting over the Utah mountains.

Only the wing tips reminded me that we were earthbound creatures. The glow of the red sunset covered the western half of the world . . . and from 32,000 feet up, a lot of world was visible.

The flaming rays touched mountains and mirrored themselves in the great Salt Lake. What a panorama! It reminded me of the little girl who was looking up at the beautiful starry sky and exclaimed, "Oh, Mommy, if the bottom side of heaven is so pretty, what must the top side look like!"

O God, how I thank You for beauty, vision, hope, eternal life.

JULY 11

For I am persuaded that neither death, nor life, nor angels, nor principalities, nor powers, nor things present, nor things to come, Nor height, nor depth, nor any other creature, shall be able to separate us from the love of God, which is in Christ Jesus our Lord.

ROMANS 8:38, 39

I think again of the blessed assurance we can have of our salvation if we will just *believe* that God has done for us what He says He has done. Our salvation is a once-and-for-all thing; it is attainable to anyone who trusts the Lord completely, honestly, and sincerely. Only the Holy Spirit can change our lives into that personal relationship, but once He has done it, He does not undo it!

Now, we can stray afar off. We can go our own willful way for a while, but somehow the Spirit woos and calls us back. When we are away there is an unhappiness within that cannot be satisfied, and God will keep on until He gets us back.

I think of young people who stray away from God—particularly of one boy who was in the armed service. He had grown away from the Lord, but he said he was walking down the street one night and heard a hymn, just a snatch of a hymn, and suddenly—just like that—he realized, *Oh, my, I am so far away from God. I need Him! I need to get back!* He had really been converted, but like so many young people he had gotten caught up in the things of the world and had drifted away. That night he followed the source of that familiar hymn, went into the little church it was coming from, and renewed and reaffirmed his vows of love and obedience to God. You see, *God* did that—He will

always do that! He will always love us and woo us and draw us
unto Himself.

"Behold God is my salvation; I will trust and not be afraid: for
the Lord God is my strength and my song. He is my salvation"
(*see* Isaiah 12:2).

Thank You, God for this BLESSED ASSURANCE!

JULY 12

*If you want a happy, good life, keep control of your tongue,
and guard your lips from telling lies. Turn away from evil and
do good. Try to live in peace even if you must run after it to
catch and hold it! For the Lord is watching his children, listening to their prayers; but the Lord's face is hard against
those who do evil.*

1 PETER 3:10–12 TLB

Morale doesn't start at the bottom and come up, it starts at the
top and comes down. How important it is for us to pray for the
heads of our government. If they turn to God and put Him first,
their morale begins to rub off and makes it easier for all people to
believe. Many people are hungry to be in an atmosphere that is
conducive to putting God first. Our country was founded with
this in mind.

There is a story of the great seal on our money. On the seal is a
pyramid. Its blocks build up, but it is unfinished at the top. It has
an eye at the top which is the eye of God. Underneath it says in
Latin, "A new order." This country was to be under a new
order—unfinished at the top, always under the eye of God. Few
people realize that this country was to be unfinished at the top
because God was to be the head of our country. How sad that we
are getting so far away from that. We are still "unfinished at the
top," but rather than being safe beneath the eye of God, we are
trusting our security and our prosperity to false powers, and ultimately, we can only fail unless as a nation we turn back to God
and place our trust in Him. "If my people, which are called by

my name, shall humble themselves, and pray, and seek my face, and turn from their wicked ways; *then* will I hear from heaven, . . . and will heal their lands" (2 Chronicles 7:14, italics added).

O God cleanse us, hear us, heal us!

JULY 13

Little children, let no man deceive you: he that doeth right-eousness is righteous, even as he is righteous. He that commit-teth sin is of the devil; for the devil sinneth from the beginning. For this purpose the Son of God was manifested, that he might destroy the works of the devil.

1 JOHN 3:7, 8

We talk a great deal about goals and how important it is to set goals. A goal is the target of your behavior. Only you can change your behavior. To change it, you work with a little piece at a time—one act at a time.

What do you want to do with your life?

I have observed that none of the very devastating, destructive habits come on us all at once. They come *one step at a time*—drug abuse, alcoholism, promiscuity—they all come one step at a time.

Why do they want to sell a youngster a can of beer out there in the world? Because it is the first step. Why do they want to sell him a joint of marijuana? Because it is the first step.

Our devastating destructive habits come one step at a time. But the good habits we have to work at—everlastingly—grab hold of them and hang on to them. I have discovered that we have to work at them every day of our lives.

> There are two natures in my breast.
> One is foul, one is blessed.
> One I love, one I hate.
> The one I feed will dominate.

And so I must feed that positive nature in my breast. I must work at it. I must be careful of what I read, what I see, the company I keep, and what I think.

O Father in heaven today, help all who read this message to feed the blessed nature in us, that one created in Your image, that has a longing to be like You.

JULY 14

Therefore is judgment far from us, neither doth justice over-take us: we wait for light, but behold obscurity; for brightness, but we walk in darkness. We grope for the wall like the blind, and we grope as if we had no eyes: we stumble at noon day as in the night; we are in desolate places as dead men.

ISAIAH 59:9, 10

These words are being written as I travel high in the sky, enroute from Salt Lake City, Utah, to Denver, Colorado.

Far below are the rugged Rocky Mountains. I cannot see them at the moment, yet I know they are there. Momentarily, they are obscured by the snow clouds beneath us.

This cannot help but remind us that our earthly sight is so limited, and eternal truths are often obscured by clouds of doubt, fear, prejudice, ignorance, and confusion.

It is easy to become confused under the high pressure and constant stimuli of today's world. It is most difficult to see and sort out eternal truths in the trappings of sophisticated America.

Father, help us to see through the confusion and distortion and know Your truths and values never change—"Christ, the same yesterday, today, and forever."

JULY 15

And Jesus knew their thoughts, and said unto them, Every kingdom divided against itself is brought to desolation; and every city or house divided against itself shall not stand.

MATTHEW 12:25

Some people have backgrounds and experiences which do not lend themselves to developing a good marriage. Some people are fearful, others are frustrated, some have suffered disappointment or are moody, nervous, naturally unlovely, or perhaps simply spiritually immature or stubborn, lacking in self-confidence. We should love them for what they might become rather than for what they are, for their potential instead of their performance. Rather than expect too much from each other in marriage, it would seem desirable for us to seek to develop a Christian disposition. This is something we are unable to do in our selves, but the Holy Spirit can work through us if we let Him control our lives. As Galatians 5:22, 23 tells us, "But the fruit of the Spirit is love, joy, peace, long-suffering, gentleness, goodness, faith, meekness, temperance: against such there is no law."

Precious Lord, love through us, grant us Thy understanding and patience. Help us to cherish and preserve the relationship You have entrusted to us.

JULY 16

... but this one thing I do, forgetting those things which are behind, ... I press toward the mark for the prize of the high calling of God in Christ Jesus.

PHILIPPIANS 3:13, 14

How important it is to learn to concentrate on the present, "forgetting those things which are behind." How easy it is to let yesterday use up today. To be successful in any endeavor in life—and certainly in the calling of God in Christ Jesus—we have to concentrate on the job at hand.

Paul said, "This *one* thing I do." So often we have to say, "These forty things I dabble in." Yes, many people are running—often looking over their shoulders from fear of what has happened in the past. Yet, Paul the great apostle says, "This one thing I do, I press forward! I keep going! I never give up!"

> *O Heavenly Father help us to remember to keep our eyes on the goal of what You have called us to do, that high calling—what You want us to be. And to concentrate and continue our efforts day-by-day. Thank You for giving us purpose in life and goals that are worthy and definite.*

JULY 17

Commit thy way unto the Lord; trust also in him; and he shall bring it to pass.

PSALMS 37:5

How many years it took me to learn the truth of this passage. For so long I tried to bring things to pass myself, by my own energy, on my own, and I found that God will let me fall flat on my face if I push the door open myself. But if He opens the door for me, I am to get up and go through it with confidence, with commitment.

So I have learned that what the Psalmist has admonished us to do is trustworthy. "Commit [it] unto the Lord, trust also in Him, and He shall bring it to pass." This does not mean that God does it for us, but He paves the way, and so often it is the difference between the success and failure of our endeavors.

Years ago, I heard the pastor of the First Baptist Church, Dr. George W. Truett, my pastor at that time, say, "The will of God is always right. Well, we do not always want what is right for us. The will of God is always best. Again, we do not always want what is best for us."

Then he added something else which made a tremendous impression on me and made a great change in my commiting to the will of God. He said "The will of God is always *safe.*" And how we always want what is safe! What security it brings to life to know that we are safe, that it will be right, and it will be best—if we truly commit our way unto the Lord, and trust in Him, and know that He will bring that which is best and safe, to pass.

Thank You, Dear Father, for help, hope, shelter, and a blessed future.

JULY 18

Now the God of patience and consolation grant you to be like-minded one toward another according to Christ Jesus: That ye may with one mind and one mouth glorify God, even the Father of our Lord Jesus Christ. Wherefore receive ye one another, as Christ also received us to the glory of God.

ROMANS 15:5–7

Here is how God will help you to handle a husband who has retired: You have to realize that you must separate "feeling" from "attitude." I cannot change my feeling that a person is lazy if he just sits in a chair. My grandmother instilled that in me; I am work-oriented. There is no way I can change that feeling, but since I cannot change it, then I have to change my attitude about it, and that I *can* do, and I *did* do. God seemed to say to me, "Mary, if sitting, relaxing, makes him happy, then the least you can do is not bother him. Thank the Lord that he is happy, and leave him alone. Let him *be* happy." Now I can accept his sitting and still love him, because I have changed my *attitude*—if he is happy, then I am happy. He thinks I am working myself to death. He tells people that he cannot get me to slow down, but I don't *want* to slow down. What I do makes me happy, so then let me do it; leave me alone and let me be happy!

He won't change. I won't change. But if we both can change

our attitudes and accept each other with our own idiosyncrasies, the feelings of irritation will quit giving us so much trouble, and we will love each other just as we are.

Dear Father, how foolish we are to let little things annoy us. Help us to learn to overlook those things and concentrate on making the people we love happy.

JULY 19

And we know that all things work together for good to them that love God, to them who are the called according to his purpose.

ROMANS 8:28

This was the favorite verse of my wonderful friend and attorney, Ralph D. Baker. Several years ago this precious friend went home to live with God eternally, but it was my joy and privilege to have worked with Ralph for twenty-three years. He was my Sunday School Superintendent, and I taught in his department for twenty-two of those years. He and his wonderful wife, Marjorie, were the models in rearing my two children. Ralph was one of the happiest Christian men I ever knew. He put his arms around the world; he taught me to love and to share and that all things truly do "work together for good to them that love God."

I have thought of this many times. When people have asked me to explain it, the best way I know is the way I explained it to my children. When you are baking bread, you have flour, shortening, milk, sometimes eggs, baking soda or powder. Any one of these might not be good at all if we had to eat it alone. Flour would certainly be dry, shortening would be worse than a dose of medicine, but put together and baked, the mixture becomes delightful bread.

And so somehow, God, the Divine Baker is able to take the various situations, happenings, growing times, grieving times, learning times, and, somehow, work them together for good, in

our lives here, but most especially in the eternity which follows
our rather short time here on earth.

> Something beautiful, something good;
>> All my confusion He understood;
> All I had to offer Him was brokenness and strife,
>> But He made something beautiful of my life.
>>>>>> GLORIA GAITHER

*Thank You, Heavenly Father, for letting me know Christian
friends who have added so much to my life and who have
taught me to be patient and to trust. And most of all, Father,
I thank You for Your overpowering love which has worked
together so much of the fabric of my own life for good.*

JULY 20

*Think not that I am come to destroy the law, or the prophets: I
am not come to destroy, but to fulfil. For verily I say unto you,
Till heaven and earth pass, one jot or one tittle shall in no wise
pass from the law, till all be fulfilled.*

MATTHEW 5:17, 18

If there is to be a society, there must be law and order. It is the
basis of a relationship with God. Jesus said He came not to destroy the law, but to fulfill it.

God commanded first that we love Him. He cannot *demand* it
because He gave us freedom of choice, but He entreats, asks, almost begs that we love Him and put Him first. God wants to
bring us into a unique relationship with Himself.

God does not try to prove His existence. He simply says, "I
AM." In geometry we learn of an axiom, a self-evident fact
which is self-proved, but which is the basis of all other proofs.
God is an axiom. He does not have to prove Himself. He *is!* To
come to God we must first believe that He *is* and then accept
Him just *as* He is.

Eternal God, how grateful we are that You are, *the alpha and omega, the beginning and the end—everything we will ever need to live victoriously on this earth, to triumph over death, and to live forever and ever with You in the place You have prepared for us.*

JULY 21

But God commendeth his love toward us, in that, while we were yet sinners, Christ died for us.

ROMANS 5:8

We cannot separate the love of God and the love of men. The more we love Him, the more we will love others. We will love ourselves in connection with Him. To love ourselves apart from Him is ego, but to love ourselves in connection with Him is to realize our value and how much He expects of us. God says we are of such value that even the hairs on our heads are numbered.

God's love is demonstrated to us in Jesus Christ. Love holds nothing back—God sent His only Son. It is hard to understand how much love that took. It is an undeserved love. We are not worthy, but, praise God, He didn't require that we be worthy, only that we accept the One who is—our blessed Lord—the beautiful, lovely, matchless, *worthy* Jesus!

Father, oh, how we love Jesus—because He first *loved us!*

JULY 22

Hear, O Israel: The Lord our God is one Lord: And thou shalt love the Lord thy God with all thine heart, and with all thy soul, and with all thy might. And these words, which I command thee this day, shall be in thine heart: And thou shalt teach them diligently unto thy children, and shalt talk of them when thou sittest in thine house, and when thou walkest by the way, and when thou liest down, and when thou risest up.

DEUTERONOMY 6:4–8

Parents have a sacred responsibility. We are responsible for teaching our children to love God. This is something that cannot be entirely left to the Sunday school teacher, the school teacher, or the pastor.

Children are one of the greatest blessings that God gives us. Talk of God's truths when you are walking with them or driving them to school. Talk of God's truths when you tuck them into bed at night, or when you sit around the breakfast table. Let your children know how much God means to you, and let them know that Christianity is real. Your actions must reinforce your words. Christianity was meant to be a part of our walking, talking, working, eating, sleeping, and playing.

Father, we have no greater desire than to teach our children to know Thee and to love Thee. Please hold our hands and lead us as we lead them.

JULY 23

And whatsoever ye do in word or deed, do all in the name of the Lord Jesus, giving thanks to God and the Father by him.
COLOSSIANS 3:17

The deeds that we do—

- Are they love-inspired?
- Are they inspired by personal pride?
- Or by another selfish motive?

Test yourself. It might be very enlightening.
The things we do—the things we *want* daily—

- Are they love inspired?
- Were they inspired by what people think about us?
- To impress somebody?
- Why do we do what we do?

Father, help us not to fool ourselves about our motives, but to genuinely search for Your attitude, Your reasons, Your way.

JULY 24

*All the special gifts and powers from God will someday come
to an end, but love goes on forever. . . . There are three things
that remain—faith, hope, and love—and the greatest of these
is love.*

1 CORINTHIANS 13:8, 13 TLB

A higher law than honesty is the "law of love." Ephesians 4
mentions "speaking the truth in love."

Somebody put it this way: A person who has divine "yeses"
and divine "noes," but cannot couple it with Divine Love, invali-
dates his authority.

You have met people like that. They have everything figured
out; everything is neatly packaged. Well, life is *not* neatly packaged. Sometimes the ribbon and paper and strings are frazzled
and torn. The person who always has a pat answer for everything
often nullifies his influence.

You have to be able to love a person when you tell him what to
do. If you cannot, you do not have the right to have authority
over that person. It is like a bank account: You have to make a
deposit of love before you can have a withdrawal of criticism or
authority. But if you put a lot of love and a lot of yourself into
the account, then you have the authority and responsibility to
help that person change in whatever way necessary for a more
productive life. We cannot criticize anyone or tell them what to
do unless we have made a deposit in their lives. To assume a
place of authority is an awesome responsibility.

O God, help us to use our authority wisely and with love.

JULY 25

*But the salvation of the righteous is of the Lord: he is their
strength in the time of trouble.*

PSALMS 37:39

A time of trouble can make us weary, weak, worried, and depressed . . . *or* it can make us more discernable, determined, and strong in our faith. My grandmother taught me long ago, "It isn't *what* happens to you in life that matters, it is *how you take it* that counts—how it leaves you."

Let us not brood upon our dangers as if we alone in all the world were suffering, but let us keep busy about our home, our business, our community, and our church—lifting the spirits of those with whom we come in contact. Become a "Spirit-lifter"— an "Ambassador of One"—with courage and strength, bearing your share of the world's burdens, going about your daily tasks with uprightness of heart!

We have much work to do, we have a great task; time is of the essence. These days of national crisis remind us more urgently of the need for a strong America.

We need a nation strong in *moral character,* strong in *military might,* strong in *financial responsibility.* This calls for work and prayer. "Work as if everything depended on *work* . . . Pray as if everything depended on *prayer!*"

We believe in WORK, and COURAGE, and PRAYER . . . and turning our attention to doing our best in the days ahead, remembering always that from the Word of the Lord, our Bible, we have God's way of saving America . . . old as history, new as today.

> *If my people, which are called by my name, shall humble themselves, and pray, and seek my face, and turn from their wicked ways; then will I hear from heaven, and will forgive their sin, and will heal their land.*
>
> 2 CHRONICLES 7:14

Remember, when God measures a person, He puts the tape around the *heart*—not the *head!*

Today, O Lord . . .
Let me stand for whatever is right and true and just and good;
Let me keep the edges of my mind keen;
Let me keep my thinking straight and true;

Let me keep my emotions in control;
Let me keep my will active;
Let me keep my body fit and healthy;
Let me put *right* before interest;
Let me put others before self;
Let me put things of the spirit before things of the body;
Let me put the attainment of noble ends above the enjoyment of
present pleasures;
Let me put *principle* above reputation;
Let me keep my mind busy with worthwhile ideas;
Let me keep my hands busy doing constructive work.

JOHN BAILLIE

JULY 26

*... and be content with such things as ye have: for he hath
said, I will never leave thee, nor forsake thee.*

HEBREWS 13:5

Life and love become more precious to us after we have spent
long days and longer nights in beds of illness. There, we are
made more aware of many things.

Several years ago when I went through the valley of suffering
and agony, it was a wonderful experience for me. I had been a
stranger to suffering, but now we are "good friends" for we have
spent some time together.

I have learned to thank God for the morning light, which He
alone can bring out of darkness. I lift my heart in gratitude for
the sheer joy of living, for loving friends and tender hands, for
gifted doctors and brilliant scientists, for work to perform and
the skill and strength to perform it.

I thank Him for the privilege of prayer—that I, weak and erring mortal, should have ready access to the heart of Him, who
with a word, created the dawn!

Above all, I am thankful for the blessed peace of forgiven sin
and the sure hope and promise of an endless life, which has been
given through the Gospel of the Resurrection of Jesus Christ, our
Lord!

I have come to understand more clearly the vanity of the temporal and the glory of the eternal ... that all good gifts have come to me from God. They were His to give, and they were His to curtail; I do but hold them in trust. Only in continued dependence upon Him, the Giver, can they be worthily enjoyed.

Blessed Father, may each day be more precious to us and viewed as a priceless gift from Your loving hand.

JULY 27

... In the world ye shall have tribulation: but be of good cheer; I have overcome the world.

JOHN 16:33

So often we feel swamped with the world and its woes. As Corrie ten Boom says, "As we look around we get distressed, if we look within, we will be depressed; so look up at Him and be at rest." Sometimes we do look around us and see the hurt and the agony, and we ask if there is any help for the broken heart, if there is any help for those who are devastated by drugs, any help for those who commit the worst of crimes and are in prison? Is there any help when the economy around us seems to be taking a downward plunge and dragging us down with it?

Then we have to remember the five times in the New Testament when Jesus said, "Cheer up": Matthew 9:2, Matthew 14:27, John 16:33, Acts 23:11, Acts 27:22. In the midst of tormenting disease and persecution and natural disasters, we can cheer up—even when the worst is yet to come—if we know the secrets of triumph. It is important to know the *problems,* the *purpose,* the *peace,* and the *power!*

So, let's look at the problems. This world hurts. That hurt touches us. Sometimes our brightest hopes become a heartache, our highest ambitions become ashes. The green, green grass of home can be decimated by the graves of those we love. We cannot ignore the fact that we *will* have tribulation.

But let us not look only at the *problems,* let us look also at the *purpose.* Suffering that is meaningless—*that* is unbearable. I think again of my sweet, precious friend, Corrie ten Boom, who through tribulation and suffering, found triumph. Tribulation is suffering with a purpose.

There is nothing that happens to us that God cannot use. A great grief is like a bonfire that burns out all the trash. Sorrows and tribulation provide depth and shadows and contrasts. Sweet, dear Corrie has the peace.

> *Dear God, help us amidst the problems to find the purpose, the peace, and the power that await us when we let You lead us through the darkness that sometimes seems to smother us, to the Light at the end of the tunnel.*

JULY 28

No man hath seen God at any time. If we love one another, God dwelleth in us, and his love is perfected in us.

1 JOHN 4:12

It is by love that God is made known. Today's verse tells us that no one has seen God at any time, but if we love one another, God dwells in us, and His love is brought to completion in us. Would you really have given your heart to God if you had not believed that He loved you? We can think about God as the great Judge who sits in righteousness and judges the world, but the knowledge of Him as the source of love, and the experience of His love for us, casts out all the fears that we might have about the way He will treat us. How crucial it is for us to realize that God is love and that He loves us. He has a plan for each of our lives, but it is a plan that is disciplined in love. Sometimes the trials and tribulations of life will upset us, but we have no fear when we come to know His love. We will stand in awe of His judgment, but the net effect of God is love. When we come to know Him and to experience His love in our lives, we will be directed to the right kinds of action toward others.

Lord, thank You for the confidence we can have in Your love for us. Help us to so live that others will know we have a Savior who loves us, and we can, in turn, love them.

JULY 29

Ye are the salt of the earth: but if the salt has lost his savour, wherewith shall it be salted? it is thenceforth good for nothing, but to be cast out, and to be trodden under foot of men.

MATTHEW 5:13

Paul reminds us that our speech should be always gracious, and seasoned with salt. Our speech can preserve and enhance *or* it can destroy. Enhancing the flavor of the lives around us can be done in all sorts of ways.

Jesus said that those who believe in Him were to be as salt. In the New Testament times, in addition to being used as a flavoring, salt was frequently used as a preservative. Did you ever try to eat popcorn or scrambled eggs without salt? Just as thousands of foods need salt for flavor, there are thousands of opportunities that cross our paths in life that require Christians to be seasoned with salt.

Dear God, help us not to be tasteless and bland in our dealings with others, but rather to add flavor and zest to their lives.

JULY 30

But seek ye first the kingdom of God, and his righteousness; and all these things shall be added unto you.

MATTHEW 6:33

Just as the admonition to seek first the Kingdom of God and His righteousness should be the objective of every individual, so it should become a double radiance for the couple who seeks that

Kingdom together. A shared faith in God is very important to an enduring, happy marriage. It expresses itself in worshiping and working together in a church where the Word of God is preached and taught.

O God, help us to seek You first, and then we will be able to-gether to establish the kind of home which will bless the lives of all involved and glorify Your wonderful name.

JULY 31

If we are to survive as a nation, we must somehow rediscover and reactivate the fierce pride in our national heritage felt by our forefathers and the principles for which many of them died.

Are you happy with our government? Write your congressmen and tell them how you would like them to represent you.

Are you critical of our president? Regardless of whether you voted for him, pray today and every day that God will place His hands upon him and guide him to wise decisions.

Do you love our flag and fly it proudly on holidays, or maybe just *any* day, because a lump still comes into your throat when you see its stars and stripes unfurled?

Pause a moment right now—pray that God will bless our country.

_____

_____

Pray that our president will be wise and good.

_____

Pray that you will be a good, responsible citizen, a real asset to these United States.

_____

_____

In the blessed name of Jesus . . . Amen.

August

AUGUST 1

Thy word have I hid in mine heart, that I might not sin against thee.

PSALMS 119:11

Many times we are confronted with the unexpected. When we have committed Scriptures to memory, they tend to come forth when we need then most.

This is August, more than halfway through the year. How much of God's Word have you hidden in your heart?

The Psalmist tells us that God's Word is a lamp unto our feet, a light for our pathway of life. How can we afford not to use God's plan of guidance by reading, digesting, devouring His Word?

Write down one of your favorite Scriptures and why it has come to mean something to you.

_____

_____

_____

This is my prayer today: that I will memorize a Bible verse a week—to hide Your Word in my heart.

AUGUST 2

Then they that feared the Lord spake often one to another: and the Lord hearkened, and heard it. . . .

MALACHI 3:16

God's language is a language of the heart, not of the tongue. The language of true discipleship is the language of obedience.

Our faith must be a firsthand discovery—not a secondhand story.

> To believe only possibilities is not faith,
>   but mere philosophy.
> If any thing can be done,
>   experience and skill can do it.
> If a thing *cannot* be done,
>   only *faith* can do it.
> Faith is fear that has said its prayers.
> Faith is not contrary to reason,
>   but rather reason grown courageous.
>   FROM *Be Somebody*

Dear Lord, may every word that comes from my mouth be pleasing unto Thee.

AUGUST 3

Wherefore God also gave them up to uncleanness through the lusts of their own hearts, to dishonour their own bodies between themselves: Who changed the truth of God into a lie, and worshipped and served the creature more than the Creator, who is blessed for ever.

                                        ROMANS 1:24, 25

"God gave them up" is a serious statement. What a horrible thing to be given up by God! I remember the verse, "Seek ye the Lord while He may be found . . ." (Isaiah 55:6). It is significant in that it is a lot easier to seek and find the Lord early in life. It is so much harder when we are grown and our hearts are hardened. In Romans 1:1–24, Paul was writing to a little group of Christians at the beginning of the decline of the Roman empire, set in a cesspool of sin. He was telling them about sin and how it grows.

Historians tell us of some of the things that were happening to Rome during that period, of the decay of morals and how the people had become so sinful and wicked. It has been called an "age of shame." Many of the emperors were homosexuals, and such sexual perversion had become an accepted thing, just as it is coming to be in our own nation today.

Sin begets sin. In the beginning, perhaps, there was honor and nobility, but **sin begets sin.** The people would not accept God as God and began to look within themselves for the answers.

In our time so many people teach others to look within themselves to try to find the answers to their problems. Their problems are then only multiplied. Socrates said, "Know thyself." Another philosopher said, "Control thyself." Jesus said, "Give *Me* thyself, and I will make of you a new life and a new creature."

It is impossible to read about these things without feeling a sense of urgency that these very things are happening in our own beloved nation. If only we could realize that the first step—not acknowledging and honoring God—opens the door for all the other sins of the world, and when the door opens, Satan comes in and claims dominion. Satan is the deceiver of the whole world, and he never changes. He is as intent on destroying America as he was on destroying Rome. Our only hope is to somehow stop the tide of sin that threatens to engulf us and to look to God and His righteousness as the standard by which we "live and move and have our being."

God help us as a small band of Christians—really the minority in America today—to keep our faith in God and let the joy of our salvation and its power be evident in all that we do and say. Help us to be an encouragement to each other and an influence for good to the unbelieving world about us.

AUGUST 4

For thus saith the high and lofty One that inhabiteth eternity, whose name is Holy; I dwell in the high and holy place, with

him also that is of a contrite and humble spirit, to revive the
spirit of the humble, and to revive the heart of the contrite
ones.

ISAIAH 57:15

ABOU BEN ADHEM

Abou Ben Adhem (may his tribe increase!)
Awoke one night from a deep dream of peace,
And saw within the moonlight in his room,
Making it rich and like a lily in bloom,
An angel writing in a book of gold;
Exceeding peace had made Ben Adhem bold,
And to the Presence in the room he said,
"What writest thou?" The vision raised its head,
And with a look made of all sweet accord,
Answered, "The names of those who love the Lord."
"And is mine one?" said Abou. "Nay, not so,"
Replied the angel. Abou spoke more low,
But cheerily still, and said, "I pray thee, then,
Write me as one that loves his fellow-men."
The angel wrote, and vanished. The next night
It came again with a great wakening light,
And showed the names whom love of God had blessed;
And, lo! Ben Adhem's name led all the rest!

LEIGH HUNT

Oh, the wonder of it all, The wonder of it all. That Jesus
should love even me. That the Holy God lives in my soul And
revives my heart. Praise His Holy Name!

AUGUST 5

. . . walk by faith, not by sight.

2 CORINTHIANS 5:7

This I say then, Walk in the Spirit, and ye shall not fulfill the
lust of the flesh.

GALATIANS 5:16

The Bible says, "... work out your own salvation with fear and trembling" (Philippians 2:12).

This sometimes confuses people. They get the idea that their final and ultimate salvation depends on how good they are or on the work they do for the Lord. This is not the meaning of this Scripture at all. Actually, the word *salvation* in the original Greek is misinterpreted here. It means *work out your conversion*—not conversion from sinner to saint, not conversion from unsaved to saved, but conversion from what we *are* in our lives to what *God wants us to be.* And this we *do* have to work at. It takes prayer; it takes Bible study. Sometimes it just takes a whole lot of giving up—surrendering of our own selfishness.

> May more of Thee be seen in me;
> May more by me be done through Thee;
> And more for Thee be done by me.
> Each day may I live more in Thee;
> Each moment walking more with Thee,
> May I grow always more like Thee!
>
> AUTHOR UNKNOWN

I think that says it pretty well, that we have to continue day after day, year after year, to be more like Jesus and to please Him in the things we do. But we are never unsaved! We are never lost! We are never *not* the Child of God! We are never *not* baptized with His Spirit! We are never *not* joined to Him! Once we honestly, really, and truly trust Him, we are His forever and ever and ever!

As Christ was raised up from the dead by the glory of the Father, even so help us to be able to walk in the newness of life.

AUGUST 6

I call heaven and earth to record this day against you, that I have set before you life and death, blessing and cursing: therefore choose life, that both thou and thy seed may live.

DEUTERONOMY 30:19

Abraham Lincoln said, "People are about as happy as they make up their minds to be."

Really, our life is a result of the choices we make. The *choices* one makes, the things one decides to do at critical crossroads, determine the progress of achievement, the successes which one attains. It is not only the choices at critical crossroads, but also the daily *decisions* of life that add up to joy—the joy of a fulfilled life, or the depressions or frustrations of an unfulfilled life.

The "law of progression" works for us all. Unfortunately for some, the "law of regression" also works. Let me illustrate: At some point in time you made a decision to do something constructive and uplifting with your time and talents, you decided to enter a new business, or continue your education, or learn to play the piano. You started out with excitement, full of plans and motivation. You did your homework, you practiced hard, you were a bundle of energy and excitement, thinking of the wonderful benefits your efforts were going to bring to you. And at first, things went well and you were a flurry of progress. But, alas, came a day the sun quit shining, obstacles came along in your path, the first flush of success seemed to fade, and results didn't seem to come so fast. That was the point of crossroad between the paths of *progression* or *regression*. So that was the crucial time in your project.

Now, if your choice was to continue, to pay the price, to weather the disappointments, to continue to learn, to continue to follow through, then good things started coming your way. Little by little, you could see the progress you were making and begin to see the final achievement that would come with your original goal. This is the "law of progression."

Each choice you make to continue, each right choice, adds a stronger base on which the next choice is made. And then, finally, your fulfillment increases, your joys begin to abound, and you are strengthened to face whatever difficulties might arise between you and that good thing that you seek.

Dear Lord, help us in the choices we make to first seek Thy face and Thy will—only then can we know that that good thing we seek to accomplish will be right for us.

AUGUST 7

Call unto me, and I will answer thee, and shew thee great and mighty things, which thou knowest not.

JEREMIAH 33:3

A closed hand can't receive. Even God Himself cannot give you or me any more than we are mentally, emotionally, and spiritually conditioned to receive.

If our hands are already full of ourselves, then God can't fill them.

FROM *Be Somebody*

Dear Lord, I want You to show me mighty things. Help me to be ready to receive.

AUGUST 8

For the love of money is the root of all evil: which while some coveted after, they have erred from the faith, and pierced themselves through with many sorrows. But thou, O man of God, flee these things; and follow after righteousness, godliness, faith, love, patience, meekness. Fight the good fight of faith, lay hold on eternal life, whereunto thou art also called, and hast professed a good profession before many witnesses.

1 TIMOTHY 6:10–12

Money is the number one problem contributing to marital disharmony. This is often due to lack of communication, but most frequently it is because of a lack of training in money matters before marriage. Even if they do not manage family finances, women should be financially intelligent. They never know when they may be cut adrift and have to manage the financial affairs previously handled by their husbands. It is not the amount of money that is handled, it is the management of that money which counts. Since emergencies will occur during your married life, you should always plan for an emergency. This is when most people get into financial trouble, when the unexpected emergency arises and there is no plan to meet it.

Dear Lord, give wisdom not only in spiritual things, but also in the practical, day-to-day matters that sometimes overwhelm us. Being a good steward also means paying our bills—help us to handle our financial affairs in a Christian way, even as we do our spiritual affairs.

AUGUST 9

But seek ye first the kingdom of God, and his righteousness; and all these things shall be added unto you.

MATTHEW 6:33

If righteousness is in the heart
—there will be beauty in the character;
If beauty is in the character
—there will be harmony in the home;
If harmony is in the home
—there will be order in the nation;
If order is in the nation
—there will be *peace in the world.*

From *Be Somebody*

Lord, change this world and let that change begin in me.

AUGUST 10

And he said, I will make all my goodness pass before thee, and I will proclaim the name of the Lord before thee; and will be gracious to whom I will be gracious, and will shew mercy on whom I will shew mercy. And he said, Thou canst not see my face: for there shall no man see me, and live.

EXODUS 33:19, 20

What is the goodness of God? People sometimes think only of God's moral goodness and tend to forget His kindness and love, His forgiveness, His consistency, His joy. He offered all of these long ago to Moses.

God told Moses that He had chosen him to be His spokesman, to do great things for God. But He also told Moses that he would never see His face. God gives us all His goodness, but we cannot in any way see His face because He is not a physical thing to see. He is Spirit, but He says, "I will make all my goodness pass before you." God told Moses that He would not yield to any pressure from Moses. He said, "I am the One that must make the decisions—not you. But *trust* me, and I will bring it all to pass."

Sometimes we need an opportunity to get away from things and be still. God can't speak to us when we are in a tailspin of our own thoughts and activities, centered on our own problems. Sometimes He is trying so hard to get through. Do you ever speak to your children and know that they're not listening? Many times! The same is true of God—He cannot get through to us until we pull aside and "be still."

I have a blind friend, John Turner, who is the dearest, most precious man. He will say, "Oh, you're looking pretty today," or "Isn't it a beautiful day?" I forget that he's blind. He never talks as though he is. He *sees,* but he doesn't see physically. This is what God is in a much bigger way. We will *see* Him, though we don't see Him physically.

Our God is knowable. He says, "Be still and know that I am God." But it is only when we stand in His righteousness that we will be able to really see Him and His goodness.

Lord, open our eyes that we might see!

AUGUST 11

Be merciful unto me, O Lord: for I cry unto thee daily. Rejoice the soul of thy servant: for unto thee, O Lord, do I lift up my soul. For thou, Lord, art good, and ready to forgive; and plenteous in mercy unto all them that call upon thee. Give ear, O

Lord, unto my prayer; and attend to the voice of my supplica-
tions. In the day of my trouble I will call upon thee: for thou
wilt answer me.

PSALMS 86:3–7

When we belong to the Lord and we find ourselves committing
acts of sin, either willfully or by neglect, it is necessary for us to
confess those sins immediately. For just as acid corrodes metal if
it is permitted to remain on it, so sin eats into the Christian life
when left unconfessed. Hebrews 4:16 tells us that we have the
right to come boldly to God's throne of grace in prayer. In 1 John
1:9, we are informed that our confession of sin provides forgiveness from God and His cleansing of our lives. By coming to God
and receiving His forgiveness, we are able to tap the immeasurable resources of His power. As a result, we will learn the lesson
of forgiveness itself. When we do, we will be able to forgive
others when they wrong us. This is the means whereby we are
empowered by the Holy Spirit and the practical result of what
the Apostle Paul wrote in Ephesians 4:30–32.

Dear Lord, thank You for the right to approach You boldly,
confident that You'll forgive us, cleanse us, empower us when
we kneel at Your feet.

AUGUST 12

Hear my prayer, O Lord, and let my cry come unto thee.
Hide not thy face from me in the day when I am in trouble;
incline thine ear unto me: in the day when I call answer me
speedily.

PSALMS 102:1, 2

People have never fully realized just how destructive a thing
worry is. It truly plays havoc with one's life. It ruins digestion. It
causes stomach ulcers. It interferes with sound sleep and forces
us to face another day unrested and irritable. It shortens our tempers and makes us snap at members of our family.

> Worry never robs tomorrow
>   of its sorrow,
> It only saps today
>   of its strength.
>
> FROM *Be Somebody*

If you borrow trouble from tomorrow and anticipate the difficulties that you see (or think you see) ahead, are you the better able to cope with them? It is a fact that "all God's chillun' got trouble," and the only thing, after all, that sets God's children apart from other people is what they *do* with trouble.

The Christian treatment of trouble is spendidly illustrated by the oyster into whose shell one day there comes a tiny grain of sand that, as an alien thing, imposes pain, distress, and presents a very real problem. What shall the oyster do? He *could* say, "Why me? What have I done to deserve this?" or, "There is no justice, all this talk of a God of love and mercy is not true!" or, "It can't be true! It isn't true! I must not permit myself to believe it!" or, "There is no such thing as pain, it is an error of the mind; so I shall just deny it and fill my mind with positive things."

But the oyster does none of these things. No, he recognizes the presence of the grim intruder and right away begins to do something. Slowly and patiently, with infinite care, the oyster builds upon the grain of sand, layer upon layer, a beautiful iridescent substance that covers each sharp corner and coats every cutting edge. And gradually, slowly, the hated grain of sand is completely obscured, buried deep in the heart of a smooth white pearl—*a thing of wondrous beauty wrapped around trouble.*

The oyster has learned, by the will of God, to turn cruel misfortunes into blessings, pain and distress into beauty, and grains of sand into pearls.

O God, may this be our everlasting goal: to turn every disadvantage into an asset. Never let yesterday use up today.

AUGUST 13

*Thus saith the Lord, Let not the wise man glory in his wisdom,
neither let the mighty man glory in his might, let not the rich
man glory in his riches: But let him that glorieth glory in this,
that he understandeth and knoweth me, that I am the Lord
which exercise lovingkindness, judgment, and righteousness, in
the earth: for in these things I delight, saith the Lord.*

JEREMIAH 9:23, 24

This is the Scripture we have written on the wall of the little
chapel in our backyard. We chose these verses because we
wanted every visitor to know the only thing in which we can
glory is in knowing God.

*O God, Omnipotent, Omniscient, Creator and Mighty . . . to
think I can know You—and that You are my Friend! Thank
You for making Yourself known to me.*

AUGUST 14

*Be merciful unto me, O God, be merciful unto me: for my soul
trusteth in thee: yea, in the shadow of thy wings will I make my
refuge, until these calamities be overpast. I will cry unto God
most high; unto God that performeth all things for me. He
shall send from heaven, and save me from the reproach of him
that would swallow me up. God shall send forth his mercy and
his truth. My soul is among lions: and I lie even among them
that are set on fire, even the sons of men, whose teeth are
spears and arrows, and their tongue a sharp sword. Be thou
exalted, O God, above the heavens; let thy glory be above all
the earth. They have prepared a net for my steps; my soul is
bowed down: they have digged a pit before me, into the midst
whereof they are fallen themselves. My heart is fixed, O God,
my heart is fixed: I will sing and give praise. Awake up, my
glory; awake, psaltery and harp: I myself will awake early. I
will praise thee, O Lord, among the people: I will sing unto*

thee among the nations. For thy mercy is great unto the heavens, and thy truth unto the clouds. Be thou exalted, O God, above the heavens: let thy glory be above all the earth.

PSALMS 57

From fear to faith all in one Psalm! David experienced the gamut of all human emotions. During this particular time in his life, Saul was king and David was fleeing for his life. David is saying to God, "O God, have pity, for I am trusting You! I will hide beneath the shadow of Your wings until this storm is past." How many times do things happen to us and we don't realize we just need to wait—it is a storm that will pass.

At a testimonial meeting one time, the people were asked to give a favorite Scripture or saying. An old man stood up and said, "And it came to pass."

He said it had sustained him many times. When good things came, he realized he had to savor them while he had them because they soon would be gone. Then, when troubles came, he could quietly endure them for they, too, would pass away.

David, in the beginning of the Psalm, didn't seem to have that assurance, for he cried, "I am surrounded by fierce lions, hotheads whose teeth are sharp as spears and arrows. Their tongues are like swords. Frantic fear grips me!" This is so much like us; we say, "O God, I know You're capable, but I'm scared to death!"

But, then we see a calm come over David, as he says, "O God, my heart is quiet and confident. No wonder I can sing your praises! Your kindness and love are as vast as the heavens, Your faithfulness is higher than the skies. . . ."

Sometimes we tell God how great He is and praise His name for all the wonderful things He does for us. The next moment or the next day, we may be down at the bottom with frantic fear gripping us. There will be no continual and everlasting peace of heart until Jesus comes again, but God promises us He will be with us and will bring us through triumphant.

O Lord, My God, how great Thou art—thank You for loving even me.

AUGUST 15

This one thing I know: God is for me!

PSALMS 56:9 TLB

God knows you by name . . . God never mistakes you in the crowd. When a person fully realizes how much he or she matters to God—then he doesn't have to go out and prove to the world how much he matters.

FROM *Be Somebody*

Dear Lord, thank You for creating me in Your image—a somebody! Help me to remember this when I tend to become discouraged. Remind me that discouragement is the devil's own tool. If Satan can discourage me, I will fall prey to all sorts of negative habits.

AUGUST 16

And all things, whatsoever ye shall ask in prayer, believing, ye shall receive.

MATTHEW 21:22

I DIDN'T HAVE TIME TO PRAY

I got up early one morning
   And rushed right into the day,
I had so much to accomplish
   That I did not have time to pray.

Problems just tumbled about me
   And heavier came each task,
"Why doesn't God help me?"
   I wondered and He answered, "You didn't ask."

I tried to come into God's presence
   I used all my keys at the lock,

And God gently and lovingly chided,
  "Why child, you didn't knock."

I wanted to see joy and beauty
  But the day toiled on gray and bleak,
I wondered why God didn't show me,
  And He said, "You didn't seek."

I woke up early this morning
  And paused before entering the day,
I had so much to accomplish
  That I had to take time to pray.

AUTHOR UNKNOWN

O Lord forgive me when I neglect to check my day's plans with You first. May I make prayer my first resource rather than my last resort.

AUGUST 17

Beloved, let us love one another: for love is of God; and every one that loveth is born of God, and knoweth God.

1 JOHN 4:7

Love of God and love of man are inseparable. They *cannot* be separated. They must come together. Imagine, if you will, a triangle. At the three points are God, you, and others, respectively. As the three points of the triangle are tied together, so are the three points of the relationship of love between God, His people, and others. As we love Him more, we will become greater. *Apart* from God our relationship centers about our ego, but *in* Him it centers about God. When we realize how much we mean to God, and how much others mean to Him, also, then we will be like the Apostle Paul when he cried out, "I can do all things through Christ who strengthens me." We will have a greater sense of our own importance, our resources, and our responsibilities to others. Christ doesn't want you to go about feeling as if you are nothing. Instead, He regards you so highly that He numbers the hairs on your head. Oh my, how precious is the truth that we are not worthy, yet we are of great worth to our Lord Jesus Christ.

O God, help us in our limited human intellect to understand how much You care for us, how important we are to You. May we love You more increasingly and love others who also matter greatly to You.

AUGUST 18

Jesus saith unto him, I am the way, the truth, and the life: no man cometh unto the Father, but by me.

JOHN 14:6

Where have you looked for security? All people look for security in life, and we seem to have entered into a period in history where security is a vapor. Countless are the people who want security in life, but do not want to work for it. When they look for work, they seek security and pensions rather than ways to make contributions. We Americans are so security-minded that we seem bent on self-destruction. But God is the only source of security. He tells us that the only way to that security is in the person of Jesus Christ.

Dear Father, we dare not trust in temporal things for they shall all pass away, but when we place ourselves in Your hands we will find the safety and security we seek.

AUGUST 19

Ye are of God, little children, and have overcome them: because greater is he that is in you than he that is in the world.

1 JOHN 4:4

The story is told in the sixth chapter of Mark about the disciples who were caught in a night storm on the Sea of Galilee. They had left Jesus on the mountain where He had gone to pray, and they were crossing the sea when a sudden windstorm came up. The disciples were toiling and rowing and getting nowhere when, out of the darkness, they saw Jesus walking on the sea. They did not recognize Him.

The troubled disciples in the wind-tossed boat supposed that Jesus was a ghost, and they were afraid.

Notice that our Lord, walking on the sea, did not say "There is no storm." He did not lecture them on the fallacy of ghosts. He did not say "The wind will blow over. Why are you so upset?" He simply said "Be of good cheer: it is I; be not afraid."

His presence makes the difference

Truly the wind is contrary in this troubled world, and individually we run into our share of storms. We do not need a pleasant religion that denies the existence of sin and evil and death. Our Lord recognized all of these and much more. He did not meet the ills of life with a pollyanna philosophy, painting the clouds with sunshine—He met them with Himself.

One of my favorite verses which has given me encouragement through the years is found in John 16:33: "... In the world ye shall have tribulation: but be of good cheer; **I have overcome the world.**"

Tribulation is a reality, but we can *cheer up,* for He has overcome all this world can hurl at us.

HE MAKES THE DIFFERENCE!

Thank Thee, Dear Lord, for Thy sacrificial life which makes all the difference in our lives.

AUGUST 20

These things I have spoken unto you, that in me ye might have peace. In the world ye shall have tribulation: but be of good cheer; I have overcome the world.

JOHN 16:33

I have a saying in my office: "Jesus never lets me down, but He never lets me off, either."

Jesus gives a peace—the only peace there is! The world doesn't have any peace to give.

Jesus does not promise a life free from tribulation, but He does promise that if we truly believe in and belong to Him, we will be overcomers! He has overcome the world!

Lord Jesus, thank You for reminding us that in You we can have peace!

AUGUST 21

And I give unto them eternal life; and they shall never perish, neither shall any man pluck them out of my hand. My Father, which gave them me, is greater than all; and no man is able to pluck them out of my Father's hand.

JOHN 10:28, 29

The Holy Spirit never lets us go. We might try to get away, but if we once belong to God, He does not disown us. He does not disjoin us. He keeps us in the hollow of His hand. We may do a lot of things that will disappoint and hurt Him and wound the Spirit, but isn't it glorious that He does not let us go!

Sometimes we have to suffer greatly, but He never lets go. Jesus says, "No man can pluck them (my sheep) out of my Father's hand." Oh, the assurance of the believer and the assurance of our safety in the hollow of His hand!

> Hidden in the hollow of His blessed hand,
>   Never foe can follow,
> Never traitor stand;
>   Not a surge of worry,
> Not a shade of care,
>   Not a blast of hurry,
> Touch the spirit there.
>   Stayed upon Jehovah,

Hearts are fully blest—
　Finding, as He promised,
Perfect peace and rest.

FRANCES R. HAVERGAL

Precious Lord, how blessed it is that, unworthy as we are, You hold us and protect us by Thy gracious hand. Make us aware and grateful of the rest we find in Thee.

AUGUST 22

This is the Lord's doing; it is marvellous in our eyes. This is the day which the Lord hath made; we will rejoice and be glad in it.

PSALMS 118:23, 24

Start this day by repeating many times, "This is the day which the Lord hath made, I will rejoice and be glad in it."

Adore Him for His greatness, *praise* Him that He is the God He is.

Give thanksgiving for His love, for care, health, home, friends, fun, and a good night's rest. Think on these great mercies until you glow with gratitude.

Give Him your life to be used for Him today. You are not your own, nothing you have is your own.

Ask for guidance through the day. Many things we cannot foresee.

Pray for others. When we get to heaven and realize all that prayer did on this earth, we shall be ashamed that we prayed so little for others and their needs.

Meditate on God's love, wisdom, power, holiness, freedom, and the joy which He gives.

O Lord, teach us to pray.

AUGUST 23

My sheep hear my voice, and I know them, and they follow me: And I give unto them eternal life; and they shall never perish, neither shall any man pluck them out of my hand. My Father, which gave them me, is greater than all; and no man is able to pluck them out of my Father's hand.

JOHN 10:27–30

God often wonders whether we have learned the habit of listening. We may be able to give a testimony of what God has done for us, but does the life we live give evidence that we are listening to God and are living by His commands?

Another lesson to be learned is that of being a good listener, listening to others, developing friendships through being willing to listen.

Be still and listen.

Dear God, help us always to hear Your voice, but seal our lips from time to time that we might listen to others and learn also from them.

AUGUST 24

. . . If God be for us, who can be against us? . . . Who shall separate us from the love of Christ? . . . For I am persuaded, that neither death, nor life, nor angels, nor principalities, nor powers, nor things present, nor things to come, Nor height, nor depth, nor any other creature, shall be able to separate us from the love of God, which is in Christ Jesus our Lord.

ROMANS 8:31, 35, 38, 39

Among our basic needs are identity, stimulus, and security. The opposites of these are being a nobody, being bored, and being anxious or fearful. Write down some of the things that you fear, then go to the Bible to find the antidote for each of them (fear—faith, anxiety—security, lack of confidence—confidence, hostility—love).

To find our identity, we must realize that we matter to God. Jesus never loses us in the crowd. Read Psalm 57 and see how God takes David from fear to faith. When we realize that God loves us, we find identity.

To love and to be loved, is to gain identity. We are stimulated by the filling of the Holy Spirit. We find security in our salvation in Jesus. Our keeping does not depend on us—**God keeps us!**

Dear God, help us to realize our worth to Thee, and then help us to live so that we reflect the confidence of one who is loved by God.

AUGUST 25

Beareth all things, believeth all things, hopeth all things, endureth all things.

1 CORINTHIANS 13:7

It is a great thing to be a believer! Believing in Jesus Christ is the greatest thing ... not only believing that Jesus Christ can do things or believing in a plan of salvation—believing in *Him!* Whatever happens we will hang on to the fact that He is true. Believing in Jesus Christ is the most important thing in our lives.

It is also important to believe in ourselves, our abilities, our future. We are in danger of putting the cart before the horse when we say that man must believe certain things before he can become a Christian. His beliefs are the *result* of his being a Christian.

We believe in ourselves because of our trust in God through Christ. Our power and success come from Him.

O Father, we believe! Help Thou our unbelief!

AUGUST 26

Let not your heart be troubled: ye believe in God, believe also in me. In my Father's house are many mansions: if it were not so, I would have told you. I go to prepare a place for you. And if I go and prepare a place for you, I will come again, and receive you unto myself; that where I am, there ye may be also.
JOHN 14:1–3

Each week memorize at least two promises found in the Scriptures. In this way you can build for yourself a Promise List inside the back cover of your Bible. These promises can mean much to you and to others as time passes. For example, Psalms 9:9 tells us that all who are oppressed may come to God, for He is a refuge in time of trouble. It goes on to tell us that all who know the Lord's mercy will count on Him for help because He has never forsaken those who put their trust in Him.

Another promise from God that has saved me a lot of heartache is found in John 16:33: ". . . In the world ye shall have tribulation: but be of good cheer; I have overcome the world." That is God's promise of peace of mind even when we are in the midst of troubles and trials, because the Lord has overcome the world.

Dear Father, help us to "stand on the promises" etched on our hearts from Your blessed Word.

AUGUST 27

Herein is love, not that we loved God, but that he loved us, and sent his Son to be the propitiation for our sins.
1 JOHN 4:10

At the mountaintop we have some wonderful experiences. We have people who have come to know the Lord personally. During one of our wonderful mountaintop retreats, a group once said to me, "You talk about God as if you know Him, and we don't know Him like that." To them, God was a judge. I tried to show them through all the Scriptures on love that God is *love* and He loves each one of us. Sometimes He shakes us up, but He loves us and has a plan for us. When we come to Him and love Him, we need have no fear of Him. When we realize how much God loves us, we realize our worth to Him—not our *worthiness,* but our *worth.*

We can't see the wind, but we can see its effect. We don't understand it, but we can appropriate it. The effect of God is love—saving, caring love—yes, disciplining sometimes, but with love. Out of that love will come the right kind of actions, the right kind of standards. *"Herein is love,* not that we loved God, but that *He* loved us, . . ."

Make this your prayer today:

Heavenly Father, I'm glad you first loved me before I even knew You. I love You, and I accept Jesus as Savior, Friend, and Lord of my life.

AUGUST 28

I can do all things through Christ which strengtheneth me.
PHILIPPIANS 4:13

People love to identify with a purpose. It gives them a feeling of belonging to and contributing to something worthwhile.

If your purpose is worthwhile enough and your belief in it is strong enough, the strength of the purpose will take over and "keep you keeping on" even when you are physically exhausted.

You may give out—but never give up.

THE CHALLENGE

Blessed is the man, indeed,
Who in this life can find;
A PURPOSE that can fill his days,
And GOALS to fill his mind!

The world is filled with little men,
Content with where they are;
Not knowing joys success can bring
No WILL to go that far!

Yet, in this world there is a need,
For men to lead the rest
To rise above the "average" life,
By giving of their best!

Would you be one, who dares to try,
When challenged by the task;
To rise to heights you've never seen,
Or is that too much to ask?

This is your day—a world to win,
Great purpose to achieve;
Accept the challenge of your goals
And in yourself, BELIEVE!

You will be proud of what you've done,
When at the close of day;
You look back on your battles, won,
Content, you came this way!

DR. HEARTSILL WILSON

Dear Jesus, may Your purpose always be my prayer.

AUGUST 29

. . . but he that is greatest among you, let him be as the younger; and he that is chief, as he that doth serve.

LUKE 22:26

Jesus gave us the formula for greatness. True greatness is not measured by headlines, the social register, or a bank statement, although it seems so by the world's standards.

Jesus said in Matthew 20:28, "Even as the Son of man came

not to be ministered unto, but to minister, . . ." He teaches us that the only way to be great in God's kingdom is to *serve*. Always know that greatness is determined by the scope of our contribution to the world around us.

O Lord, keep us humble and help us to forget ourselves. Make us willing to be the one behind the scenes. Help us to serve.

AUGUST 30

And God shall wipe away all tears from their eyes; and there shall be no more death, neither sorrow, nor crying, neither shall there be any more pain: for the former things are passed away.

REVELATION 21:4

It was early morning on the day I had to go for extensive dental surgery. I was more than apprehensive about this day, for I had had dental work done in the past year that was difficult and painful.

Then I thought of how many people across this land face surgery or illness or pain much more serious than mine. For them all, Heavenly Father, I pray.

I pray for all people who will have to stay in bed today, who cannot get up and walk around, and work and serve, and feel free to do what they need or want to do.

I pray for the people who will serve them—the doctors, the nurses, the technicians. I pray today for surgeons—that their hands will be steady, their heads clear, and their hearts compassionate. I pray for all the people in hospitals around this earth and especially in our own city and nation.

Then I think of little children. Our own older granddaughter was in a children's hospital for over two years of her very young life. I cannot forget the difficult times for all of us when we would have to leave her there, knowing that she was in good hands, medically, but too young to understand why she could not be with her family. And I realize there are little children who will stay in hospitals for many years.

Heavenly Father, we look forward to the day when, with Your own hands, You will wipe away all tears, You will touch all little bodies, and they will be whole again. I pray that, if I am ever ill, I will be a good patient, I will exhibit Your patience and Your love, even through difficulty. I thank You for people who care about me and who will minister to me if I am ill. Again my heart goes out to the many elderly people who do not have this kind of care.

And so, dear Heavenly Father, today I pray that I will be a good child.

In a world of television, newspaper, and magazine commercials, I pray that today I will be a commercial for You, dear Lord—a living commercial.

And I come early this morning confident in Your care, knowing that You will hear and answer all because of Jesus.

What a beautiful name, a healing name, the precious name of Jesus.

AUGUST 31

And let us not be weary in well doing: for in due season we shall reap, if we faint not.

GALATIANS 6:9

Summer is quickly drawing to a close. Vacations are over, the thermometer is finally showing some signs of dropping, and it seems we have hardly asked the question, "What am I going to *do* with them all summer?" when, suddenly, it is time to get the children ready for school again. And we are reminded again that time is such a fleeting thing.

How have you used *your* summer? I hope you've made it a family time, as leisurely a time with those you love as your schedule could permit.

Did you make the opportunity each day to draw aside for time with the Lord and with our daily thoughts through these devotionals? If in your hectic summer pace you found that impossible, take the time today to go back and read the ones you missed, praying that God will bless them to your heart and grant you a special understanding of any truths He might wish to impart to you through them.

Capsule the summer by making a list of the three most important things you accomplished and a second list of what you think were the three best things that happened to your children.

My List:
1. _____
2. _____
3. _____

My Children's List:
1. _____
2. _____
3. _____

Teach me, O Lord, to outgrow my self-centeredness—to lose sight of myself in love and concern for others.

September

SEPTEMBER 1

But made himself of no reputation, and took upon him the form of a servant, and was made in the likeness of men: And being found in fashion as a man, he humbled himself, and became obedient unto death, even the death of the cross.

PHILIPPIANS 2:7, 8

Jesus gave up all His rights and came to be our servant! He grew tired, hungry, and even sleepy.

Men have tried to destroy Him . . .
But don't you know you can't destroy Him?
What would you use for Power?
All power belongs to Him!
If you try to destroy Him by rejecting or ignoring Him—
Before you know it—you will hear a still small voice saying:
> "Behold, I stand at the door and knock—if any man hear my voice and open the door, I will come in to him, and will sup with him—and he with me."

If you try to destroy Him by fire He will refuse to burn—
If you try to destroy Him by water, He will walk on the water.
If you try to destroy Him by a strong wind, the tempest will lick His hand and lay down at His feet.
If you try to destroy Him with the law—you will find no fault in Him.
If you try to destroy Him with the seal of an empire—He will break it!
If you try to destroy Him by putting Him in a grave—HE WILL ARISE!

At His birth, men came from the East. At His death, men came from the West and the East and West met in Him. HE IS LORD. HALLELUJAH—and the Lord Omnipotent Reigneth!

S. M. LOCKRIDGE

Dear God, how could we, unworthy and undeserving as we are, be so blessed as to become joint heirs with One such as this—Wonderful Counselor, King of kings, Lord of lords! Thank You for loving us and giving us Your blessed Son!

SEPTEMBER 2

Ye have not chosen me, but I have chosen you, and ordained you, that ye should go and bring forth fruit, and that your fruit should remain: that whatsoever ye shall ask of the Father in my name, he may give it you.

JOHN 15:16

Our concept of God will determine our concept of ourselves and of others. The Bible defines sin as lawlessness, lying, and the like. Sin is transgression of God's will—it is unbelief. Essentially it is missing the mark of God's will for your life.

The most basic example of unbelief and transgression is selfishness. Selfishness, in the final analysis, is putting your own will against the will of God. The most important decision you can make for your life is to believe—to choose a right relationship with God. Unbelief is to center your life on yourself and, thus, to miss the mark of God's will for your life in this world.

Father, we are so selfish! Help us to turn our thoughts away from ourselves and toward You and Your work in the world.

SEPTEMBER 3

I can of mine own self do nothing: as I hear, I judge: and my judgment is just; because I seek not mine own will, but the will of the Father which hath sent me.

JOHN 5:30

God created Adam and Eve and gave them a free will so they could choose whether or not to love Him. He also gave us a free will, and we must see that the same is developed in our children. We can set an atmosphere, but we cannot determine the will of another individual. We can lead them to God and attempt to show them their need for God. We can also show them the love and forgiveness of God through our own lives, but we must remember that they will determine their own destinies. Each person has his own free will. The way we respond to God's revelation of Himself to us is our own personal responsibility.

Lord, help us to use our free will to find and to do Your *will for our lives.*

SEPTEMBER 4

Praise ye the Lord. Praise the Lord, O my soul. While I live will I praise the Lord: I will sing praises unto my God while I have any being.

PSALMS 146:1, 2

In addition to confession of sins, we should develop a prayer life in order to simply praise God for His blessings. Among those blessings are the numerous things mentioned in the Psalms. Then we can praise God for Himself, just praise Him for being God. We can praise Him for our nation, our church, our family, friends, and whatever else He has given to us. This purpose for prayer is simply an expression of our gratitude to the Lord for the daily blessings He richly showers upon us.

*Lord, teach us to praise more and beseech less, knowing that
in the end we'll gain the greater blessing.*

SEPTEMBER 5

*Children, obey your parents in the Lord: for this is right. . . .
And, ye fathers, provoke not your children to wrath: but bring
them up in the nurture and admonition of the Lord.*

EPHESIANS 6:1, 4

After our relationship with God and with the mate He has
given us, the most important relationship in our lives is that with
our children.

How terribly important and vital that is—important in their
younger years and later, when they go to school and become
teenagers.

A successful parent works himself out of a job, but never out
of a *relationship.* You have to let your children go free, yet give
them restraints and love all the time. They must have restraints
until they are mature and responsible, but love will build a fence
around them and give them the foundation they need upon
which to build their own lives.

Love is such a fragile thing, it must be handled with prayer.
And our love, like sunlight, should surround our children and
give them illumined freedom.

Our children need our *presence* far more than they need our
presents! Spend quality time with your children—answer the
"first tug." Teach your children to have self-confidence. Give
them a good self-image. They are *somebody,* created in God's
image . . . God has a plan for their lives. Oh, how important it is
that every young person feel like somebody! When they realize
that they are created in God's image, that His likeness is theirs—
though conceived in earthly fashion, they have been born of the
Divine—there is no hill they cannot conquer, no height they may
not reach. When they find out how much they matter to God,
they won't have to go out and prove anything to the world.

Gracious Lord, today especially, we need Thy guidance and strength so that we may be able to lead our precious children in Thy way.

SEPTEMBER 6

Every man's work shall be made manifest: for the day shall declare it, because it shall be revealed by fire; and the fire shall try every man's work of what sort it is.

1 CORINTHIANS 3:13

If I must spend my days at work, let it be work that I love. Make it more than glamor or dazzle, make it more than crazy days of funny people or being worn to a frazzle. Let it be a chance to express all the things I feel inside so that at the end of the day, it never ceases to amaze me that they call it work and they actually pay me.

If it is to be, it is up to me.

Father, thank You for the privilege of work, but especially, thank You for giving us a zest for working when we have found the thing we love to do. Help everyone who is boxed in to a job that is drudgery to somehow tune into a new thing that would bring joy and fulfillment to his life.

SEPTEMBER 7

There is nothing better for a man, than that he should eat and drink, and that he should make his soul enjoy good in his labour. This also I saw, that it was from the hand of God.

ECCLESIASTES 2:24

Labor day—a special day set aside to recognize the working people of America.

This includes you and me. Look back—think. If there was one thing the pilgrims and our founding fathers had, in addition to their faith and trust in God, it was the *desire to work*. Night and day they toiled, and God blessed their efforts.

On this great day each year, we honor and congratulate the workers of America. They have toiled and built what we have today—our America.

It seems strange that what built this country—hard work and real success—is becoming distorted today, and the idea that work is outdated seems to be prevailing. Many today would like to start at the top and work their way down to all leisure time and no work at all, but this is not the answer.

What is work? It is God-ordained from the beginning:

• Adam was told to work the garden;
• Moses was busy with his flocks;
• David was caring for his father's sheep;
• Peter and Andrew were busy casting a net into the sea.

From the beginning, **God intended that we should work.**

Work is that human activity that provides the goods and services in our economy. We would not enjoy the good life with which we are blessed today without the work, the physical and mental effort put out by those who really understand what is important and what counts.

Money received without productivity is destructive. There is no easy way. Work is an opportunity!

Thank You, Lord, that I have work to do. Whether I leave the house each morning to pour my energy and effort into the job You have given me, or stay behind in the home to toil at my assigned task there, help me to labor as unto Thee and to realize that work will reward me richly and bring me self-control, diligence, strength of will, cheerfulness, and contentment that the idle will never know.

SEPTEMBER 8

He wrote them to teach his people how to live—how to act in every circumstance, . . .

PROVERBS 1:2 TLB

King Solomon wrote Proverbs "to teach his people how to live—how to act in every circumstance, for he wanted them to be understanding, just and fair in everything they did. . . . 'I want those already wise to become wiser and to become leaders by exploring the depths of meaning in these nuggets of truth,'" he said.

How wonderful it is that our Creator did not leave us drifting about in this world without signposts, without guidelines. The Book of Proverbs is not a list of promises, but, rather, examples and admonitions. The key word, of course, is *wisdom*. There is a difference between having knowledge in your head and having the *wisdom* to use it pleasingly and skillfully to the pleasure of God.

The great yearning of us all is to know how to act in every circumstance, how to live. We are bombarded with advertisements from television and from newspapers and magazines on how to live, how to find happiness: **Proverbs is a handbook that will teach us how to live.**

Lord, thank You for not leaving us adrift without direction. Help us to follow Your signposts to fruitful, productive lives.

SEPTEMBER 9

He wanted them to be understanding, just and fair in everything they did.

PROVERBS 1:3 TLB

What does it mean to be understanding? How many times do we "understand" our children into failure? How many times do we "understand" the people we work with into failure?

What does it really mean to be understanding? Many definitions come to mind. For one, to be able to see things as the other person sees them . . . as the old Indian saying goes, to be able "to walk a mile in the other person's moccasins." One can almost say that it is "standing under the circumstances so you can see them as they see them, being able to think where they are coming from."

And yet, we are admonished to "trust in the Lord with all your heart and lean not on your own understanding." It took me a lifetime to realize that I did not have to understand everything. There are things we will not be *able* to understand, and that is when we really have to trust our God to know what is best for us and to work things out in His own loving, caring way. Not all things that happen to us are good, but if we give them to God, He can work them out for our ultimate good.

Dear Father, thank You for opening to us the things we need to know but guiding us through the areas that are beyond our understanding.

SEPTEMBER 10

He wanted them to be understanding, just and fair in everything they did.

PROVERBS 1:3 TLB

Think of these two words—*just* and *fair.* Stop and write down what you think it means to be *just.* And then write down your definition of *fair.* God, our Heavenly Father, is not only just, but He is also fair, and in addition to that He has mercy.

What is God's definition of *being just?* What is His idea of *being fair?* King Solomon was the wisest man who ever lived, and his justice in dealing with his people was well known. It was an example of fairness.

We all remember the story of the two women who brought one live baby and one that was dead to King Solomon, each claiming the live baby. To settle the dispute, he ordered his aide to bring a sword, cut the baby in two, and give half to each woman, knowing of course, that the true mother of the living baby would come forth and say, "Please, no, let her have the baby. I'd rather let her have the baby than see my baby die." So he found which was the true mother and gave the baby to her.

We must ask the Lord every day to help us make fair decisions and just decisions and treat people equally. We must think of each person as a child of God, someone who is somebody and who deserves our respect and love and concern.

Heavenly Father, as we look at the people around our world, help us to think of each person as very important to You and as very important to our world, and help us to treat each with justice and fairness in all dealings and see each as somebody.

SEPTEMBER 11

How does a man become wise? The first step is to trust and reverence the Lord!

PROVERBS 1:7 TLB

What a wonderful admonition this Scripture is for every person, and most especially for the men in your life, for every man in our world.

Oh, there is such a need for men to be wise!

If the men in our nation, the men in our government, the men in authority, the men on our Supreme Court, would read this verse and practice it—oh, what a difference there would be in our nation!

Proverbs teaches, "With wise counselors, there is safety in the nation. Without wise leadership, the nation is in trouble" (*see* Proverbs 11:14).

Everlastingly, God admonishes us to trust and listen to the Lord first. To trust means to trust even when we do not understand. To reverence means to put the Lord and His desires, His laws, commandments, and precepts first, and at the center of our being.

Everyone has to build a life around something or someone that doesn't change, and God Himself is the only Person that does not change.

O Lord God, our prayer is that all of our national leaders might be pierced to the heart to trust and reverence You. O Lord God, that we truly might put God first in every facet of our national life, and in our individual and family life.

SEPTEMBER 12

Yes, if you want better insight and discernment, and are searching for them as you would for lost money or hidden treasure, then wisdom will be given you, and knowledge of God himself; you will soon learn the importance of reverence for the Lord and of trusting him.

PROVERBS 2:3–5 TLB

How many times we have all desired insight and discernment. We want to be able to look past the surface of a situation and see the real cause. We want to be able to look behind the front of an organization or a group of people and see the purpose. We want to be able to look within ourselves and examine our motives, and find whether they are selfish or unselfish. And God promises that if we are searching for these as for lost money or hidden treasure, then wisdom will be given us and the knowledge of God, Himself. Oh, how we all desire this! How many people do we know who say, "Yes, I would like to know God." Well, we have good news: **Our God is knowable!** He says, "Come unto me, . . ." (Matthew 11:28, 29). But it begins, as the writer of Proverbs says, with "the importance of reverence and trust in the Lord."

Do you really trust Him? Do you trust Him with all of life? With your family? With your finances? Oh, that you might say, "Yes, I trust Him! I trust Him completely!"

Dear God, today we desire to trust You with our lives, with our families, with our finances. Teach us the knowledge of Yourself as You want us to learn.

SEPTEMBER 13

For the Lord grants wisdom! His every word is a treasure of knowledge and understanding. He grants good sense to the godly—his saints. He is their shield, protecting them and guarding their pathway. He shows how to distinguish right from wrong, how to find the right decision every time. For wisdom and trust will enter the very center of your being, filling your life with joy.

PROVERBS 2:6–10 TLB

Oh! What promises we find here in God's Word! The Lord grants wisdom. His every word is a treasure of knowledge and understanding. God has revealed Himself to us through His works and His Word in the revelation of His Son, Jesus Christ.

How many times we look around at His works and, as at our beautiful mountain retreat, we see the blue, blue sky, and the fleecy clouds as they float along, the tall pine and fir trees, and the handsome, large blue jays. All around are majestic mountains and a sense of the majesty of the Creator. And yet, we seldom get to know God just through His works.

And so He has prepared for us His Word, and it is through reading His Word over and over, studying it, asking questions, and seeking answers that He gives wisdom to us. His every Word is a treasure of knowledge and understanding.

Thank You, God, that You gave us Your Word, as well as the majesty of Your works. Create within us a deep, earnest desire to get to know You better, and to read Your Word daily, knowing that You will honor the seeker, and reward the asker.

SEPTEMBER 14

He grants good sense to the godly—his saints.

PROVERBS 2:7 TLB

I have five grandchildren. As the oldest grandson went off to college, I prayed daily that God would grant a shield of protection around him. I will pray this for all of them as they each go off to school . . . that God's shield will be their protection, guarding their paths from the temptations that are constantly being thrust at our young people: temptations to listen to the permissiveness that permeates our society, to follow man-made social values instead of God's design for living, temptations to get high on many things—from liquor, to marijuana, to cocaine—other than those that God has planned as best for the body, mind, and soul of His creation, His greatest creation—the human being.

Oh, how we need to pray for our young people! We need to let them know that we care, and that we as adults are doing our best to make the world better for them. How we need to strive to do this and become models rather than critics.

O God, I pray today for all young people of our nation and our world. As they seek to find the right pathway for their lives, I pray that You will send someone, some adult, into their pathway, that will be the right kind of a model through which they might come to know You and to see You as Lord of life and King of kings.

SEPTEMBER 15

He shows how to distinguish right from wrong, how to find the right decision every time. For wisdom and trust will enter the very center of your being, filling your life with joy.

PROVERBS 2:9, 10 TLB

Oh, how many times we have all wished that we could know how to make the right decision every time.

There are many facets of decision-making. I have learned through the years that you should be sure to get all the facts you can, because no decision is any better than the facts on which it is based. Get all the input you can, too, but don't delay forever. You come to a point where you have to decide. You have to think, not only about whether the decision is right or wrong, but about the effect it is going to have on many people. I have learned that it is not enough that the decision be right, it must also be communicated properly and at the right time for people to understand it.

It is not easy to be in a decision-making situation, and yet it is something we all face. Decisions that people make affect their very lives—how important it is that they be right!

Precious Lord Jesus, give us Your joy. You have said that You have come so that our joy might be complete. Through You, we want that true joy.

SEPTEMBER 16

He shows how to distinguish right from wrong, how to find the right decision every time.

PROVERBS 2:9 TLB

What are the most important decisions in life? The first decision would have to be *What will I do about Jesus Christ?* All other decisions are based upon this one.

The second decision is *Who will I marry?* Of course if we are already married, we know how much this decision has influenced our whole lives.

The third decision is *Where will I live? Will I live where I grew up, or will I live someplace else?* Of course this includes, and would be influenced by, the fourth decision which is *What will I do with my life? What will I choose for my profession, my career— my purpose in living?*

The fifth decision would be *Will I let God make these decisions for me?* I have learned in life to make a few big decisions that will take care of a whole lot of little decisions, and this takes a lot of the anxiety out of living. For instance, long ago I made the decision to tithe, so I do not have to agonize every Sunday morning over what to put in the envelope for God's people and God's work. That decision is already made for me. Sometime while growing up, we make the decision to be honest or not to be honest, so we do not have to agonize over how to treat people or whether to cheat or not, because we made the decision to be honest. It takes care of a lot of little things; it takes care of a lot of the anxiety of life. Of course the first decision has to be *What is God going to mean in my life? What will I do about Jesus Christ, His Son, in whom, He says, is life—life everlasting?*

Have you made that decision about Jesus Christ? Have you accepted Him as Lord and Master? Have you accepted Him, first, as Lord and Savior? Have you accepted His forgiveness?

Dear Jesus, because You came and lived and gave Your life for me that I might have life everlasting and forgiveness for my sins, I accept this as a precious gift. And because You rose again to life everlasting, I ask to be buried with You in baptism and rise anew in the fullness of life that I, too, might be with You forever and ever. I accept forgiveness for my sins, which I cannot cleanse myself. I want to walk with You, and live for You, and be Your servant. Help me, Jesus.

SEPTEMBER 17

My son, never forget the things I've taught you. If you want a long and satisfying life, closely follow my instructions.
PROVERBS 3:1, 2 TLB

How grateful I am that our God is all the embodiment of truth, and yet He is the embodiment of kindness. He put these two virtues together—truth and kindness. Otherwise we might tend to use truth as a club and forget to be kind.

How important it is to be kind and how difficult, sometimes, to learn this lesson. I think of Shakespeare's words in *Twelfth Night:*

"None can be call'd deform'd but the unkind." This reminds me
of a verse I learned long ago:

> I have wept in the night
> For the shortness of sight,
> That to another's need made me blind—
> But I never have yet
> Had a twinge of regret
> For being a little too kind.

As the little girl prayed: Make the bad people good and the
good people kind. How many times we forget that someone
needs our kindness more than our judgment.

*God, help us to be kind, to reach out to others in love and un-
derstanding.*

SEPTEMBER 18

*If you want favor with both God and man, and a reputation for
good judgment and common sense, then trust the Lord completely; don't ever trust yourself.*

PROVERBS 3:4, 5 TLB

The Bible does not say "do not use your understanding," but
we *are* told not to lean on it. How many times it says in Proverbs,
"Get understanding." That was one of the first things He said.
Certainly we are to learn to be understanding and to have understanding, but not to lean on it, not to trust ourselves completely.

If we learn to put God first, He will direct our paths and He
will give us success beyond anything we could imagine.

How do we put God first? So many believers really want to,
and yet, because we are innately selfish, we have to everlastingly
work at it. One of the best ways I know to put God first is to take
one day at a time and to start each morning with a time of
thanksgiving to God our Creator, to Jesus Christ our Savior, and

to the Holy Spirit, our Comforter and Director. If we start every day that way, we will be better equipped to put God first in every decision and plan we make during the day and in all we think and do.

I am a fellow struggler in this lifelong journey to put God first, and yet I know that when I really do it and ask His plans—rather than make the plans and ask Him to bless them—I have the extra power of the Holy Spirit, I have the extra strength, I have the extra energy of the source of all energy in my endeavors.

Dear God, teach us how to put You first—because we really do love You.

SEPTEMBER 19

Honor the Lord by giving him the first part of all your income, and He will fill your barns with wheat and barley and overflow your wine vats with the finest wines.

PROVERBS 3:9, 10 TLB

Giving God the first part of all the increase was the epitome of the providence of food and substance in the day in which Proverbs was written. I cannot stress too much my own personal belief in tithing. You can read in my earlier books, *Think Mink* or *You Can Too* how I learned to tithe in a time of very limited income and very large responsibilities. Yet, it seemed to me that God was saying, "Mary, you are not doing such a hot job of it yourself. Why don't you give Me a chance?" And so my two children and I sat down and we made a pledge to tithe. The only way we could do that was to put our tithe in the envelope first, before any necessities were taken out of my paycheck. Somehow the God of all resources honored our trust—God always keeps His promises!

So, if you want financial security—not necessarily abundance, but security—I would urge you to begin now to honor the Lord with your substance, and "prove the Lord if He will not open the windows of heaven, and pour you out a blessing so there will not be room enough to receive it" (*see* Malachi 3:10). But more important is the promise in the New Testament: "For where your treasure is, there will your heart be also" (Matthew 6:21).

Lord, if we can trust You with our salvation, can we not also trust You with our finances? Help us to trust You in all *things.*

SEPTEMBER 20

Wisdom gives: A long, good life, Riches, Honor, Pleasure, Peace.

PROVERBS 3:16, 17 TLB

In our search for wisdom, we must everlastingly remind ourselves what wisdom is. Wisdom is more than knowledge. Wisdom comes from God . . . "The fear of the Lord is the beginning of knowledge . . ." (Proverbs 1:7).

How does a man become wise? The first step is to trust and reverence the Lord. In Psalms 53:1, the Psalmist said, "The fool hath said in his heart, There is no God." How easy it is for man to believe that his own intelligence is so superior that if he learns enough about the world, about other people, about science, about the body, he will be able to solve all problems and assure peace, prosperity, freedom, and happiness.

History reveals that it does not work that way. Along with the wonderful creative genius of mankind that comes from our Creator God, we live in a fallen world, and we have the stain of sin and selfishness in our blood stream.

There is an old verse that says:

> For some men die in shrapnel,
> And some go down in flames—
> But most men perish inch by inch,
> In play at little games.
>
> ROBERT D. ABRAHAMS

*O God, how we pray that, instead of playing at little games,
we will seek Your wisdom, reverence Your ways, and learn
from Your Word ... all because of Jesus.*

SEPTEMBER 21

*Don't withhold repayment of your debts. Don't say "some
other time," if you can pay now.*
                                            PROVERBS 3:27, 28 TLB

Who is my neighbor? We have neighbors close and neighbors
far, and we are to be kind and gracious to them, we are to be
helpful—and, certainly, we are not to plot against them.

It is very easy in some parts of the country, where there are
high-rise apartments and people are really unknown to their
neighbors, to become self-sufficient and selfish. But there are still
places where it is the unwritten law of the land that when you see
anyone in distress you stop and give aid. Neighbors are truly
neighbors there. When I grew up as a little girl in the country, if
someone's barn burned down, all of the men of the community
would get together and rebuild it, and the women would cook
delicious food and feed the workers. In just a few days there
would be a new barn where there had been only ashes. No one
would think of paying anyone for his work, it was a neighborly
act of love. The people who rebuilt the barn knew if some misfortune happened to them, their neighbors would come to their
aid.

Somehow we yearn for those times when helping one another
was the thing to do. Now, because of our modern life, we are
often isolated from our neighbors, and, yet, I believe God wants
us to go out of our way to help and to form a community of love
wherever we live.

*Lord, help us today to go out of our way to find somebody
who needs our help.*

SEPTEMBER 22

*"Learn to be wise," he said, "and develop good judgment and
common sense! I cannot overemphasize this point."*
PROVERBS 4:5 TLB

How much our world today needs common sense! Cliff Barrows made the statement that his wonderful father had his "C.S.
degree"—the degree of common sense! He had been called upon
to help underprivileged nations develop agricultural methods
that would produce more grain and fruit—all because of his love
of God. He had true wisdom, good judgment, and common
sense.

Unfortunately, many of our colleges are turning out students
who have great book knowledge but a shortage of common
sense.

Some of our greatest common sense can be learned from the
Book of Proverbs, and that is why we use it so consistently. Many
times we can find the right way to do something, we can find the
answer to a problem by applying this test to the solution. What
would be the most sensible way to solve this problem? What will
work? How will it affect people? Will it bring another problem
with the solution?

Many times I have observed that one tiny little fact tosses out a
great big theory. Look for the sensible way to solve a problem,
not necessarily the one in theory.

Our grandmothers, who came across these prairies to settle the
great heartland in the west of America, and our forefathers, who
built this nation, did not have the advantage of great universities
or the time to spend in getting degrees. But they did have a tremendous amount of common sense and a commitment to hard
work. We could learn a lot from them.

*O Lord, help us today to cut through the theories and the
constant knowledge that pounds at us and find Your wisdom
and common sense, so that we might master the art of living
that will honor You and bless others.*

SEPTEMBER 23

Determination to be wise is the first step toward becoming wise! And with your wisdom, develop common sense and good judgment.

PROVERBS 4:7 TLB

How much we miss in life . . . how many errors we make from wrong assumptions and lack of observation. One author says:

We go through each day like people in dark tunnels armed only with flashlights. We get through the tunnels fairly efficiently, but we've only seen the narrow paths illumined by our lights.

This makes us realize how insensitive we really are to other people . . . to their needs . . . to their wants and desires . . . and backgrounds . . . and feelings.

We speak from *our* background . . . and *our* feelings . . . and *our* interpretation . . . to other persons—and the other persons LISTEN from *their* background . . . with *their* feelings . . . with *their* interpretations . . . and it is almost a miracle that we ever understand one another at all.

It certainly seems that we are going through a dark tunnel armed with only a flashlight, and yet, we *do* get through, and at times, ideas *are* communicated with tremendous force. This is why we build good homes, great companies, great buildings and bridges, and even launch men into space.

Certainly it makes us stop and think, however, that we must constantly work at understanding people and being understood.

It takes the **faith** to believe, the **vision** to see, and the **courage** to act.

Father, it is You who have given me another day of life. Unless You help me, I'll mess up some of today. Please control my tongue—keep me from saying things that irritate or hurt

or make trouble. *Control my thoughts against any negative
or destructive ideas. Help me to be Your voice today through
Jesus Christ, my Lord.*

SEPTEMBER 24

*I would have you learn this great fact: that a life of doing right
is the wisest life there is. If you live that kind of life, you'll not
limp or stumble as you run. Carry out my instructions; don't
forget them, for they will lead you to real living.*

PROVERBS 4:11–13 TLB

We hear a great deal these days about what is real versus what
is plastic. **God is real!** His creation is real! His Word is real!

We see His hand in all His works, but we hear His voice in the
Book of His Word. This admonition, that living a life of doing
right is the wisest life there is, has been proved to be true down
through the centuries of all the Judeo-Christian nations, and
even in some that did not recognize the source. The saying,
"Honesty is the best policy" and the golden rule, "Do unto others
as you would have others do unto you," express it in different
words, but however you say it, it is still the truth of God's Word:
A life of doing right is the wisest life there is.

*Lord, help us to be right and help us to be wise, and we will
claim Your promise that these will lead us to real living.*

SEPTEMBER 25

*Above all else, guard your affections. For they influence
everything else in your life.*

PROVERBS 4:23 TLB

How true it is that what we put at the top of our priority list of
affections will control or influence the rest of our lives. Somebody once said that you could go through a person's check regis-

ter, note all the check stubs for a year, and get a profile of that person's priorities. How careful we have to be about what we put on the list of our likes and loves.

This would also apply to the people we place first on our priority list of affection. I think all of us would desire to have our blessed Lord as the first on our list because He commanded His disciples to "Love the Lord thy God with all thy heart, and with all thy soul, and with all thy strength . . ." (Luke 10:27).

So many times we fall so far short of this, for living the Christian life is not easy—in fact, it is impossible without the control of the Holy Spirit. I am a very confident person, and I believe in having a good self-image and self-confidence, but I have to make it very clear that my self-confidence comes from the fact that **my God is able.** He is the source of all wisdom, the source of all supply. My confidence comes from believing in *Him,* believing that He created me to be *somebody,* believing that He created me with genius in His creative image, as well as His spiritual image, believing that if I continuously tap the source of His energy and wisdom, *I can do all things through Christ Who strengtheneth me!* Or, it may read *"which* strengtheneth me" meaning that I can do all things through Christ, and that this reliance on Him strengthens me, gives me confidence, and also brings me back to continually seek His will, His wisdom, and fall in love with Him again every day.

> *O God, forgive me for the times I have placed my affections on things of this earth. Forgive me for the times I have thought more of others than I have of You. Forgive me for the times I have wanted to please others more than I have wanted to please You. And O Father, because I am Your child, I can come boldly and ask forgiveness, and ask for Your help to do better today and in the tomorrows of my life.*

SEPTEMBER 26

Look straight ahead; don't even turn your head to look.
PROVERBS 4:25 TLB

People usually fail for lack of faith, not lack of ability.

A few years back a gallant woman, Florence Chadwick, after successfully swimming the English Channel, became the first woman to attempt to swim the twenty-one miles from Catalina Island to the California coast. Thousands of television fans watched her battle all night through icy water, fog, and schools of sharks, only to be pulled from the water a mile short of her goal, exhausted, humiliated, chilled, and defeated.

Florence, in evaluating her two experiences, remembered that at the point in her English Channel swim when she felt she had gone as far as she could go, she begged to be taken from the water. Just at that moment, she and her father sighted land and that gave her the push she needed to go on and make it. But in her unsuccessful attempt to cross from Catalina, fog obscured the land ahead. When they told her it was only a mile away, she *didn't have the faith to believe what she could not see.* What she lacked was *faith,* not ability.

Two months later, with renewed faith, Florence Chadwick turned her defeat into victory, and not only became the first woman to swim the Catalina Channel despite recurring fog, but beat the men's record by two hours!

Precious Lord, help us to keep our eyes on the goal, our hearts on You, our Friend and Redeemer.

SEPTEMBER 27

Drink from your own well, my son—be faithful and true to your wife. Why should you beget children with women of the street? Why share your children with those outside your home? Let your manhood be a blessing; rejoice in the wife of your youth.

PROVERBS 5:15–18 TLB

How I pray for our young people to keep themselves honorable and true to the plan of our Creator. I pray daily for my young grandsons that God will be preparing the right wives for them, if it is His plan for them to marry. And how I pray for my granddaughters. For the one who is already married, I pray for the strength and joy of her marriage. And how I pray for my youngest granddaughter. She is so beautiful and clean and sweet, and I pray that God is preparing a man somewhere just for her—if that is in His plan. If not, I pray she will find the joy and fulfillment of God's plan for her life. I am so grateful that there are organizations, along with the youth programs of our churches and colleges, such as the Fellowship of Christian Athletes. This organization has been a blessing in the lives of my family, our grandchildren, and many others.

I believe in our young people. I invest in young people. They are going to rule some day, and I want their education to be in the wisdom of Almighty God and their commitment to be to excellence in all areas.

> Turn your eyes upon Jesus,
> Look full in His wonderful face,
> And the things of earth
> Will grow strangely dim
> In the light of His glory and grace.
> HELEN H. LEMMEL

How I do pray, O Heavenly Father, that You will put Your arms around all the children of this nation and of the world. I pray that every young person I meet today will know, without a particular word or action, that I love You, dear Heavenly Father, and that I love them. Because You have loved me, and taken care of me so wonderfully through the years . . . I thank You.

SEPTEMBER 28

Take a lesson from the ants, you lazy fellow. Learn from their ways and be wise! For though they have no king to make them work, yet they labor hard all summer, gathering food for the winter. But you—all you do is sleep. When will you wake up?

"Let me sleep a little longer!" Sure, just a little more! And as you sleep, poverty creeps upon you like a robber and destroys you; want attacks you in full armor.

PROVERBS 6:6–11 TLB

When will we wake up? What a lesson for us today . . . and in this generation. I grew up in the generation of the work ethic. My grandmother raised me on the farm most of my life after my mother died. She believed in work. She believed that laziness was a sin with a capital *S*. But more importantly, she taught me to love work. She taught me that it was a royal thing to work and to serve. She liked the old proverb, "Early to bed, early to rise, makes a man healthy, wealthy, and wise."

She taught me the joy of working and also the lesson that if you do not learn to work, you will have a hard row in life, for life is made up of serving and working and laughing and worshipping. All of us heard this little prayer when we were growing up:

> Now I lay me down to sleep
> I pray the Lord my soul to keep,
> If I should die before I wake,
> I pray the Lord my soul to take.

This verse does not dwell on death, but on the everlasting providence of God, that whatever happened we would be in His care. There is a second verse which most people in America have forgotten. We all need to be reminded . . .

> Now I wake me up to work,
> I pray the Lord I will not shirk . . .
> If I should die before tonight,
> I pray the Lord my work's all right.

We use a verse in our company that goes like this:

> If you work for the thing you believe in
> You are rich, though the way is rough,
> If you are working only for money,
> You can never make quite enough.

O God, help us to make our work worthy. May it be an honor to You and a blessing to others.

SEPTEMBER 29

For there are six things the Lord hates—no seven: Haughtiness, Lying, Murdering, Plotting evil, Eagerness to do wrong, A false witness, Sowing discord among brothers.
PROVERBS 6:16–19 TLB

God names the seven deadly sins:

- Haughtiness
- Lying
- Murdering
- Plotting evil
- Eagerness to do wrong
- A false witness
- Sowing discord among brothers.

It is our practice to list them vertically and then next to them to list the opposites, which would be the things pleasing to the Lord.

- Haughtiness—you may want to write your own definition, but my definition for the opposite of haughtiness is "the serving heart." Haughtiness is the feeling that I am better than you, henceforth you must serve me. Sometimes we can be haughty over our experience, haughty over money, haughty over knowledge, haughty over position. The one real way to avoid that is to have a "serving heart" with whomever we might be, or wherever we might be.
- The opposite of lying, of course, would be telling the truth.
- The opposite of murdering would be valuing a human life.
- The opposite of plotting evil would be looking for ways to be good to people.

• Eagerness to do wrong ... would be opposite to delight in doing right.

• The opposite of a false witness would be a truthful witness.

• Sowing discord among brothers—this we call *gossiping,* and I have an abhorrence of gossip. In fact it is one of the tenets of our company that we have no alcoholic beverages at any Home Interiors' functions, and we try to avoid gossip, because gossip can be as deadly as drunkenness.

I heard the following definition of gossiping: "Gossiping is sharing negative information about a person or a situation with someone who is neither a part of the problem or the solution."

Proverbs 11:13 (TLB) says, "A gossip goes around spreading rumors, while a trustworthy man tries to quiet them."

Verse 20 of chapter 26 (TLB) says, "Fire goes out for lack of fuel, and tensions disappear when gossip stops." When someone in whose company I am brings up a bit of gossip that is destructive or derogatory about someone else, I have found the best way to stop it is to simply say, "You know, you and I are both intelligent people, and I believe we can find something more constructive to talk about." That usually ends it right there, because gossip can be deadly, it can be destructive, and it hurts everyone it touches. We must continue everlastingly to ask ourselves, *Is this true? Is it beneficial to all concerned? Is it fair? Will it build people?* If it does not, then keep it to yourself.

> *Heavenly Father, today make me aware of the destructiveness of idle talk and gossip. Help me to guard my tongue and watch every word I say, and may it please You and build others. Sometimes I might need a divine clothespin to keep my mouth shut when I want to talk. Help me to guard my tongue for Jesus' sake.*

SEPTEMBER 30

There is so much good, common sense in the Proverbs—so much practical help in how to live and how to behave.

Go back through this month and pick out the Proverb that has made the greatest impact on your life thus far. Write it down:

_____

_____

_____

Memorize it—say it over and over as you drive along and do your work today.

Then, for the next month, in addition to the particular Scriptures accompanying our devotionals each day, read one chapter of Proverbs. There are exactly enough to read one chapter each day in October. Read them in *The Living Bible* and you will find them as timely, fresh, and applicable as today's newspaper, but with far more lasting, life-changing benefits. Try it for a month, and it will bless your life—I guarantee it!

October

OCTOBER 1

For the value of wisdom is far above rubies; nothing can be compared with it. Wisdom and good judgment live together, for wisdom knows where to discover knowledge and understanding. If anyone respects and fears God, he will hate evil. For wisdom hates pride, arrogance, corruption and deceit of every kind.

PROVERBS 8:11–13 TLB

There is a wisdom that lifts human life above arrogance, above corruption, above pride, above deceit, and certainly above the misuse of sexual energies. Sexual immoralities prove degrading to the individual. They damage the capacity for genuine love responsibilities, impair human relationships, and reduce God-given sex drive to an animallike experience.

We have been so misled by current media and literature that we think there should be no rules or regulations concerning sexual energies. But life *itself* imposes rules and regulations, and experience teaches that lasting love relationships depend upon learning from our Creator how He planned the perfect sexual relationship. We live in a fallen world, and there is no perfect person or perfect situation, but He says, "I, Wisdom, give good advice and common sense. . . . I love all who love me. Those who search for me shall surely find me. . . . My paths are those of justice and right. Those who love and follow me are indeed wealthy. I fill their treasuries" (Proverbs 8:14, 17, 20, 21 TLB).

Then in Proverbs 9:10 (TLB) it says, "For the reverence and fear of God are basic to all wisdom. Knowing God results in every other kind of understanding."

If we do not come to God in worshipful submission, we will be overcome with the problems and frustrations of life.

O Lord, we pray that we might return to the moral values which made us strong and great and seek the wisdom You have for us.

OCTOBER 2

For the reverence and fear of God are basic to all wisdom. Knowing God results in every other kind of understanding.
                                                PROVERBS 9:10 TLB

There will be days when you feel that you have really blown it, and days when you can't quite get it "to gel." On such days you have to come back to the basics: "For the reverence and fear of God is basic to all wisdom. Knowing God results in every other kind of understanding."

I well remember my sweet friend, Tom Landry. Several years ago, when his Dallas Cowboys had lost a game they should have won, he said that after the game he was going over everything in his mind. Why did they lose the game? They should have won it! He thought of every player and examined his relationship with him—*Is my relationship intact with the quarterback?*—How was his relationship with all their families? How was his relationship with Jesus Christ? With his son Tom? With the rest of his family?

After deciding that his relationships with the people who were important in his life were intact, he resolved that, if he just kept on doing what he knew to do, everything would come out right—*as long as the relationships were intact.* That year they won their first super bowl!

So the basic issue is this: **"Knowing God results in every other kind of understanding."**

Lord, help us to get back to the basics and trust You for understanding and wisdom in our dealings with others.

OCTOBER 3

Happy is the man with a level-headed son; sad the mother of a rebel. Ill-gotten gain brings no lasting happiness; right living does. The Lord will not let a good man starve to death, nor will he let the wicked man's riches continue forever. Lazy men are soon poor; hard workers get rich. A wise youth makes hay while the sun shines, but what a shame to see a lad who sleeps away his hour of opportunity. The good man is covered with blessings from head to foot, but an evil man inwardly curses his luck. We all have happy memories of good men gone to their reward, but the names of wicked men stink after them. The wise man is glad to be instructed, but a self-sufficient fool falls flat on his face. A good man has firm footing, but a crook will slip and fall. Winking at sin leads to sorrow; bold reproof leads to peace.

PROVERBS 10:1–10 TLB

The Bible has much to say about instruction, constantly pointing out that it takes instruction, discipline, and work to give us the skill to live our lives beautifully and effectively. Proverbs does not propose to change the world. It teaches us how to have the skill to live in it—you might say to live positively in a negative world. I read in a current issue of *Time* magazine about the tremendous rate of suicide along Chicago's wealthy lake coast line. The behavioral psychologists were trying to figure out why the rate was so high among these young people who had been given every opportunity, everything that life could offer. Yet they talked of suicide as easily as buying a new pair of socks.

God help us when we rear young people and do not teach them that God has a plan for their life, that He is the real reality, that there are challenges to be met, there is an excitement and an exhilaration in knowing God and having the power of His Holy Spirit within us that puts intoxication in the shade. God forgive us for not teaching young people the joy of work, the value of service. There is so much work to be done, so many people to serve.

OCTOBER 4

*We all have happy memories of good men gone to their re-
ward, . . .*

PROVERBS 10:7 TLB

When you go to Big Sky, Montana, and you worship in the
Soldier's Chapel there, you find these words dedicated to the
young men who died to defend our beautiful land and to protect
our precious freedom:

> They grow not old as we who are left grow old.
>   Age shall not weary them or the years condemn;
> At the going down of the sun and in the morning
>   We will remember them.

Just today I received some mail from the Disabled Veterans,
and I thought again how easy it is while going about our busy
duties to forget not only the ones who paid the supreme sacrifice
of life, but those who are disabled and are living in hospitals or
institutions.

O God of Hosts, be with us yet, Lest we forget, lest we forget.

OCTOBER 5

*We all have happy memories of good men gone to their re-
ward, but the names of wicked men stink after them.*

PROVERBS 10:7 TLB

Have you ever thought to thank God for the precious gift of
memory? Oh, it is one of God's most pleasant gifts to His human
creatures. Memory can bless or burn—according to how we
use it.

Like all God's gifts, it was intended for our good and joy. We
are in the memory-making business every day. In our homes and

work we are building memories for our children, our loved ones, ourselves.

We would do well to hold the beautiful memories in our hearts; we would do better to blot out those that are detrimental to progress.

Dear Father, help us to remember only the good, only the true, only the beautiful.

OCTOBER 6

Hatred stirs old quarrels, but love overlooks insults.

PROVERBS 10:12 TLB

Today's verse in Proverbs reminds us of that wonderful thirteenth chapter of 1 Corinthians (vv. 1–7, 13 TLB), where Paul tells us that although we have all kinds of gifts and all kinds of talent, and we could do mighty and great things—if we did not love others, we would only be making noise. "Love is very patient and kind, never jealous or envious, never boastful or proud, never haughty or selfish or rude. Love does not demand its own way. It is not irritable or touchy. It does not hold grudges and will hardly even notice when others do it wrong. It is never glad about injustice, but rejoices whenever truth wins out." And Paul finishes with these words, "If you love someone, you will be loyal to him no matter what the cost. You will always believe in him, always expect the best of him, always stand your ground in defending him. . . . There are three things that remain—faith, hope, and love—and the greatest of these is love."

I can never read these words, or write them down, but that I have to fall on my knees and ask God to help me have this kind of love, for I do not stand up well in this test. I am often impatient; I am sometimes touchy; I am sometimes critical about the inaccurate work of others. I *am* loyal; I would defend someone to death—but oh, how hard it is to live up to this example of love: overlook insults; don't get your feelings hurt; don't push the rejection button when somebody criticizes you; be open for instruction and criticism. We just have to stop and pray that God will help us, that more and more of His Spirit will control us, and less and less will self be on the throne.

Our very nature is selfish. Our very attitude is "he can't do this to me." And so it takes the power of the Holy Spirit, daily, moment by moment, to teach us to love. When we walk with love, we walk under God's protection. When we step out of the love walk, we step into the territory of the enemy—Satan. And out there he can get at us and harass us, and make us unhappy, make us miserable to be with and to live with.

Our faith in God is a beginning principle, and a *continuing* walk.

O God, help me to walk in love today—in Jesus' love.

OCTOBER 7

A wise man holds his tongue. Only a fool blurts out everything he knows; that only leads to sorrow and trouble. . . . Don't talk so much. You keep putting your foot in your mouth. Be sensible and turn off the flow!

PROVERBS 10:14, 19 TLB

How easy it is to read these words . . . and how hard it is to live them out! I have always said that God was trying to tell us something when He gave us two ears and one mouth: We should listen twice as much as we talk.

There have been many books about the art of listening. And one of the biggest complaints that teenagers have of their parents is, "They don't listen to me."

Perhaps today we can try a little experiment. Each time someone starts to talk to you today, *stop* and *listen* intently, giving them your complete attention, putting out of your mind what you want to say next. Listen with your eyes, your mind, with your face, and your attitude. Listen to what he or she is trying to tell you. Listen to the words . . . and especially if it is a woman, listen to what she *really* means. Women seldom say what they mean, or mean what they say.

When a woman says to her husband, "You don't love me any more," she does not want him to agree with her, she wants him to reassure her that he *does* love her. Women need lots of reassurance.

And so we have to listen to what the heart is saying, not just to the words. Understand where the words are coming from. If it is from hurt or disappointment or rejection or sorrow . . . I am so grateful that God listens. He said, "Call unto me and I will hear you." He is never too busy. My real Boss is never out. I can call Him anytime, person-to-person collect, and He listens.

And I am also glad that God never said to me, "Mary, you are talking just like a woman." No, God my Father listens! And I am trying to learn to listen, too.

Today, let's listen to the voice of our families, our co-workers, and the Holy Spirit.

OCTOBER 8

The Lord's blessing is our greatest wealth. All our work adds nothing to it.

PROVERBS 10:22 TLB

In our organization, we have adopted today's verse to remind us continually that the Lord's blessing, His guidance, His help, His providence, is our greatest wealth. Of course we have worked hard. Many, many hundreds and thousands of people are working hard, but I have seen hard work come to naught. I have seen difficulties happen that erased many years of hard work, and I have also seen much good work lost for want of a little more.

And, so, we give God the glory, we give Him the credit. We praise His name for His guidance, His providence, His love, His care, His blessing for us.

Sometimes I sound real cocky, for I am self-confident, but, let me tell you, my cockiness, my confidence, my strength—all are because I worship a big God. The God that is within me is greater than the difficulties or the problems or the situation without, and so His blessing is truly my greatest wealth, and the greatest wealth too of our company, our family, and the larger family of associates and friends.

We sing a chorus at our mountain retreat that goes like this:

> I love the Father, I love His only Son
> I love the Spirit. I love the three in one . . .
> For He created me; redeemed and set me free,
> Praise Him, praise Him, praise Him!

Thank You, Father. Thank You, Jesus. Thank You, Holy Spirit.

OCTOBER 9

Reverence for God adds hours to each day; so how can the wicked expect a long, good life?

PROVERBS 10:27 TLB

How often we all have made the comment, "I don't have *time.* I didn't have the *time* to do thus and so. Where does the *time* go? I never have enough *time.*"

God has a word for that. He understands our limitations. He is not limited by clocks or calendars as we are here on this finite planet.

Oh, how many of us would like to add hours to each day. We think if we could just have twenty-five hours a day, we would do more.

There is a book called *The Tyranny of the Urgent,* written by Charles E. Hummel and published by InterVarsity Press. It is the best book on time management that I have ever seen. Just to quote a couple of paragraphs:

> When we stop to evaluate, we realize that our dilemma goes deeper than shortage of time. It is basically the prob-

lem of priorities. Hard work does not hurt us. We all know what it is to go full speed for long hours totally involved in an important task. The resulting weariness is matched by a sense of achievement and joy. Not hard work, but doubt and misgivings produce anxiety. As we review a month or a year, we become oppressed by the pile of unfinished tasks. We sense easily that we may have failed to do the important. The whims of other people's demands have driven us under the reef of frustration. We confess quite apart from our sins, we have left undone those things which we ought to have done, and done those things which we ought not to have done.

Several years ago an experienced cotton mill manager said to me "your greatest danger is in letting the urgent things crowd out the important." We live in constant tension between the urgent and the important. The problem is that the important task rarely must be done today, or even this week. Extra hours of prayer and Bible study, a visit, careful study of an important book. Those projects can wait, but the urgent task calls for instant action, endless demands and pressure, every hour of the day.

A man's home is no longer his castle, no longer a place away from urgent tasks, because the telephone reaches the walls with imperious demands. The momentary appeal of these tasks seems irresistible and important, and they devour our energy. But in the light of time's perspective, their deceptive prominence fades. With the sense of loss, we recall the important task pushed aside. We realize we have becomes slaves to the "Tyranny of the Urgent."

What is the answer? One of the first places to start is embodied in the words an old missionary wrote in her Bible:

> You ask me what is the will of God
>   And I will answer true . . .
> It is the nearest thing that should be done
>   That God can do—through you.

It might be tending a child, preparing a meal with love and beauty, seeing that the family has clean sheets and clean clothes, answering the phone call of a friend who needs encouragement, helping a co-worker feel better about her work, comforting a husband whose job has grown monotonous and tedious ... or comforting a husband whose job has just been lost.

Lord, how we do pray that we will not overlook the important or the urgent. So teach us to number our days that we may rejoice in them.

OCTOBER 10

The Lord hates cheating and delights in honesty.
                                          PROVERBS 11:1 TLB

How interesting it is that of the 535 men and women who make up the Congress of the United States of America, there is a higher percentage of men and women who have been convicted of crime than there is in the poorest ghetto in the United States.

All about us we read of crime in high places, low places, and in between, of cheating in college, of how the policy of "honesty being the best policy" has become eroded in our beloved nation. We have found that there are many people who do not know what the word *honest* means. They often think it means that one would not steal money out of the cash register. But honesty has such a wide and beautiful meaning.

First of all, we have to be honest with ourselves—look at ourselves as we really are, refuse to accept our own excuses for failure or for avoidance of duty. And then we must be honest with our families. Being honest with our children—this is a tough one. We want them to think we are honorable people, upright, and yet we know the pettiness that we often cover up. It is tough to say "I am sorry, I was wrong; please forgive me," to your children or your mate. How much cleaner we feel when we can be honest with our families.

Second, be honest with God and say "I failed today. Please

forgive me. I want to do better." So many people carry a burden of guilt around, day into night and night into day, when our loving Heavenly Father—because of Jesus—is waiting to take the guilt away and cover it with forgiveness.

Psychologists tell us that most of the people in institutions are there because of guilt—guilt that they carry as a burden. Oh, how sad! Guilt is a burden a believer does not need to have, for Jesus came and died on the cross so that we might be forever cleansed of guilt when He bore all our sins in His own body.

Thank You, Jesus, for cleansing me. Oh, how many times I come to pray: O God, forgive me. O God, cleanse me. O God, show me. Help me today to be Your person here on earth— with my family—with my associates—in my community.

OCTOBER 11

Without wise leadership, a nation is in trouble; but with good counselors there is safety.

PROVERBS 11:14 TLB

How we pray for our nation in these difficult days—days of inflation, days of turmoil, days when all around us the nations of the world are changing. Those that were once our friends are now our enemies; those that were once our enemies are now claiming to be friends. How we need wise leadership! How we need men and women who are godly, not just in word, but in deed, who come daily to the throne of grace and ask for God's wisdom—wisdom in making decisions, wisdom in looking ahead, wisdom in guiding a nation.

Wisdom has been described as the reverence and awe a person ought to feel when he comes into the presence of God. That is the beginning of wisdom. God is the Creator. God is in this world, and it is only in atheism that we lose the key to the uniqueness of life.

It depends upon a man's soul whether he sees God in the firmament of His handiwork, whether he comes to God for the direction of his life, his duty, his job, his responsibility. And O God, how true it is that the leaders of our nation need good counselors—counselors who are wise and good in the ways of Almighty God, who have submitted their egos to the searching light of the Holy Spirit.

Lord, how we pray that You will raise up men and women today to be Your leaders in this beloved land of America.

OCTOBER 12

It is possible to give away and become richer! It is also possible to hold on too tightly and lose everything. Yes, the liberal man shall be rich! By watering others, he waters himself.
PROVERBS 11:24, 25 TLB

How true it is that you cannot outgive God. God has all the resources. God invented giving. God loves to give. God has a plan that has never been bettered.

Again I talk about tithing. This is giving your tithe to God and then, above that, being generous with those who need it, those who are in difficulty, or those with whom you can share to add joy to their lives.

I am so grateful that God has taught me to have a generous heart. This was also taught to me in my childhood. My grandmother and grandfather always shared with others; no one was ever turned away from our table or our home.

I have found in my life that God's blessings are very abundant, and I am so everlastingly grateful that I really want to share them with every person everywhere. I have to remember that it is God's money, and, as His steward, I have to try to share it in a way that will honor Him and bless others.

I always remember that it was just one little boy's lunch—just enough to feed one little boy—that was given to Jesus, and it fed a multitude.

"Little is much when God is in it." The obedience is mine, the miracle is His!

Dear Jesus, help me to be loyal to You today as You work Your work through me with Your provisions.

OCTOBER 13

A worthy wife is her husband's joy and crown; the other kind corrodes his strength and tears down everything he does.
PROVERBS 12:4 TLB

Mrs. Norman Vincent Peale wrote a book several years ago on how to be a good wife. Something she said in it has stayed in my mind: "Learn your husband. He is unique. He is not like any other husband in the world. Learn your husband."

Learn your husband. Learn what pleases him and try to do more of it. Learn what displeases him and try to do less of it. Also learn his strengths and his weaknesses and do not be afraid to confront in love his weaknesses, because you are to be his helpmate, the one who shores him up when he is weak, and leans on him when he is strong.

I think of the group of women together at a luncheon. A young bride there was speaking to an older woman and she said. "I am rather confused. My husband wants me to lean on him, he wants me to trust his strength, his energy, and his wisdom—and yet he depends on me so much of the time. I am confused as to what I should do." The older and wiser woman said, "It is like this. You lean on him on one side and prop him up on the other."

Certainly I pray that every one of us who is a wife will build up her husband, build up his ego constantly. Sometimes I put it this way: He has an ego. The greatest enemy to men is ego, and the greatest enemy to women is fatigue. But if you puncture his ego, down he goes. So you might as well learn early, if you are a wife, that you must everlastingly pump up his ego, so you just get to pumping. "I am tired of this. Why doesn't he pump me up for a while?" Sometimes you will feel like this, but I know from experience that God rewards us when we follow Him and try to build up our husbands instead of trying to tear them down.

Dear Father, make me conscious of my husband's needs and help me to be a strength to him.

OCTOBER 14

A worthy wife is her husband's joy and crown; the other kind corrodes his strength and tears down everything he does.
                                              PROVERBS 12:4 TLB

One of the best little books I have ever seen for women was *Ms means Myself,* written by Gladys Hunt. She insists that women are whole people, not defined by what they do, but by what they are as unique individuals. Every woman has the potential for more basic personal freedom and fulfillment than she now experiences. Discerning what is really valuable will continue to be the heart of the issue. The answer is not unisex, equal tyranny, or the demise of male chauvinism. A woman's freedom grows out of quality relationship with God, and thus with herself.

God, oh, how I do pray that more wives will read these verses from Proverbs and wisely ask God's help in building up their home.

OCTOBER 15

It is better to get your hands dirty—and eat, than to be too proud to work—and starve.... Work hard and become a leader; be lazy and never succeed.
                                          PROVERBS 12:9, 24 TLB

God ordained work to be a necessary part of the human existence. When Adam and Eve disobeyed God, even work suffered, because up until that time, it had been all joy. Adam was given the job of taking care of the Garden of Eden. Because we are in a fallen world, part of the result was that work is difficult. Yet, I have learned that work is really a blessing, and even hard work can be a blessing.

We hear a great deal these days about meaningful work—and yet, if our hearts are right, and if our desires are in delighting the Lord, most any work can be "meaningful." There is a story of a man who kept the boilers in one of the river boats in Mark Twain's time, and he kept them so beautifully clean and shiny. Someone asked him why he spent so much time on those old boilers, and why they were so beautiful, and why they shone so, and why he took such a pride in them. He answered, "I have a glory." His glory was doing his job, his very best job, making those old boilers shine.

I have always set a lot of store by hard work, and I have done a lot of it in my lifetime. For the most part, I loved every bit of it. I thank my grandmother for teaching me the joy of work, and the excitement of seeing the job well-done, and the earned rest after a day's work. I love the song, "We'll work 'till Jesus comes, and we'll be gathered home."

Lord, how grateful we are to be able to work! Help us to approach our tasks with joy and zest.

OCTOBER 16

Anxious hearts are very heavy but a word of encouragement does wonders!

PROVERBS 12:25 TLB

Most things in life tend to tarnish. Silver must be polished. Brass must be rubbed often to have a sheen. Even stainless steel must be carefully kept.

We must not allow life to become ordinary. We have to continually be on guard, or life can become so dull.

That is the thing I have learned about success—you have to do it all over again every morning. We all need to breathe a new sense of privilege and opportunity into daily tasks.

All around us are people who need the touch of love and compassion and caring. When we share HOPE, when we share ENTHUSIASM and COURAGE and BEAUTY with each other, we are sharing it with someone made in the image of GOD.

When this knowledge really grips you, it will generate a drive within you; you will find it generates a "double radiance" for you and for those around you.

I am reminded of an old definition of *worry:* "Worry is an old man with bowed head carrying a load of feathers which he thinks are lead."

There are many weary strugglers for whom the fresh enthusiasm of life has been lost and a dullness has set in as they seem to struggle beneath their "loads of lead."

How precious is the gift of encouragement . . . of praise . . . of hope.

Thank You, dear Lord, for the gift of hope.

OCTOBER 17

Anxious hearts are very heavy but a word of encouragement does wonders!

PROVERBS 12:25 TLB

Oh, how grateful I am that the good Lord has given me the gift of *encouragement.* How many times I have learned that what most of this world needs is a little encouragement—a dose of hope. Oh, how wonderful it is to form the habit of encouraging people. I am grateful—I am so everlastingly grateful—that somehow God has given me this gift. I have tried to use it in a way that would be to His honor and a blessing to others—to encourage people along life's road.

Yes, give a little love and kindness. Lift up someone whose

burden is heavy. Walk beside them, give a little word of encouragement. Oh, how many times it comes at just the right moment.

Thank You, Lord, for Your special gifts to us. Help us to be aware of the feelings of those around us and to extend a hand of hope and encouragement.

OCTOBER 18

Despise God's Word and find yourself in trouble. Obey it and succeed.

PROVERBS 13:13 TLB

It bothers me that there are so many people in this nation today that have never had an opportunity to fall in love with God's Word. We give *The Living Bible* to all our managers and employees, and many times we have had them say, "This is the first time I have had a Bible in my hands."

I have a goal, I have a desire, I have a purpose. I am called to live in perfect relationship to God so that my life produces a longing after God in other lives—not admiration for myself.

GOOD CHEER

Have you had a kindness shown?
Pass it on.
'Twas not given for you alone—
Pass it on.
Let it travel down the years,
Let it wipe another's tears,
Till in heaven the deed appears—
Pass it on.

Someone has said that no smile is so beautiful as the one that struggles through tears. If we only use our afflictions and troubles aright we can soften and enrich our natures by our sufferings, our disappointments, or we can turn them into instruments of torture.

O precious Jesus, this is my prayer and goal. If I can just create a desire, a longing to know Him, to get to know Jesus better through His Word. To know God, to learn of Him, and consequently, to learn about ourselves. This is my goal. This is my purpose. This is the purpose of this book, these meditations, of everything. Oh, to create a longing to know God better.

OCTOBER 19

An unreliable messenger can cause a lot of trouble. Reliable communication permits progress.

PROVERBS 13:17 TLB

We work in our business to become reliable communicators so that progress and growth might be permitted. I learned a long time ago there are certain nonconductors of electric power, and there are certain nonconductors of spiritual power—nonconductors that keep communication from coming through.

Hate is a nonconductor of spiritual power. Resentment is a nonconductor, bitterness is a nonconductor; and unreliability is a nonconductor.

Oh, how we are communicators—every one of us is a communicator. When we walk into a room, we communicate either love or hostility. We communicate an "upness" or a "downness." We communicate encouragement or discouragement. We communicate a positive outlook or a negative outlook. We communicate God's love or apathy. We communicate confidence or anxiety.

Dear God, I pray that each of us will become a reliable communicator and that there will be no nonconductors to inhibit God's love, God's message, God's truth, and the joy that can come from loving and sharing.

OCTOBER 20

*If you refuse to discipline your son, it proves you don't love
him; for if you love him you will be prompt to punish him.*
PROVERBS 13:24 TLB

Many books have been written on how to discipline children
and how to bring them up in the love and admonition of the
Lord. God's Word in Ephesians has much to say to fathers and
mothers, but especially to fathers.

All through His Word we are taught that discipline with love
teaches a child that he is cared for—that somebody cares how he
grows up, that there are limits.

A young teenager used to stay at our house a lot. Once, I asked
him whether his parents knew that he was there, for it was growing late. Did he plan to go home or spend the night? Had he
asked his parents if this was all right? He answered, "Oh, no,
they don't know where I am, they don't care." I learned from
that: A teenager—any child—recognizes that **if parents care,
they set limits.** There are disciplines; there are standards, there
are rules of the family. They have hours to come home, hours to
be in, and they have family standards to be met.

We have a whole generation that has grown up in this permissive society, and so many times they do not know what is expected of them. Consequently, they feel at war with themselves
and with society.

I remember Ruth Graham saying that during the resurfacing
of a highway near her home in North Carolina, there was a period of time when there were no white lines down the center or
the sides. She observed that people felt ill at ease, they did not
know whether they were in the right lane or not, and they were
not nearly as comfortable as when the lines were there. She put it
this way: "We have turned our young people loose on the high-
ways of life without any white lines to guide them, no speed
limits, and wondered why there are so many wrecks in their high
speed cars."

*Dear God, Your Word says that if we refuse to discipline our
children it proves we do not love them. Help us to be prompt
to discipline and care about them and set standards and teach
them Your discipline and Your plans.*

OCTOBER 21

*A wise woman builds her house, while a foolish woman tears
hers down by her own efforts.*

PROVERBS 14:1 TLB

Jeanie Hendricks tells women that if they are wives, and have
good husbands, every morning they should hold a thanksgiving
service for them.

How true! And how many, many times in this modern world, a
woman corrodes her husband's strength and tears him down.

My heart goes out to the many foolish women who are tearing
down their houses, who are more concerned with "rights" than
with responsibilities, who are more concerned with "What am I
going to get out of it?" than with "What can I give to this relationship?" They are more concerned with equality than with liberty. Maybe it is because I have seen people equally angry,
equally bitter, equally hateful, that I am much more concerned
with liberty than equality—the *liberty* to become the woman
that God wants me to be, to become the wife that God wants
me to be.

It is not easy to be a wife in today's world, with its constant
pressure not to be submissive to another person. I learned a long
time ago that a wife is to be submissive to her husband's *needs,*
not his will. Be submissive only to the will of God! Put God first,
and somehow He will work things out and help you be submissive to your husband's needs.

Today, I hear young women say, "But I don't love him any
more. He does not make me happy." Oh, how sad! They have
gone into marriage for the wrong reason. It is so true that if we
expect somebody else to make us happy, we will be disappointed.
Happiness comes from loving service. Happiness comes from fol-

lowing through, sometimes in doing things you do not like to do, sometimes from just doing duty rather than wishes. But the real joy of a relationship never comes from being selfish and wanting our own way all the time.

God, may we be less concerned with "rights" than we are with our husbands' needs and our responsibilities to them.

OCTOBER 22

Reverence for God gives a man deep strength; his children have a place of refuge and security.

PROVERBS 14:26 TLB

We should pray for the men of our land, that they have deep strength, that children have a place of refuge and security.

My wonderful friend, Ralph Baker, guided our company in its early days, and was my Sunday School superintendent for twenty-two years. The greatest Christian friend I ever had, he went home to be with God in the middle of a step ten years ago. My sweet friend put his arms around the world. His reverence for God was continuous and everlasting. He had a precious wife and reared a wonderful family who are now grown with homes of their own. This reverence for God gave him deep strength. Not only his children, but I, and my children, and others, found him to be a place of refuge and security. I thank the Lord that I knew him and had the privilege of having him for a friend.

Many times when I have worked all day and have decisions to make, I run them by the test of *What would Ralph think? What would he do? How would he determine what decision to make for our company?*

I am so grateful that we had him during the early years, and that he was the architect of our corporation. Most of all, I thank the Lord for letting me teach in his department for twenty-two years and have the privilege of knowing this man for whom, truly, the Lord was a fountain of life.

Dear God, this reminds us, of course, that the good we do lives after us in the lives of many people. I thank You for that knowledge.

OCTOBER 23

Godliness exalts a nation, but sin is a reproach to any people.
                                          PROVERBS 14:34 TLB

All thinking people are concerned these days with the erosion of morality in our own precious United States of America. I am reminded again of the words of Tocqueville when he came to America:

I sought for the greatness and genius of America
In her commodious harbors and great rivers,
... and it was not there.

I sought for the greatness and genius of America
In her fertile fields and boundless forest,
... and it was not there.

I sought for the greatness and genius of America
In her rich mines and her vast world commerce,
... and it was not there.

I sought for the greatness and genius of America
In her public school system and her institutions of learning,
... and it was not there.

I sought for the greatness and genius of America
In her Democratic Congress and matchless Constitution,
... and it was not there.

Not until I went into the churches of America and heard her Pulpits flame with righteousness did I understand the *Secret* of her *Genius* and *Power!*

America is great because America is good, and if America ever ceases to be good—America will cease to be great.

O God our help in ages past, our hope for years to come—our shelter from the stormy blast, and our eternal home. . . . How we do pray that America will return to the God of her fathers, and that once more our nation can be called "good." You have told us "If my people who are called by my name, will turn from their wicked ways and call unto me, I will hear and heal their land." God help us.

OCTOBER 24

Today we're just going to "walk through" Proverbs 15 (TLB) and savor some of its richer verse:

Verse 1: A soft answer turns away wrath,
     but harsh words cause quarrels.
Verse 4: Gentle words cause life and health;
     griping brings discouragement.
Verse 13: A happy face means a glad heart;
     a sad face means a breaking heart.
Verse 15: When a man is gloomy, everything seems to go
     wrong; when he is cheerful, everything seems
     right!

All of these verses serve to remind us of the song written by Ella Wheeler Wilcox:

   Laugh and the world laughs with you,
    Weep and you weep alone
   For the sad old earth must borrow its mirth
    But has trouble enough of its own.

Lord Jesus, help us to stay true to You, even though we might suffer because of it. We know Your plan finally ends in good—thereby happiness.

OCTOBER 25

We can always "prove" that we are right, but is the Lord con-
vinced? Commit your work to the Lord, then it will succeed.
The Lord has made everything for his own purposes—even the
wicked, for punishment.

PROVERBS 16:2–5 TLB

How easy it is to rationalize what we do and convince ourselves that it is right, but we really can't fool God. So often we
judge others by their actions—but, we judge ourselves by our intentions. How many times we make resolutions and we intend to
do better, and for a while we do—then we blow it! We lose our
tempers and say something we shouldn't.

How true it is that we really can't do it alone. I have written in
my Bible these words: "Our part is to persevere in obeying God.
Go as far as you can." Thus we learn for ourselves that the Lord
leads us.

It is sometimes difficult to learn the difference between the
pride of achievement—pride in our work—and self-centered
pride. I have always believed that God wants us to do our best
for Him, and anything done for Him—whether it is a book or a
tract, a magazine or a film, a song or a visit—should be given our
best.

I have agonized over this book, this cup of daily meditations,
for I want to do the best for God. And yet I know—little is much
when God is in it.

And so I just pray that He will take the thoughts that are sometimes so difficult to express ... and I earnestly pray that "the
words of my mouth, and the meditations of my heart, be acceptable in thy sight, O Lord, my strength, and my redeemer"
(Psalms 19:14).

When I talk to a group and people come up with words of
praise there is always that nagging temptation just for a moment
to accept the praise for myself. Then I think of Corrie ten Boom
who would take the words from people as a flower, and each
night she would take the flowers, the words of praise or the special response, and offer them as a bouquet to Jesus the Lord.

Dear Lord, I pray that my work is all right . . . for Jesus' sake.

OCTOBER 26

When a man is trying to please God, God makes even his worst enemies to be at peace with him.

PROVERBS 16:7 TLB

I have counted on the promise of today's verse when someone was moving against us. I have found that it is really easy to love your enemies—until you have one, and then it takes the grace of God to accomplish it. Sometimes it takes a while for God to work out a difficulty with another person. I remember something my grandmother always said to me, "When you are right, time is on your side."

Many times when I have been criticized and treated unfairly, I have remembered these words, remembered that life is not always fair, but if you are right, time is on your side. More importantly, you are on God's side! And God will work things out in His own beautiful way.

Dear Father, through Thy love and goodness, help us to stay on Your side and bring others with us.

OCTOBER 27

We should make plans—counting on God to direct us. . . . God blesses those who obey him; happy the man who puts his trust in the Lord.

PROVERBS 16:9, 20 TLB

Make big plans when you plan with God—as God directs you. Always remember the words of Hudson Taylor: "God's work—done in God's way—will never lack God's support."

*Gracious Father, help us to plan our work and work our plan
all in Thy name.*

OCTOBER 28

*The Lord demands fairness in every business deal. He estab-
lished this principle.*

PROVERBS 16:11 TLB

Businesses that are successful—that are a blessing to others—
are established on the principles that God has laid down. I have
observed that there is no business that has been truly successful
over a long period of time, and that has been a blessing to others,
that hasn't been built on the principles that God laid down for
His people. Many times the people involved may not even know
that they are following God's principles and may not even acknowledge Him as their Heavenly Father, yet the principles by
which the people truly succeed are found in His Book.

*Father in heaven, guide us with diligence in our business and
in Thy business.*

OCTOBER 29

*Idle hands are the devil's workshop; idle lips are his mouth-
piece.*

PROVERBS 16:27 TLB

How many times I remember my precious little grandmother
repeating today's verse, reminding me that if I was not busy
doing something constructive, Satan or his little imps would
tempt me to do something destructive.

We always had so much work to do as kids that we did not
have time to get into mischief. I guess that is a good thing, for I
had a great imagination. I am so grateful that my grandchildren
are being taught to work and are being given many responsibil-

ities, jobs to do from the time they are little. My son Don's two boys have worked in the warehouse for several summers, and this summer my granddaughter, Christi, worked in the warehouse for our company. All are being taught the value of work and the temptation of idleness.

I mentioned earlier the high suicide rate among the children of the affluent, and I thought, *How sad!* When we were growing up you never heard of a young person taking his life. We were too busy trying to survive. There was so much work to do. Of course we did not have television. A psychiatrist who treats depressed teenagers on Chicago's North Shore indicates that television leads children to expect quick answers and undermines their ability to tolerate frustration. Programs present serious problems and then solve them in half an hour. Life just does not work that way. Other experts blame the breakdown of the extended family, the vise of the narcissist culture.

In the post-Vietnam disillusionment with politics, it was heartbreakingly sad that the young, with so much of life ahead of them, would have such idle hands and idle minds that their thoughts would turn inward to utter depression.

Gracious Lord, keep our hearts, and minds, and mouths tuned to Thy will; keep us busy in Thy way.

OCTOBER 30

It is hard to stop a quarrel once it starts, so don't let it begin.
PROVERBS 17:14 TLB

The Scriptures admonish us, "Don't let the sun go down on your wrath" (*see* Ephesians 4:26). What wonderful advice for all of us! Don't let a quarrel begin. I have talked with many counselors who deal in marital difficulties, and they say that even after bitter fights a husband and wife often cannot remember what little thing triggered the argument.

I once read that there are some rules which you must follow if you do not want a quarrel to get out of hand:

- Don't ever bring up the kinfolks of your mate.
- Don't use the word *never,* as in "You *never* do this," or "you *never* do that."
- Don't use the word *always,* as in, "You are *always* late," or "You are *always* on the phone."

I wish I knew much more about how to help people who have gotten in the habit of quarreling. Again I just have to come back to God's Word, because it teaches forgiveness, it teaches love, and it teaches how practical it is to keep silent. The Bible teaches it is better to be slow-tempered than famous, it is better to have self-control than to control an army.

Gracious Lord, even as we have been forgiven, help us to forgive others. May we always be gentle and ready to forgive.

OCTOBER 31

Fall is in the air. Just as it is time to rake up all the leaves and clean up our yards, getting ready for Winter, we should mentally and spiritually rake up all the bits and pieces of knowledge and inspiration we have gleaned thus far from our mornings together with the Lord—just "touching base" with Him, seeking His wisdom and guidance, learning of His love and care for us.

We never know when the wintertime of loss or disappointment might come into our lives, and we need to be fortified to face such times with our storehouses full of His strength and wisdom to see us through.

- Practice the Presence of the Lord. . . .
- Claim His promises for your own. . . .

- Ponder the truths we've covered together. . . .
- Envelop yourself with His warmth and know, "If winter comes, can spring be far behind?"

He *will* make the sun to shine again, but better yet, He will bring joy and beauty even in the glistening snow of wintertime.

November

NOVEMBER 1

It is hard to stop a quarrel once it starts, so don't let it begin.
PROVERBS 17:14 TLB

Don't constantly criticize, complain, or condemn. Occasionally you can swallow your pride without getting indigestion. Don't let the sun go down on your wrath. Whenever you do get into a quarrel, don't go to bed angry, settle it somehow. As Proverbs 21:9 (TLB) says, "It is better to live in the corner of an attic than with a crabby woman in a lovely home." Every woman and man should try to develop a Christian disposition. Most of the problems that bring about a miserable disposition arise from an inherent selfishness. These dispositional weaknesses are nourished by self-pity, jealousy, introverted petulance, and self-centeredness. There are many reasons for irritability. Some are physical, such as fatigue, hunger, strain; others are spiritual, which means that not enough time is spent with the Lord.

> Are you sure you are right?
>   how fine and strong,
> But were you ever just as sure,
>   and wrong?

Dear God, remove from us traces of a critical spirit and grant us instead a determination to exhibit a sunny, positive, loving disposition, slow to anger, quick to forgive.

NOVEMBER 2

Ability to give wise advice satisfies like a good meal!
                                                    PROVERBS 18:20 TLB

Someone once said that you can be "wise or otherwise" and the entire study of Proverbs teaches us to value wisdom. Wisdom seeks to find the good in other people. However, the way some look for fault, you would think there was a reward for finding it. Wisdom possesses strong convictions and expresses them with mercy and graciousness. I have learned it is much wiser not to give advice unless asked. And again, people will not always take your advice.

Wisdom speaks carefully and gently. In Colossians 4:6 it says to let your speech always be gracious, seasoned with salt, so that you may know how you are to answer everyone. I have learned that if I am going to seek advice, I should seek it from someone who has achieved what I want to achieve, and has built the kind of relationships that I want to build.

We have a saying in our business, "Be sure the person you are following has arrived at, or is going toward, the destination where you want to arrive." One of the reasons—one of the *main* reasons—that I go to the Bible for wisdom is because it is the source of all wisdom and truth. How many times we go to the wrong source and get misinformation and follow it to our unhappiness. So the ability to give wise advice satisfies both the person who receives it and the person who gives it, and this ability comes from listening long to the Word of God, learning from the wise and noble, reading the wisdom literature, and studying the lives of people who have made their lives count.

Heavenly Father, today we pray that we will always listen to the right source and go to the right source for answers.

NOVEMBER 3

A man may ruin his chances by his own foolishness and then blame it on the Lord!

PROVERBS 19:3 TLB

It is very difficult for any of us to accept the responsibility for our own foolishness. We either blame it on someone else, or, when that fails, blame it on the Lord, moaning about our "bad luck," or our "fate." I have found that if we truly see God as Someone who, not only *knows* what is good for us, but *wants* what is good for us and will *lead* us into what is good for us, we can trust His wisdom and then give Him the glory and the credit for our achievements, our successes, our happiness, our blessings, our joys. I have seen many people who, by their own foolishness, get themselves terribly into debt and then want somebody to bail them out and pray for God to help them out of their terrible dilemma.

God forgives us for our sins and our mistakes, but we have to live with the results of them. How many times we make plans and then ask God to bless them, instead of asking God to help us make the plans first and then following His direction.

Today, O Lord, we pray that we will seek Your way first, that we will make prayer our first resource rather than our last resort.

NOVEMBER 4

A father can give his sons homes and riches, but only the Lord can give them understanding wives.

PROVERBS 19:14 TLB

How true today's Proverb is! How important it is for both the young man and young woman to seek to find their life's mate in the places where God can give them understanding mates, where God can lead them and guide them into making a right choice.

The choice of a mate is the second most important choice in life. The first most important choice is to live for Jesus Christ instead of self. Once we have made the choice to let God be master, certainly we would want His direction in choosing our life's mate, our life's work, choosing the paths we walk daily.

As parents, one of the greatest things we can give our children is the knowledge and assurance that God loves them, God has a plan for their lives, God seeks to direct them, and the only real success in life is to follow His way.

Heavenly Father, we pray today that all young people, as they struggle with the temptations of life and the pressures of peers, will seek Your way and Your wisdom in every choice of life, and most especially in the choice of a mate.

NOVEMBER 5

When you help the poor you are lending to the Lord—and he pays wonderful interest on your loan!

PROVERBS 19:17 TLB

How wonderfully and beautifully true—you cannot outgive the Lord! It is interesting to look deeply into how we can help the poor. I think of the old adage, "Give a man a fish and he eats for a day—teach him to fish and he eats for a lifetime."

In our business we have tried to apply this principle and have worked hard and long to build a company that would provide jobs with dignity, that would provide opportunity for many who would otherwise be called handicapped, that would provide opportunity for people who do not have all the benefits of education or skill—and God has blessed our efforts beyond anything that we could ever imagine. Truly He pays wonderful interest, plus the glorious satisfaction we get from helping to raise the standards of living for many people, helping to raise the economy of our nation, and helping to provide an atmosphere for the growth of persons. God has given me opportunities to serve, and

I am everlastingly grateful that I learned early how to work, how to serve, how to share. I have been terribly broke at times—what the world would call poor—but I have always tried to remember that both poverty and riches are of the spirit. One is never really poor when he has health, the assurance of God's love, and freedom.

Thank You, Lord Jesus, for this land of freedom. May we continue to work and strive to keep it free.

NOVEMBER 6

Wine gives false courage; hard liquor leads to brawls; what fools men are to let it master them, making them reel drunkenly down the street!

PROVERBS 20:1 TLB

We have a purpose in our company: to build people up, to create an atmosphere that provides for the growth of persons. And so, from the beginning, we have had the principle of no alcoholic beverages at any Home Interiors' function at any time. We also hold to the principle that we will not have gossip which tears, hurts, or destroys. Both are equally destructive. Not long ago I heard that a waiter had given his card to my pastor, and on it he had written a little note that said, "I am so glad I can serve you, for when you or Mary Crowley come in, I know I do not have to serve liquor. One time she was in here with a group of people, and she said 'No, thank you, we just get high on enthusiasm.' "

How pleased I was to hear that I had made an impression on this young man. We never know who is watching us, who is following after us, who will remember our words. I thank the Lord that He gave me the wisdom to say the right thing and to be able to refuse alcoholic beverages with a cheerful remark, for I think it is important how we learn to say no. Learn to say no in a way that will not put people down, but will somehow lift them up. My heart hurts when I think of the times I have not had the sense to say the things in the right way. So I just pray for wisdom, for graciousness, and for the ability to lift people's hearts up and truly get them high on enthusiasm.

Someone said a long time ago that the filling of the Holy Spirit gives an intoxication that puts any other intoxication in the shade.

Dear Lord, just let us be filled with Your spirit today and so intoxicated with genuine love, tenderness, courage and enthusiasm, that all will know that You have the best plan for every life in every way.

NOVEMBER 7

Most people will tell you what loyal friends they are, but are they telling the truth?

Proverbs 20:6 TLB

I am only ONE, but I AM ONE! And what can one "I" do for a better America? I can be of good courage. Fear paralyzes and intimidates and is contagious. Fear tends to cause panic and destroy reason. I must not spread an atmosphere of fear. I must develop *courage* through *faith in God* in my own home and family!

I can instill and practice before my family *respect* and *obedience to the law*—laws of the city, state, county, and federal government, also, laws of God, better known as the Ten Commandments.

I can create the feeling of courage and love and law wherever I go—not preach, but *practice* optimism, confidence, sincere love, respect, and concern for every individual.

I can pray daily for our nation's leaders. Pray that they will seek God's guidance, be a "leaven of good will," make a real contribution to a better America.

Heavenly Father, only through Thy will in our lives will we be able to be what we should be to our fellowman. Help us to truly see him as a brother.

NOVEMBER 8

We can justify our every deed but God looks at our motives.
PROVERBS 21:2 TLB

How this Proverb makes us all turn and look at our motives in the light of God's yardsticks and standards. Since I deal a lot with motivation and have been given the joy, the privilege, and the opportunity to motivate thousands of women to become their best selves, to be what God wants them to be, and to achieve, to be winners over doubt and discouragement, to have a good self-image, I have learned that two-thirds of motivation is motive.

God looks at our motives. He looks at *why* we do things. He looks at what motivates us daily for success, what motivates us to give, what motivates us to act.

It is dangerous to believe one thing and do another. The pull in between is going to catch you. There is no greater conflict than believing one thing and trying to act another way.

God has a wonderful therapy. It is called confession, forgiveness, and restitution.

> *I pray today that my motives will be right, for it is so human to rationalize our behavior and justify our deeds. Dear God, make me a real Christian today.*

NOVEMBER 9

It is better to live in the corner of an attic than with a crabby woman in a lovely home. . . . Better to live in the desert than with a quarrelsome, complaining woman.
PROVERBS 21:9, 19 TLB

How I have had to learn that being critical makes it very difficult for other people to live with you. And I have also learned that no matter what you say, if you say it several times, it sounds like nagging. I can remember when I used to ask my dear husband to mow the lawn when he was sitting reading on his Saturday off, and he would grunt and continue to read or say, "Yes," and go on. Then I would ask him again; then I would tell him again; then I would remind him again. I finally began to realize that the reminding was beginning to be nagging. So I said to myself, "Mary, you are smarter than this. The lawn does not matter to him. He does not like to mow the lawn, and you can hire someone to do the lawn, and leave him be."

It is very easy to fall in the habit of nagging, and it is very tough on everybody else. I well remember learning early to avoid the three c's: Don't criticize, condemn, or complain. And, yet, how hard it is to live up to that!

Dear God, today help me to not become a nagger. Help me to watch the habit patterns of my talk, and help me to remember not to criticize, condemn, or complain so that I can be a pleasant, joyous person to live with and be around.

NOVEMBER 10

For as he thinketh in his heart, so is he. . . .

PROVERBS 23:7

What a person thinks about God affects his life-style. Whether or not he believes in God definitely matters. The kind of person he becomes is determined by his belief or unbelief in God. Our concept of God affects our treatment of other people, either for ill or for good.

Oh, that He might live through us in such a way that those with whom we come in contact might see Him shining through our lives! Let us not be like the fool who said in his heart there is no God.

Lord, we do so want to be the kind of person You would have us be. Strengthen us to find the way You have charted for us and day-by-day to walk in it.

NOVEMBER 11

But if anyone keeps looking steadily into God's law for free men, he will not only remember it but he will do what it says, and God will greatly bless him in everything he does.

JAMES 1:25 TLB

Today is November 11, a day we used to call Armistice Day. Now we call it **Veterans Day.** It is a good day for all of us to remember how high is the price of FREEDOM and to appreciate our opportunities in America.

God is indeed good to us! The road is not always easy; often there have been obstacles and detours. But life is always fruitful—friends, family, and most of all, the love of God make it all worthwhile. We all make mistakes, errors are part of an active life. The important thing in approaching a New Year is to analyze the mistakes of the past, profit from them, right them when we can, hope we are forgiven by those whom we have wounded or wronged—then, forget the mistakes and carry into the New Year only the hopes for the future and joys of today.

May the heart of man seek out the heart of God until armistice will reign supreme.

NOVEMBER 12

You are a poor specimen if you can't stand the pressure of adversity.

PROVERBS 24:10 TLB

Sooner or later all of us will face adversity. Character is not *built* in a crisis, it is *revealed.* How important it is to build a reservoir of wisdom, encouragement, and hope. Repetition builds reputation. What we do daily is building up a life.

No man or woman of the humblest sort can really be strong, gentle, pure and good without somebody being

helped and comforted by the very existence of that goodness.

PHILLIPS BROOKS

*Dear God, help us to redeem the time wisely. Help us to live
every moment of our lives. Help us to look to You as we build
our reservoir of character and perseverance, and not play at
little games.*

NOVEMBER 13

*Fire goes out for lack of fuel, and tensions disappear when
gossip stops.*

PROVERBS 26:20 TLB

Gossiping is a deadly sin, and yet how many people gossip and
do not think about what they are doing. I have seen Christian
people who would gossip about others, hurt their reputation, and
cause dissension, maybe even a split, in a church. How sad—how
horribly sad!

So I think of these words, "Tensions disappear when gossip
stops." Don't gossip! Don't gossip!

I mentioned before that I have a definition of gossiping:
"sharing negative information about a person or situation with
someone who is neither a part of the problem nor of the solution." In fact, remember in Proverbs 6 gossiping was one of the
seven deadly sins that God hates. Sowing discord among the
brothers—oh, how God hates gossip! I have seen it tear friends
apart, tear families apart; and I have seen women who could not
wait to spread gossip, and yet, in their own minds, they convinced themselves that they were good, godly women doing their
"duty."

*Oh how I do pray that I will never be guilty of letting idle
words fall that would damage or hurt somebody's reputation
or their opportunity to grow in God's grace and goodness. So
I pray Lord, slow me down. Inspire me to send my roots*

down deep to the soil of life's enduring values. Let me learn to put down roots into God's marvelous love so that I may grow tall in His grace. Lord, fill my mouth with worthwhile stuff and nudge me when I have said enough.

NOVEMBER 14

When there is moral rot within a nation, its government topples easily; but with honest, sensible leaders there is stability.
PROVERBS 28:2 TLB

How we pray for our blessed nation, and how we pray that our own influence will be that of right. I heard a marvelous man from Israel say, "No nation or society or culture rises any higher than the standards of its women."

Since I work with thousands of women, and I speak as a woman, how earnestly I pray and how hard I work to keep our standards high in our family life, in our business life, and in our personal life.

I believe in America. I believe it became great because of its faith in God, its hope of independence, its love of freedom. I want to keep this land with its glorious past, founded by our fore-fathers on the principles of God's Word, safe and free for my grandchildren, for all children in this nation, with an opportunity for them to become what they can be. I want a free choice, not a free handout. I prefer an opportunity to prove my abilities on the job rather than the irresponsibility to demonstrate frustrations.

O God, our help in ages past,
    Our hope for years to come,
Our shelter from the stormy blast,
    And our eternal home!

Under the shadow of Thy throne
    Still may we dwell secure;
Sufficient is Thine arm alone,
    And our defense is sure.

Before the hills in order stood,
  Or earth received her frame,
From everlasting Thou art God,
  To endless years the same.

A thousand ages in Thy sight
  Are like an evening gone;
Short as the watch that ends the night,
  Before the rising sun.

ISAAC WATTS

NOVEMBER 15

A man who refuses to admit his mistakes can never be successful. But if he confesses and forsakes them, he gets another chance.

PROVERBS 28:13 TLB

Somebody said long ago that the one most important word is "you." The least most important word is "I." The two most important words are "forgive me." The two most important sentences are "I love you" and "I am sorry."

And so, again, I am reminded to admit mistakes, ask for forgiveness, and seek another chance. And aren't we everlastingly grateful that our God is a God of the second chance, and the third, and the fourth, and on and on—He gives us another chance time and time again. He forgives us, loves us, guides us, and cares for us.

Forgive me, Lord, for the times I have disappointed You. Thank You for today, which is another chance. Help me to make today a good day for all who come in contact with me.

NOVEMBER 16

O God, I beg two favors from you before I die: First, help me never to tell a lie. Second, give me neither poverty nor riches! Give me just enough to satisfy my needs! For if I grow rich, I

may become content without God. And if I am too poor, I may
steal, and thus insult God's holy name.

PROVERBS 30:7–9 TLB

How interesting it is to think on these petitions: First, never to
tell a lie. We have to everlastingly be conscious of truth. One of
the wonderful things about telling the truth is that you don't
have to try to remember what you said.

Second, having neither poverty nor riches, just enough to satisfy our needs, for if we grow rich we may become content without God.

The temptation to become self-satisfied and to feel that one
has made it and does not need God often accompanies the life of
ease and prosperity. So the wise man is asking God for enough to
satisfy his needs, giving God the credit and the glory and the
thanks. At the same time, realizing that if one is without the basic
needs of life, and especially if one sees his family suffering because of this, there is a temptation to steal, or to demand, or to
take.

This should be a good standard for us in our economic plan-
ning and in building a society that will give every person an opportunity to work and earn the money for their basic needs, and
then the opportunity to earn more and share it with someone less
fortunate, but *never* to hoard. All through the Scriptures, we are
warned against hoarding or possessing for possession's sake.

I think of Abraham with all his possessions, including his most
treasured possession—his beloved son, Isaac, whom he was willing to sacrifice to God. After God spared Isaac, Abraham still
had all his possessions *and* Isaac, plus the wonderful knowledge
of his obedience. An added blessing was the freedom of knowing
that although he still had everything, he did not possess them,
nor did they possess him.

Emerson said it best—"Things are in the saddle and are riding
mankind." We seek to develop an appreciation for things beautiful, but never the love of the things themselves. *People* were
made to be *loved* and *things* were made to be *used,* and we get in
trouble when we reverse the order and begin to love things and
use people.

*We pray with the wise man, give me just enough to satisfy my
needs and help me not to be tempted by too much or too little.*

NOVEMBER 17

*If you can find a truly good wife, she is worth more than pre-
cious gems. Her husband can trust her, and she will richly satisfy his needs. She will not hinder him, but help him all her life.*
                                      PROVERBS 31:10–12 TLB

Many times today's Proverb has been misunderstood. First of
all, a truly good wife is the most wonderful thing a man can have.
She is worth more than many gems, any possession, or any success. Most of the women that I know and with whom I work and
associate want to be truly good wives if they are already married.
If not, they want to know how to become truly good wives someday.

A good wife's husband can trust her, and she will richly satisfy
his needs. I am so glad that God understands, and I know that
we are to submit to the will of *only* our Heavenly Father and not
to the will of our husbands, for their will can be selfish. So God
tells us to submit to His will and to our mate's needs.

Then, of course, comes the big question of how to know the
difference between our mate's *needs* and his *will*. I have discovered that usually if it is the *will*, it can be selfish. That does not
mean that we cannot have selfish needs, for we can, but if they
are very real needs, each person must realize that at that particular moment a need must be met.

These verses go ahead to say, "She will not hinder him, but
help him all her life." Certainly this does not mean that she will
be a doormat, but it does mean that she will be a partner and that
she will be a helpmate. And this of course means that he, in turn,
should help her.

*Lord God, every one of us that is a wife would pray that she
would be the kind of a woman who would satisfy the needs of
her husband and be a help to him and never a hindrance, but*

be that precious gem of great worth—never worthy, but of great worth.

NOVEMBER 18

She finds wool and flax and busily spins it. She buys imported foods, brought by ship from distant ports. She gets up before dawn to prepare breakfast for her household, and plans the day's work for her servant girls.

PROVERBS 31:13–15 TLB

A lot of people have read this and said, "Well, of course, she can do all those things because she has servants." And it *was* the custom in that day to have servants. However, in our modern world, we, too, have servants, but they are mechanical: We have washers and dryers, we have dishwashers, and we have water in the house—many wonderful servants. In my early childhood, I lived on the farm and we had to pump water from the well and carry it to the house. We had to wash clothes in an iron pot with a washboard and boil them in an iron pot in the backyard.

All of us who have lived long enough, or in that particular situation, know how wonderful it is to have mechanical servants to help us with our daily housework and to keep the clothes and the house clean. We appreciate having electricity and running water and the things that go with modern living.

It is interesting, too, that our wife in today's Scripture was a gourmet cook. She bought imported foods and fixed them beautifully and lovingly for her household. She was also very wise in the management of her household and in seeing that they had clothes made of fine wool, or whatever might have been the particular fabric necessary for her family and the climate in which they lived.

Love is expressed many ways in a home. Love is expressed in clean clothing, in good food beautifully served and lovingly prepared, in clean rooms and beautiful accessories on the walls to say interesting people live here, people who care live here, and every person is somebody.

As we say in our Home Interiors' Code of Ethics, "We believe in the dignity and importance of women, believe that everything a woman touches should be enobled by that touch. We believe that the home is the greatest influence on the character of mankind. We believe that the home should be a haven, a place of refuge, a place of peace, a place of harmony, and a place of beauty."

And so we pray, O Lord, that we will each build the kind of home that has the kind of attraction power that brings our husbands home at the close of day, our children home at close of play, and is a place and a source of contentment, of joy, of learning, and of loving.

NOVEMBER 19

She goes out to inspect a field, and buys it; with her own hands she plants a vineyard. She is energetic, a hard worker, and watches for bargains. She works far into the night!

PROVERBS 31:16–18 TLB

It is interesting to me to see in this description of a truly good wife that she is also a business woman. She is knowledgeable about vineyards and the right kind of grapes to plant. She is knowledgeable about real estate. She certainly understands what is a good field, as she has the wisdom and practicality to inspect it and to make a decision as to whether or not to buy it.

She is capable of making decisions, and certainly she is not a doormat nor does she have to ask her husband everything about every decision. He trusts in her (verse 11). Her husband can trust her.

She has studied and learned, and she knows what constitutes a good buy. She looks for bargains, and sometimes she works far into the night.

She is a woman; she has a brain; she makes decisions; she is an equal. This is God's plan for a wife. It is always wonderful to be able to come back and find again in His Book the pattern as He wants it to be.

Many is the time when people have asked me about women's liberation. I have to truthfully tell them that I was liberated over 2,000 years ago by Jesus Christ, Himself. Actually, go back to Proverbs and you see again God's plan.

A truly liberated woman is not afraid of leadership. She does not hide her intellect, her ideas, or her abilities by feigning humility.

If she is liberated as God planned for her to be, and as He has arranged for her to be, she has come to terms with herself. She can be who she is with sensitivity to the needs of others.

Heavenly Father, thank You for liberating me and for creating me with intellect, with ideas, with sensitivity to the needs of others and to Your love. I praise Your name! Help me to become what You want me to be.

NOVEMBER 20

She sews for the poor, and generously gives to the needy. She has no fear of winter for her household, for she has made warm clothes for all of them. She also upholsters with finest tapestry; her own clothing is beautifully made—a purple gown of pure linen.

PROVERBS 31:19–22 TLB

It is exciting to read God's plan for a virtuous woman, an example of the diversity of a woman's life as God frees her to be a woman—the diversity and the balance of a lifetime. A woman who fears God, has a business, speaks up with wisdom and kindness, cares for her family, and is sensitive to the needs of others less fortunate. She loves to look her very best, so she selects clothing beautifully made of quality material. Her home also shows the measure of her devotion and her commitment to excellence, so she upholsters with the finest tapestry that she can possibly fit into the framework of her budget.

Lord, we pray that we as women might seek the excellence set before us in Your Word and make our lives exciting, alive—a testimony to Thee.

NOVEMBER 21

Her husband is well known, for he sits in the council chamber with the other civic leaders. She makes belted linen garments to sell to the merchants.

PROVERBS 31:23, 24 TLB

God's woman, described in today's Proverb, not only is in real estate, but she is also a saleswoman, using the skill of her hands and her mind; and she is not ashamed to sell to the merchants. This has been appealing to me because my own life is so entwined with the joy of selling and service—commitment to excellence and the opportunities of leadership.

You see, if you have leadership ability, you will be using it all of your life. Your sensitivity to others will determine *how* you will use it and *where* you will use it.

So, God's woman is sensitive to the needs of the poor and of her husband and the merchants in the city. What a woman! Truly she is the example of the diversity in a woman's life.

Heavenly Father, thank You for giving us this example and showing us the many talents, many opportunities, and the many ways a woman can be free to become what You want her to be. Thank You.

NOVEMBER 22

She is a woman of strength and dignity, and has no fear of old age. When she speaks, her words are wise, and kindness is the rule for everything she says. She watches carefully all that goes on throughout her household, and is never lazy.

PROVERBS 31:25–27 TLB

Certainly here are the attributes and the strength that every woman would want. Strength and honor and beauty are her clothing. She exercises for strength, she looks her best, she is careful about her diet, she watches carefully all the money that comes and goes through her household, and she is never lazy.

How interesting this description is. It certainly would help us to remind ourselves to be up and about our duty, to take care of our household—whether it is an apartment, a single room, a cottage, or a large dwelling. It helps us to be careful with money and with words, and to look and be our very best. One of the things that disturbs me greatly is the many hours of idle time spent watching daytime dramas by so many women nowadays. Soon the fantasy world takes over and discontentment with present circumstances begins to enter the mind. This could well be one of the causes of many separations and divorces.

God help us to redeem our time more wisely. We have the freedom to live the way that we should live and can live. God help us to want to live a life of productivity, of achievement, of careful management.

NOVEMBER 23

Her children stand and bless her, so does her husband. He praises her with these words: "There are many fine women in the world, but you are the best of them all!" Charm can be deceptive and beauty doesn't last, but a woman who fears and reverences God shall be greatly praised. Praise her for the many fine things she does. These good deeds of hers shall bring her honor and recognition from even the leaders of the nations.

PROVERBS 31:28–30 TLB

What a beautiful finish to a rich description! God promises us that if we will follow His blueprint, if we will follow His pattern, then, as women, as God has freed us to be, we will receive honor and blessing, and we will not have to worry about getting old.

Skin can age and wrinkle, and bodies can weaken and cease to be young and beautiful, but God promises us that if we will fear and reverence Him, we will receive the honor, the praise, and the blessing that is due us as God's women.

As we finish Proverbs, I hope, dear reader, that you will pray with me. . . .

O God, thank You for this book of wisdom. Thank You for the richness in every page. Thank You for the closing tribute to woman, and O God, thank You for giving us this freedom, this place of stature, this place of importance, this place of equality. And O God, with that, help us to remember that we have the liberty to become what You want us to be, what You plan for us to be. Cleanse us, show us, use us, O God.

NOVEMBER 24

Charm can be deceptive and beauty doesn't last, but a woman who fears and reverences God shall be greatly praised.
PROVERBS 31:30 TLB

As a woman, you owe it to yourself, and to others, to **be somebody to someone!**

As a woman, you are an interesting combination of the IDEALISTIC and the PRACTICAL. A proper balance between the two is desirable and necessary.

A woman with a great aspiration but no roots may find herself bankrupt and disillusioned. On the other hand, to succumb to the drab routine of practical, everyday living can rob a woman of her sparkle and charm!

Diapers and dishes . . . dishes and diapers . . . day in, day out . . . the monotony of humdrum activities takes its toll. This woman is tired and bored. She is in a rut where her only diversion is self-pity.

How easy it is for such a woman to settle down in the status quo, and how deadly to her personality and self-development!

You must grow—or shrivel. You must have a source to draw from and an outlet of expression!

PERSONAL GROWTH IS A CONTINUAL PROCESS. ONE NEVER GRADUATES FROM THE "SCHOOL OF LIFE."

Dear Lord, help us to humble ourselves to Thy will and yet realize our great worth. Lead us to keep a proper balance in Thy will.

NOVEMBER 25

Bless the Lord, O my soul, and forget not all his benefits.
PSALMS 103:2

Soon we will gather in family groups across the land to express joy and thanks for the blessings we have received as a nation, as a community, as a family, and as individuals.

So much of the time we rush from plane to plane, city to city, appointment to appointment . . . and it has always been so. For centuries, men and women have gone forth from their homes to work, to serve, to play. Whether in the end it was "worth it all" has always depended on whether a person found time as the years went by for those things far more important than money or power—FAMILY, HOME, and CHURCH.

If the demands of your job or the pace of your life have chained you to a clock that is getting bigger than you are, pause to remember: In any human life there are only so many hours, none of which may be reclaimed once they have ticked by. You have all the time there is . . . to each is given an equal amount daily. Make every minute count.

This is a busy, busy season. It is necessary to pause and count our blessings in order to keep from getting frustrated by the many demands upon our time. Pause to realize, too, that it only takes a minute to pray, only an hour or two to go to church on

Sunday, yet the benefits reaped from even such brief dedication to God can be eternal.

Here are some—there are many others—of our symbols of greatness and courage: George Washington at Valley Forge, Thomas Jefferson, the architect of the Declaration of Independence; and the sunken Arizona with 1,100 American boys entombed beneath the blue waters of Pearl Harbor in Hawaii. Our symbols challenge us to cease scurrying about like so many fiddler crabs fearful to be far from our holes in the sand . . . to learn to have more faith and less fear!

And so . . . let us all with hearts united this Thanksgiving week say with the sweet singer of Old Israel, "The Lord is my shepherd, I shall not want!" With confidence in the future and with thanksgiving for the hope that is tomorrow.

Dear Heavenly Father, accept our humble gratitude for Thy bountiful blessings to us as a nation, a family—as individuals.

NOVEMBER 26

God be merciful unto us, and bless us; and cause his face to shine upon us.

PSALMS 67:1

This is the time of year when we begin to think more deeply of our blessings. This month our nation has a whole day set apart and dedicated to giving thanks. We call it **Thanksgiving Day.**

We are all familiar with the story of the first Thanksgiving— pumpkin pies and turkeys and pilgrims have become identified with our childhood memories of Thanksgiving Day. The picture that still glows in memory is of the pilgrim families gathered around a bountiful table with their heads bowed in a prayer of thanks to God for having survived the hardships of the first year in a new world: the extreme weather, the ravages of illness, and the loneliness of living in a strange land.

Now our nation again has reason to bow in a prayer of thanksgiving for survival. Let us give thanks for the bounty of providence which has made possible the growth and promise of our land. Let us remember that our God is the God of all men, that only if all men are free can liberty be secure for any. Let us join in vigorous concern for those who now endure suffering of body, mind, or spirit, and let us seek to relieve their distress and to assist them toward health, well-being, and enlightenment.

Finally, let us dedicate ourselves and our nation to the highest loyalties which we know. Let us breathe deeply of the clean air of courage, preparing ourselves to meet the obligations of our day—in *trust,* in *gratitude,* and in the supreme *confidence* of a people who have accomplished much, united under God.

Let us count our blessings this Thanksgiving Day.

May we on this special day, Dear Lord, come before Thy presence with thanksgiving and with singing.

NOVEMBER 27

In every thing give thanks: for this is the will of God in Christ Jesus concerning you.

1 THESSALONIANS 5:18

If one should give me a dish of sand and tell me there were particles of iron in it, I might look for them with my eyes and search for them with my clumsy fingers and be unable to detect them. But let me take a magnet and sweep through the sand, and I would see how the magnet would draw to itself the most invisible particles by the mere power of attraction!

The unthankful heart, like my finger in the sand, discovers no mercies, but let the thankful heart sweep through the day and, as the magnet finds the iron, so will the thankful heart find some heavenly blessings in every hour.

The iron in God's sand is gold!

O God, may ingratitude never creep into our attitudes, may we stand in awe, rather, of all the wondrous things You have poured out on us.

NOVEMBER 28

*But God, who is rich in mercy, for his great love wherewith he
loved us, Even when we were dead in sins, hath quickened us
together with Christ, (by grace ye are saved;) And hath raised
us up together, and made us sit together in heavenly places in
Christ Jesus.*

EPHESIANS 2:4–6

Man has conquered space, heights, armies, and diseases, yet
the art of daily living baffles us all. Sometimes we just wonder
how we're going to get through the week or through the day.
What is required to live triumphantly? We need to lean on God
and learn of Him.

The only road to recovery for us is to know the reality of the
unchanging, forgiving, redeeming love of Christ. Sins must be
confronted and confessed.

God's love is the secret to the right relationship with others.
When we can see Him as He really is, we can begin to look at
others, not as *we* see them, but as *He* sees them.

The only way we can recover from unforgiveness is to let God
do it through us. The love of God is the secret of the ability to
forgive, of recovery from sorrow.

God's love is as real as the power He offers. The God who
created the world and flung the stars into space is *my Friend.* He
is interested in *my* tears and *my* heartaches and *my* loves. What a
beautiful picture of God we have when we see His power, majesty, omnipotence, and also his lovingkindness, graciousness,
tenderness, and compassion to every individual. When we really
see that, we can live triumphantly, confidently, victoriously,
leaning on Him, drawing our strength and power from Him.

*Father, help us to live triumphantly, knowing Your unlimited
power is ours to use if we'll but claim it.*

NOVEMBER 29

And we know that all things work together for good to them that love God, to them who are the called according to his purpose.

ROMANS 8:28

If we do not have ourselves lined up right with the Lord, there can be no complete identity. Romans 8:28 does not tell us that all that happens to us is good. It says that all things *work* for our good if we turn them over to God.

Ten young people came to our session of Explo '72 in Dallas. One of the young people told how he had invited Christ into his heart a year before. He said, "I would like to tell you I have had the greatest year of my life, but it wouldn't be true. In many ways, I have had more problems. If you haven't met the devil face-to-face, maybe you're going the same way he is! But I have the assurance that Jesus is with me and that I will be victorious."

I once received a letter from a new Christian. She was relating to me all the things that had happened to her since she had found the Lord. She said, "Why is it that so many problems are coming my way? Is God testing me?" I don't know whether God was testing her, but she could rest assured the devil was working hard and fast to fill her with doubts.

We must trust God that in all these things we are *more than conquerors* and that *nothing* can separate us from His love or have victory over us. This is a promise to hang onto when we feel that things are going against us. God is all-powerful. We cannot separate ourselves from His love. We can get out of harmony, out of focus—and how many times we do. David did and Paul did. But we cannot stop God's love for us.

When you love someone, doesn't that give identity to them? You love your children, your family members. When you tell them you love them or think about them, do you think about a generalized group? No. You think about them *one* by *one—this* child or *this* mother, or father, or brother. I have talked to people who have big families and are asked how they can love all of the family members individually. You can't have too many children to love. You love them individually—one at a time. That gives identity to each one. God loves you and me so much more. He gives identity to each of us.

Thank You, Jesus, for giving me identity—for loving and saving even me.

NOVEMBER 30

It might seem too obvious or simple, but what better way could we end November than by reflecting on the goodness of God to us, counting our blessings. One page could not begin to contain them all, but, after thinking of your many blessings— "mentally naming them one by one"—choose the six at the very top of your list and write them down:

1. _____
2. _____
3. _____
4. _____
5. _____
6. _____

Now, thank God for each one individually and praise Him for being a God of such love and generosity. How often we fail to feel grateful for all the good things that come to us—we take them for granted as a "right" to be expected. God, forgive us and make us always conscious of our blessings.

December

DECEMBER 1

The heavens declare the glory of God; and the firmament sheweth his handywork.

PSALMS 19:1

This is the time of year when harvesttime is all about us, when yearlong efforts pay off in bountiful crops, and the gracious God who created our world adds a touch of autumnal beauty.

Our part of the world is aflame with brilliant colors of russet reds, golden yellows, and burnt oranges painted by the Lord God Himself! As I revel in such abundant beauty, I am aware there are others who are unmindful of its glory, who never really open their eyes to see. Then I am reminded of these lines by Edna St. Vincent Millay:

> The world stands out on either side
> No wider than the heart is wide;
> Above the world is stretched the sky,—
> No higher than the soul is high.

How true it is . . . that "none is so blind as he who will not see."

BEAUTY IS IN THE EYE OF THE BEHOLDER.

O God, help us to open our eyes to see the beauty You put all around us—all the things You have created just to make Your children happy!

DECEMBER 2

Give, and it shall be given unto you. . . .

LUKE 6:38

Read this verse over five times, and it will really begin to speak to you.

Recently, in a Bible study with a longtime friend of mine, Geneva De Loach, a new truth was revealed to me: The world of men will return blessings unto you for giving abundantly. What an exciting thought.

I have a pair of small silver shovels on a chain around my neck. They were given me by a student we were sponsoring. One is very tiny and the other is a little larger. The story behind the shovels goes like this: A philanthropist was asked, "How can you give away so much and have so much left?" He answered, "I really don't know, but I guess it is like this—I shovel it out and God shovels it in . . . and He has a bigger shovel!"

O God help us to give with joy—and good measure.

DECEMBER 3

Rest in the Lord, and wait patiently for him: fret not thyself because of him who prospereth in his way, because of the man who bringeth wicked devices to pass.

PSALMS 37:7

The sin of our time is not idleness, but rather being too busy, which causes us to fret. There are many things we want to do, and there are some things we *must* do—

- Earn a living wage
- Keep up household chores
- Share a ministry of our faith through our church fellowship
- Provide opportunity for growth and recreation

- Care for our families
- Care for an elderly parent

Life has a sense of incompleteness from within and pressures from without. They confuse the mind; they break the body. Work or worry is something that robs us of the poise and power we would like to have daily.

Remember: "Worry never robs tomorrow of its sorrow, it only saps today of its strength."

OVERHEARD IN AN ORCHARD

Said the Robin to the Sparrow:
  "I should really like to know
Why these anxious human beings
  Rush about and worry so."
Said the Sparrow to the Robin,
  "Friend, I think that it must be
That they have no Heavenly Father
  such as cares for you and me."

ELIZABETH CHENEY

Father, if Your eye is on the sparrow, then I'm sure You're watching me, so help me not to fret and worry. May I rest in Thee, knowing "Thou wilt keep him in perfect peace whose mind is stayed on Thee."

DECEMBER 4

For I know whom I have believed, and am persuaded that he is able to keep that which I have committed unto him against that day.

2 TIMOTHY 1:12

Our God is *knowable.* Isn't that glorious!

So many people are searching for God. We can *know* Him. One of the best ways is to read His Word.

The continual change in our lives will come as we walk in

grace, and read the Bible, and pray. Sometimes we wonder why God didn't just make us perfect to begin with, or when we became Christians—why didn't God just make us permanently good? If He had, there would not have been the growth in grace that makes us continuously dependent upon Him. We would have had our own goodness all the time and would not have to depend on Him day after day to make us good, to mold and shape us into His likeness. But one day, "We shall see Him as He is, for we shall be like Him!"

O GLORIOUS DAY!

For the blessed assurance of Thy everlasting safekeeping, we are truly grateful.

DECEMBER 5

But whoso looketh into the perfect law of liberty, and continueth therein, he being not a forgetful hearer, but a doer of the work, this man shall be blessed in his deed.

JAMES 1:25

Your rights—we hear it on every hand, but the time has come for all women, church women, Christian women, liberated women, *all* women, to find a word from God. We need a word from God for women.

We want and need to know how to become our best selves . . . how to be the women God intended for us to be. I am much more interested in *liberty* than I am in equality—the *liberty* to be the woman that God intended for me to be. I do not worry about liberation, because I was liberated over 2,000 years ago, and yet, I understand discrimination. I have been on the other end of it, and I know that many times there has not been equal opportunity. Unfortunately, this has often been man's idea, because Christian men have not always stood up for the liberty of women, the liberty in God's sight. I think this is the reason Women's Lib has come on so strong.

Yes, I believe in liberty . . . the liberty for all people, both men and women, to be their best selves, unfettered by the restraints of men, limited only by any bounds *God* might impose in leading them to become the persons He would have them be.

My prayer today is the echo of the words of the hymn, "Living for Jesus."

> Living for Jesus a life that is true,
>   Striving to please Him in all that I do;
> Yielding allegiance, glad-hearted and free,
>   This is the pathway of blessing for me.
>   THOMAS O. CHISHOLM

DECEMBER 6

Cause me to hear thy lovingkindness in the morning; for in thee do I trust: cause me to know the way wherein I should walk; for I lift up my soul unto thee. Deliver me, O Lord, from mine enemies: I flee unto thee to hide me. Teach me to do thy will; for thou art my God: thy spirit is good; lead me into the land of uprightness.

PSALMS 143:8–10

Tell God that you are willing to be made willing to do His will. God wants to break our wills, but not our spirits. All of us are so human and so inclined to want to do things our own way, that it is most difficult for us to say, "Lord, I want to know and to do Your will for my life." Sometimes, God has to "bottom us out" so that we will find rest and trust only in Him. For us to be made willing to do His will opens the doorway for Him to do far above all that we ask or imagine. This is the message of Hannah Whitall Smith's book, *The God of All Comfort.* There are times when we are so determined to do God's will for our lives in our own way that He has no alternative but to break our wills and then proceed with His plans for our lives. Oh, how much agony and heartache we could avoid in life if we would be willing to be made willing to do God's will!

*Dear God, help us to be willing to be made willing and then
we shall trust You to bring us to the place of truly walking in
Your will for our lives.*

DECEMBER 7

*Brethren, I count not myself to have apprehended: but this one
thing I do, forgetting those things which are behind, and
reaching forth unto those things which are before, I press toward the mark for the prize of the high calling of God in Christ
Jesus.*

PHILIPPIANS 3:13, 14

Since we are human, we make mistakes. The fact that we make
a mistake is not as important as our reaction to it. It is interesting
to note the amount of time that is wasted explaining *why* we did
what we did, instead of admitting we were wrong in the first
place.

Sometimes an error affects the constructive effort of an individual for days, causing additional mistakes to be made. It is best
to admit a mistake quickly, so there will be no burden carried
forward to interfere with the task of the moment. It is usually not
the work of the day that breaks down our mental, emotional, and
physical health, but the *extra burden* we have accumulated because of our mistakes or disturbances through the days in the
past. Remember again this favorite quotation: "Worry never
robs tomorrow of its sorrow; it only saps today of its strength."

Worry is often the fear that we will make a mistake, that we
have already made one, or that we will make another one. When
we are *free* to think clearly without the pangs of a previous mistake affecting us, we are less apt to make another error. Never be
hesitant to admit when you are wrong. The world needs honest
people. Who knows all? An old Hebrew axiom says, "Everything
in one package, nobody's got."

*Father, help us to "forget those things that are behind" and
go on in a positive way, confident that You know our frailties
and failures but love us nonetheless.*

DECEMBER 8

I have fought a good fight, I have finished my course, I have kept the faith.

2 TIMOTHY 4:7

Whatever else you think . . . **think that you can!** WIN WITH-OUT BOASTING . . . LOSE WITHOUT EXCUSES.

There are two kinds of people in the world—*self-starters* and *self-stoppers!*

Many people never give themselves a fair start, because they have the habit of making excuses rather than the habit of making good. They are the *self-stoppers*. It is easy to find excuses for not doing things, but it is a habit loaded with danger! It is giving up without even trying! It undermines the self-confidence. It encourages a pessimistic attitude.

The weather is a perennial excuse for self-stoppers. It is too hot, too cold, too wet, too stormy, too threatening—to do that unpleasant task, *or* it is just too nice a day to be working! Don't accept your alibis. Winners never accept their alibis! They make a habit of overcoming obstacles. Someone once said, "If Columbus had turned back, no one would have blamed him, but they would not have remembered him either."

You know, when we practice being "go-givers" and give of ourselves, our energies, our enthusiasm, life has a way of compensating us by returning to us a hundredfold. Become a "go-giver" and you will reap the rewards of a "go-getter."

Remember Columbus and sail on . . . and on . . . and on.

Dear Lord, help us keep the faith and finish our course in Thy name and for Thy sake.

DECEMBER 9

Beloved, let us love one another: for love is of God; and every one that loveth is born of God, and knoweth God.

1 JOHN 4:7

To know God is to love Him, and to love Him is to really know Him. There are many people with great human compassion. It is amazing that they do not realize that this compassion comes from God, whether they know Him or not. **God is the origin of love.** He is not only the origin of love—love comes *from* and leads *to* God. Love makes us kin to God. God says let us practice loving each other, for love comes from Him. All human love is not godly love, but all feelings of unselfish love come from God. We may express it to our children and not even know Him. We may express it to other people and not even know Him. But, whether we know Him or not, in the human heart, all love comes from God.

We can have great human compassion, but it is only by knowing God we can begin to love as He loves. There is a difference. It is easy to love those who love us, that is only natural. God says even the heathen do that. But, without God, can you truly love someone who despitefully uses you? No. That is alien to human nature; it has to come from God's love through us. There are people who irritate us, people who frustrate us, people who aggravate us. The only way we can live with them or tolerate them or put up with them—let alone *love* them—is to begin to see them as God sees them, and let His love and grace flow through us to them. When God lives in our hearts, then, and *only* then, can we really love as He wants us to love.

Dear Lord, teach me to want to love the unlovely. Thank You for loving me when I am unlovely. I pray that You will love others through me.

DECEMBER 10

Ye have heard that it hath been said, Thou shalt love thy neighbour, and hate thine enemy. But I say unto you, Love your enemies, bless them that curse you, do good to them that hate you, and pray for them which despitefully use you, and persecute you.

MATTHEW 5:43, 44

Love has a dual relationship to God. It is only by knowing God that we are able to love as He would have us love. We can love someone, we can have great human compassion, parental love and brotherly concern, but it is only by knowing God that we can love as He loves. The more like God we become, the more tolerant we will become of those who do not love us.

For us to have God's love, we must know what it is. To know what it is, we must know Him who is its Author. It is when God dwells in our hearts that we are able to love as He expects us to love. It takes God's grace for us to see others as God sees them, and to love them as He loves them.

Lord, give us the grace to see people as they can be *and not as they are, but to love them in their unlovely, unfinished state, even as You also love us.*

DECEMBER 11

Come unto me, all ye that labour and are heavy laden, and I will give you rest. Take my yoke upon you, and learn of me; for I am meek and lowly in heart: and ye shall find rest unto your souls.

MATTHEW 11:28, 29

Where have you looked for happiness, joy, and inner peace? Happiness cannot be found in a place, whether it be a house, resort, or any of the other places people continue to look. Nor can it be found in *things,* such as power, wealth, social standing, popularity, or prestige. Many who achieve these things often finish their lives as disillusioned, disappointed, and frustrated people. They look for happiness, joy, and inner peace in the wrong places and in the wrong things. As the great St. Augustine wrote, "Thou awakest us to delight in Thy praise; for Thou madest us for Thyself, and our heart is restless, until it repose in Thee."

Father, may we look always to Thee and find in Thee our joy and peace—may a genuine love for You be the status symbol we so proudly display.

DECEMBER 12

*And the angel answered and said unto her, The Holy Ghost
shall come upon thee, and the power of the Highest shall over-
shadow thee: therefore also that holy thing which shall be born
of thee shall be called the Son of God.*

LUKE 1:35

Jesus was born *into* this world, not *from* it. Our Lord's birth
was an advent; He did not come from the human race, He came
into it from above. Jesus Christ is not only the *best* human being,
He is a being who cannot be accounted for by the human race at
all. He is God incarnate. The Lord came into history from the
outside, so He must come into us from the outside. In the New
Testament the concept of the new birth is something that enters
into us, not something that springs out of us.

*Dear Father, may we know the true meaning of why Christ
came, who He was, and who He IS today.*

DECEMBER 13

*And when she could not longer hide him, she took for him an
ark of bulrushes, and daubed it with slime and with pitch, and
put the child therein; and she laid it in the flags by the river's
brink.*

EXODUS 2:3

From the moment of birth when the doctor clamps the cord, it
is clear that being a parent involves letting go. The important
questions are, How much should we let go? How much freedom
should we give our children? In today's Scripture, it is obvious
that Moses' mother had to let go of her son in the most dramatic
fashion. As soon as she knew she had given birth to a boy, she
knew that giving him up was inevitable.

First, we must give our children to the Lord. Second, we must feel the responsibility of teaching our children the truths of the Bible so they will be prepared for the freedom we give them.

As parents, we are to work ourselves out of a job—but not out of a *relationship*. Also, it is wise to remember a quote from Ruth Graham in regard to our children: "Be patient with me—God isn't finished with me yet."

Father, prepare us to "let go" of our children when the time to do so comes, but reassure us that YOU *never let go—that even though they stray away, they will always be within reach of Your loving hands.*

DECEMBER 14

. . . Believe ye that I am able to do this?

MATTHEW 9:28

Our extremities are God's opportunities. He never sends us anywhere that He does not go before us.

God is always seeking our *availability* and not our ability. He opens the doors, but we must walk through with faith and trust.

God gives us peace, quiet, and confidence when we lean on His everlasting arms, for He is the source of all strength.

Our Heavenly Father, help us to be still and know You are our God.

DECEMBER 15

Make a joyful noise unto the Lord, all ye lands. Serve the Lord with gladness: come before his presence with singing. Know ye that the Lord he is God: it is he that hath made us, and not we ourselves; we are his people, and the sheep of his pasture. Enter into his gates with thanksgiving, and into his courts with praise: be thankful unto him, and bless his name.

For the Lord is good; his mercy is everlasting; and his truth endureth to all generations.

PSALMS 100

This is a wonderful time of year! A time of excitement, increased activity, football fever, Thanksgiving holidays, and a much anticipated Christmas!

We all need to keep our attitudes positive and cheerful! It makes a great difference in our whole day. For example, there are two kinds of people: one who wakes up and says, "Good morning, Lord!" and the other who wakes up and says, "Good Lord, it's morning!"

Dear Lord, may we all make every moment of these wonderful, crisp, alive days count for Thee.

DECEMBER 16

Search me, O God, and know my heart; try me, and know my thoughts: and see if there be any wicked way in me, and lead me in the way everlasting.

PSALMS 139:23, 24

There are certain dates that stand out in each of our memories—some with joyful responses, some sad.

The date December 16 was my mother's birthday, and, although I never knew my mother, I remember the date with a strange melancholy feeling.

Then, in 1980, my brother was buried on December 16. Mother had died shortly after he was born, and since he was only sixteen months younger than I, we were really "babes."

I was the more fortunate. I lived with my grandmother for the next five years of my life, while Charlie went to live with an aunt for a while and was never in one place very long.

His poem, "Searching," which was printed on his memorial service, says so much about his life. I reprint it here for any of our readers who might be searching also. Your search can only find TRUTH and FULFILLMENT in JESUS CHRIST, the SON OF GOD.

> I'm always searching, searching for a
>   place I've failed to find—
> A place of pure contentment, with a
>   quiet untroubled mind;
> Altho' I've always hoped, I've failed
>   to find it yet
> But how I'd love to go—someplace
>   where I'd forget
> My troubles, woes, and hardships, that
>   dwell in human mind
> To leave those things forever, and go
>   where I should find
> Peace, joy, and comfort—a place of
>   perfect rest;
> So God has made us Heaven, where
>   we'll be forever blest.
>
> CHARLES W. WEAVER

Thank You, Lord, that You are an absolute and that we can depend on You.

DECEMBER 17

For who hath known the mind of the Lord? or who hath been his counsellor? Or who hath first given to him, and it shall be recompensed unto him again? For of him, and through him, and to him, are all things: to whom be glory for ever. Amen.
                                                        ROMANS 11:34–36

You have to begin at the beginning if you are going to find the source of things—the source of wisdom—and you have to start with whether this is a personal or impersonal universe.

When you look at a table or a fireplace, you automatically know that somebody built it, somebody planned it, somebody thought it up. Behind everything you see—whether it is a mud pie a child is making, a chocolate cake in the oven, or a sky-scraper towering in the heavens—you know there was a mind that conceived it and then made it.

Then look at the universe, which is complex beyond our un-derstanding, and you have to accept, if you are a rational, think-ing person, that there was a mind that conceived it, and the mind means that there was a personality, and the personality means there was a person!

This leads you to the fact that there had to be a Creator, and—wonder of wonders—we can know Him. He did not leave us floating around unknown or unable to know Him. He has re-vealed Himself to us and forever draws us to Himself so that we might know Him and have fellowship with Him.

Lord, thank You that You have made Yourself known to us and given us the privilege of sweet fellowship with You.

DECEMBER 18

For if by one man's offence death reigned by one; much more they which receive abundance of grace and of the gift of right-eousness shall reign in life by one, Jesus Christ.

ROMANS 5:17

If I could send you each a personal gift on the wings of Christmas it would be *awareness*. All year long we talk about en-thusiasm and its importance in successful business and living. Awareness is really "enthusiasm with a heart." Awareness of the real Christmas spirit is becoming a lost art like conversation and family reading time. All around we hear people say, "Thank goodness Christmas comes only once a year!" "I'll be glad when it is over." "I hope I live through it!"

What are we doing to Christmas? What are we doing to this

starlit season that there should be no room in our heart for wonder and joy?

The Child in the manger at Bethlehem grew up to say to a too-busy woman one day, "Martha, Martha, you are anxious and troubled about many things." I think He would say the same to us today. So—

> Let us *seek* the gift of awareness,
> *Savor* all the magic—all the warmth of hearts,
> Really *listen* to the music—*hear* the words of the Christmas story,
> *See* the beauty of Jesus in the eyes of children as they mirror the light of a Christmas tree, and
> *Feel* the loneliness that aches in the hearts of many, remembering that sorrow is more poignant at Christmastime—the season of joy and cheer.
> Let us *stop, look,* and *listen* this Christmas and hear the singing of the angels so long ago—A song of *hope, peace,* and *good will.*

However discouraged we may be at other times about the future, about the fate of the world in which we live ... for a little while may we catch a vision of the world the way God meant for it to be, the way it could be, and we will be more aware of the part we can have in making it so.

Dear Father, for Thy Son, our Savior and Lord, we praise Thy name. May we ever be thoughtful to keep "Christ" in Christmas.

DECEMBER 19

Only they would that we should remember the poor; the same which I also was forward to do.

GALATIANS 2:10

All around us we hear the music of Christmas—"'Tis the season to be jolly"—and certainly this is true. Yet all of us know there are people who, either because of illness or accidents or loneliness, have little to make them jolly.

I would like to think that everyone of us could look around and find someone with whom to share Christmas. Everyone benefits from sharing—the giver and the receiver.

It is an old song, but it is so very true—"Make someone happy, make just *one* someone happy ... and *you* will be happy, too. ..."

If you really want the true secret of continuing joy and success, it is simply this: If your *purpose* is right, and what you want is right, you will get what you want out of life *if* you help other people find *their* true and rightful purpose in life and get what *they* want out of life.

May this Christmastime be especially meaningful as you share your home, your love, and your material blessings with others around you. And as you gather your loved ones around you and sing the age-old carols, you might particularly notice the words of the third stanza of "It Came Upon a Midnight Clear":

"For Lo! the days are hast'ning on, By prophets seen of old ...
When with the ever-circling years shall come the time fore-
    told ...
When the new heaven and earth shall own The Prince of
    Peace—
Their King ... And the whole world send back the song which
    now the angels sing. ..."

O Heavenly Father of our Lord Jesus and of me, may I truly share Your love with someone I meet today.

DECEMBER 20

And let the peace of God rule in your hearts, to the which also ye are called in one body; and be ye thankful.

COLOSSIANS 3:15

This poem has meant a great deal to me. May it be an inspiration for your life.

READY FOR CHRISTMAS

"Ready for Christmas," she
    said with a sigh
As she gave a last touch
    to the gifts piled high.

Then wearily sat for a
    moment to read
Till soon, very soon, she
    was nodding her head.
Then quietly spoke a voice
    in her dream
"Ready for Christmas,
    what do you mean?

"Ready for Christmas
    When only last week
you wouldn't acknowledge
    your friend on the street?
Then ready for Christmas
    while holding a grudge?
Perhaps you'd better
    let God be the Judge."

She woke with a start
    and a cry of despair.
"There's so little time and
    I've still to prepare.
O Father! Forgive me,
    I see what you mean!
To be ready means more
    than a house swept clean."

Yes, more than the giving
    of gifts and a tree.

It's the heart swept
    clean that He wanted to
see, a heart that is
    free from bitterness and sin.

So be ready for
    Christmas—and
ready for Him.
                                        MYRTLE HAYNES

Dear God, help us to ready our hearts for the gift of Thy precious Son.

DECEMBER 21

. . . the God of peace shall be with you.
                                        PHILIPPIANS 4:9

How often during the "getting-ready-for-Christmas days" we find ourselves living under the pressures, rather than in the peace of God.

How I personally have to pray more, "practice the Presence" more, stop and assess priorities more during the days before Christmas.

Do you need to join me in this prayer for peace today?

Dear Lord Jesus, I thank You for the many joys of Christmas. I thank You for the music of Christmas, for the sweet-scented pine boughs used for decoration, for the joy of baking cookies for delighted children, for the fun of shopping for others.

Help me to keep ever in mind why I am doing these busy things—that it is all to celebrate Your coming to our earth to live in our humanity and to see life through our eyes.

Help me not to become irritable or cross with others because of my "busy-ness." I love You, Lord Jesus, and I really do want to celebrate Your birthday in a way that will honor You.

DECEMBER 22

And we have seen and do testify that the Father sent the Son to be the Saviour of the world.

1 JOHN 4:14

Sometimes we tend to get lost in the traditional lore of the Christmas season—the Christmas tree, the visit from Santa Claus, and the feverish giving of gifts. Yet, if we truly worship the Christ Child in our hearts, we can make each tradition become a part of the deeper meaning of Christmas.

The Christmas tree will inevitably and properly suggest the One who grew to manhood to bear "our sins in his own body on the tree, that we might die to sin and live to righteousness" (*see* 1 Peter 2:24).

Family reunions will point to the truth that where two or three are gathered together, there Christ is, in the midst, as well as to the family of the Redeemed. The dinners and the parties will speak of the Christ who hallowed feasts when He walked this earth and who constitutes the "living bread which came down from heaven" (John 6:51).

The centrality of children at this blessed season should remind us that childlike faith before the mysteries of the Incarnation is a requisite for participation in His Kingdom.

Even Santa Claus, who comes from a land of snow-white purity to give gifts to those who have nothing of their own, proclaims to all who have ears to hear the message of the entrance of God into our sinful world to "give gifts to men."

Christmas thus calls for total appropriation and reconsecration. Human love manifests divine love, and we can truly share the love and worship of Christ as we sing our heartwarming carols, as we trim our trees, and as we share our love with gifts—both given and received.

O Lord, may the deeper glory of Christmas invade our hearts and give a glow to our homes and families.

DECEMBER 23

The Lord himself shall give you a sign; Behold, a virgin shall conceive, and bear a son, and shall call his name Immanuel.
ISAIAH 7:14

God shook the world with a BABE—not a bomb!

This dynamite of truth keeps repeating itself in my mind as I think of Christmas, "And this shall be a sign unto you; Ye shall find the *babe* ... lying in a manger" (Luke 2:12, italics added). The manner of His coming—as a *baby*—has many important, significant meanings for us who recognize and accept the Baby as Jesus Christ, Savior and Lord. He was a Baby, winning His way into our hearts, never forcing His way. A baby doesn't stand up in his crib and force us to love him. He wins his way into the hearts of his mother and father until either parent would die for him if necessary.

Christ came as a *Baby,* not as a full-grown man; He *never* comes full-grown into our understanding. Many seek for a complete knowledge of God and His universe and His mysteries before they will accept Christ into their hearts, but He *never* comes full-grown into our understanding. As He came into the world of mankind that night long ago in Bethlehem, so He comes into our hearts and minds as a Baby and grows and develops in our understanding.

Oh, the wisdom of God in the manner of His coming, so that all might see and understand, and come to a full knowledge of the Lord.

Dear Father, open our hearts and our understanding so that we may know that You are Lord and we are Your people, as You taught in Jeremiah 24.

DECEMBER 24

And the angel said unto them, Fear not: for, behold, I bring you good tidings of great joy, which shall be to all people. For unto you is born this day in the city of David a Saviour, which is Christ the Lord.

LUKE 2:10, 11

It is that grand, glittery, and glad time of the year—the week before Christmas, when in the midst of the rush and confusion, the luscious smells of baking, the joyful sound of Christmas carolers, the eager faces of children, we find ourselves caught up once again in the glory that is the Christmas season.

Time rushes by so swiftly. Thanksgiving yields to Christmas, and once again we return to the cradle of Bethlehem that held in human form the incarnate God who was made flesh and dwelt among us. How swiftly the days will pass and in four short months we will, in memory and symbolism, go to the Cross of Calvary where this same Son of God offered Himself as an atonement for men's sins and opened the gates of paradise to all men. His sacrificial death was crowned by His Resurrection which demonstrated victory over death, and Satan, and hell— and His Ascension into heaven to the Heavenly Father. This is the greater story of Christmas, but not all of it.

We wait for the consummation; God has not finished His work; His Son, Jesus Christ, will come again from heaven. Whereas, the first coming was humble and lowly, this time He will come in power and great glory! Sin will be abolished. The earth will be renewed. Men will learn to live in peace with each other. The sword will become a plowshare and the spear a pruning hook. Men will not learn war anymore.

Every Christmas people pause from their normal, selfish pursuits—from the tension and anxiety of daily living, from the monotony of thinking of self, from the desire for power and fame, from the senseless killing of one another—to pay tribute to the honorable Babe of Bethlehem and, knowingly or unknowingly, to bear testimony to the hope of an "age of peace" when Christ shall return.

Father, what can we say but "Thank You" for so great and unspeakable a gift!

DECEMBER 25

And suddenly there was with the angel a multitude of the heavenly host praising God, and saying, Glory to God in the highest, and on earth peace, good will toward men.

LUKE 2:13, 14

Merry Christmas! Yes, the words *Merry Christmas* will ring out cheerily and spontaneously from the lips of millions of men, women, and children throughout the world. Yet, there are unnumbered millions who do not know about, and many more who do not share in, the celebration of the birthday of Jesus Christ, the Son of God, Lord of heaven, and Savior of men.

Yet, even they are drawn to the flame of the spirit of Christmas, because of the kindness and unselfishness it brings to the world for one day.

Is it not odd that this kindliness and unselfishness, which we find so impractical for 364 days in the year, become on Christmas Day as natural and as easy as the prattle of a child or the throb of a father's heart?

Life is somehow too calculating and too demanding, until for a single day we resume, almost without realizing it, the faith and the simplicity of little children at play.

World peace and world amity, which pose such staggering problems, with twisted hatreds and tortured fears, seem on Christmas Day to become startling in their promise of a good world for everybody ... everywhere. The Babe in the manger grew up to be the Carpenter of the dusty ways of a tiny country under the heel of an occupation army. He talked of a kingdom not of this world. He talked of riches which were neither silver nor gold. He cared more for men's souls than for their substance. *Things,* He said, are merely lent to us for a few days or a few years, at most. But *faith* and *hope* and *love*—these same feelings we demonstrate and express once a year at Christmastime—endure forever. Once a year the day comes when it seems that Jesus was right—His way suddenly has no angry theology in it. Nobody wants to damn anybody for being generous, and gracious, and thoughtful on that day.

O Lord, do You suppose we could stretch out the Christmas spirit over two days instead of one . . . over a week . . . over a month . . . or a year? If we could, in all our dealings with people, at home and around the world, what an impact we could have on the hearts and minds and lives of individuals of the world!

Grant us the grace to earnestly make the effort and lend us Your strength to carry through.

DECEMBER 26

. . . [Jesus said], Inasmuch as ye have done it unto one of the least of these my brethren, ye have done it unto me.

MATTHEW 25:40

The holidays are tough for anyone who is all alone—an alcoholic man or woman who is not welcome at home, a prisoner serving time, an elderly person in a nursing home, a recently divorced man or woman, a teenage runaway angry with his family.

During the holiday season, Lord, help us to remember these people who are so alone. Help us to reach out to welcome those who need companionship. Help us to write to someone, or to visit someone, or send a gift or a note of encouragement to someone who is lonely.

I read in a survey that 60 percent of all the women in America are lonely. That is a lot of lonely people. Help us to remember, not only at Christmastime, but all the time, those who might be lonely.

Help us, Father, to do what Jesus would have us do, not only at Christmastime, but every day of the year—to remember those who are lonely.

DECEMBER 27

And the Word was made flesh, and dwelt among us, . . .

JOHN 1:14

God is continuously seeking lost and lonely souls who have
fallen into moral despair. He wants to use our hands and minds
to reclaim the possibilities of the world's spiritual failures. He
wants to use our voices to encourage those in need of His assured
love and forgiveness.

He loved us enough to live among us to show us the way—He
spent His life on earth setting an example for us to follow.

*Father, into Thy hands we commend ourselves and those we
love. Keep us mindful that nothing can separate us from Thy
love.*

DECEMBER 28

Call unto me, and I will answer thee, . . .

JEREMIAH 33:3

This verse has great meaning for me, especially on the anniversary of this day.

In 1977, my son, Don, and his family were returning from a ski
trip. Don was piloting the plane, and when they left Colorado the
weather report was not bad for Dallas—but the fog closed in
quickly just about landing time.

Don is an excellent pilot, but he crashed short of the runway.
Most of the family was jolted but unhurt—one son, Ronnie, was
badly cut on the top of his head; but Don had critical injuries in
the ankle and foot and frontal injuries to his face and head.

I recall God's peace as I wrote it in *You Can Too* for all who
might need help in time of crises during these days. Don did recover, and I did thank the Lord for the preservation of our family.

About 5:00 A.M. Don was wheeled from recovery to the Intensive Care Unit, where Linda and Ronnie were already sleeping soundly under sedation. The nurses let me stand by Don's bed.

As I listened to the sound of Don's breathing machine and the beep of his heartbeat monitor in the semidarkness of the ICU, I was not his "business partner." I was simply a mother standing by the bed of her son. I was praying, sometimes silently, sometimes audibly, for our Heavenly Father to save his life and mind—not just because he was so sorely needed by his family (that was my first request), but, praise the Lord, the Spirit helped me to pray for his healing so that all might know that our Heavenly Father loves and cares, and that He is able—that His Name might receive honor and glory.

All through that long dawn in the ICU, I stood by Don's bed, my heart full of gratitude for his being alive. At the same time, I was wracked with pain for his hurt—seeing him lying so still, with the tracheotomy tube in his throat and other life-giving tubes attached to his helpless body. It was as if God spoke to my heart: "I understand, Mary, I understand. I, too, saw My Son broken and bleeding and hurt and helpless. I understand, I care, and I'm here!"

What a peace flooded my soul and what assurance flooded my spirit!

There's not a heartache that He does not share, there's not a place that He is not there.

DECEMBER 29

Fear thou not; for I am with thee: be not dismayed; for I am thy God. . . .

ISAIAH 41:10

LOOK BACK .... THANK HIM
LOOK AROUND .... SERVE HIM
LOOK FORWARD .... TRUST HIM
LOOK UP .... EXPECT HIM

These four lines would be good to remember as we claim every new day—looking back with thanks, looking around to serve, looking forward with trust, and *always* looking up.

Thank You Lord for daily provisions, for daily help, for daily opportunities to love and to serve.

DECEMBER 30

A land that the Lord your God personally cares for! His eyes are always upon it, day after day throughout the year!
                                          DEUTERONOMY 11:12 TLB

The verse before this tells us that it is a land of hills and valleys. It is not all smooth nor all downhill. If life were all one level, the dull sameness would oppress us; we want the hills and the valleys. We ought not to rest content in the verdant valleys when the summit view awaits us.

One of my favorite hymns, "Higher Ground," has these words:

> I'm pressing on the upward way,
> New heights I'm gaining every day;
> Still praying as I'm onward bound,
> "Lord, plant my feet on higher ground."
>
> My heart has no desire to stay
> Where doubts arise and fears dismay;
> Tho' some may dwell where these abound,
> My prayer, my aim, is higher ground.
>
> I want to scale the utmost height
> And catch a gleam of glory bright;
> But still I'll pray till heaven I've found,
> "Lord, lead me on to higher ground."
>   JOHNSON OATMAN, JR.

We cannot tell what the New Year will bring—joy, success, trial, sorrow—but we *can* trust that the Father comes near to take our hands and lead us on our way today.

Our Father, we praise Your name as we commit our future to You.

DECEMBER 31

. . . put off the old man with his deeds; And have put on the new man, which is renewed in knowledge after the image of him that created him.

COLOSSIANS 3:9, 10

In the ancient Greek games, the victor was not necessarily the runner who crossed the finish line first, but the one who ran the distance with his torch still burning.

As we come to the close of this year and look back at our achievements, let us hope that we have kept our torches burning and run the distance to the finish of the year . . . winners!

Will Rogers once said, "So live that even when you lose, you are still ahead."

Now we come to the beginning of another year, each new day and hour a gift of life.

None of us knows exactly what each new day will bring, but we should all live confidently, expecting the *best*—

I DO NOT KNOW WHAT THE FUTURE HOLDS,
BUT I KNOW WHO HOLDS THE FUTURE.

The sorrows of our lives would break our hearts and destroy us if they came all at once, and the joys of our lives would so overwhelm us that we could not contain them. But God is so wise that He divided our lives into time segments of moments, hours, days, and years. How can we best divide that wonderful thing called *time* into service, achievement, and happiness? The best

way is to LIVE EVERY MOMENT AS BEST WE CAN . . . and
trust God for the results.

> *As we look across the span of time to another year, Dear*
> *Lord, create within us a new life that will bring honor and*
> *glory to Thy name throughout each day which You may give*
> *to us.*

The year is over. Its days are all behind us. Whatever we could
have accomplished or contributed is history now, and in spite of
all our good intentions, we've left so much undone.

But, the wonderful thing is—tomorrow we can make a brand
new beginning. We can start a fresh, clean, unblotted page!

Looking back, we have surely grown. If we have been faithful
even in just following these devotionals, we have spent time with
the Lord. We have looked at ourselves and felt despair, but we
have looked at Him and felt hope and confidence and found
Love and Peace and Joy and Forgiveness. During this wonderful
Holiday Season, who could wish for more?